Christmas 1992

OUTBACK HEROES

OUTBACK HEROES

Patsy Adam-Smith

An imprint of CollinsAngus&Robertson Publishers
A division of HarperCollins*Publishers*

Miles and Quart-pots

Throughout *Outback Heroes* I have kept the old Imperial measurements used by pioneers and familiar still to many readers. Readers who think in metric units will be able to use the conversion table below.

Patsy Adam-Smith

Conversion Table

Quantity	Conversion factors
Length	1 inch = 25.4 millimetres
	1 foot = 30.5 centimetres
	1 yard = 0.914 metre
	1 mile = 1.61 kilometres
Mass	1 ounce = 28.3 grams
	1 pound = 454 grams
	1 stone = 6.35 kilograms
	1 hundredweight = 50.84 kilograms
	1 ton = 1.02 tonnes
Area	1 acre = 0.405 hectares
	1 square mile = 2.59 square kilometres
Volume	1 pint = 568 millilitres
	1 quart = 1.14 litres
	1 gallon = 4.55 litres
Temperature	degrees Centigrade = $\frac{5}{9}$ (degrees Fahrenheit -32)
	$37.8\,°C = 100\,°F$

CORNSTALK PUBLISHING
An imprint of CollinsAngus&Robertson Publishers Pty Limited

First published in Australia in 1981 by Lansdowne Press, Sydney
This Cornstalk edition published in 1992 by
CollinsAngus&Robertson Publishers Pty Limited (ACN 009 913 517)
A division of HarperCollinsPublishers (Australia) Pty Limited
25–31 Ryde Road, Pymble NSW 2073, Australia

Copyright © Patsy Adam-Smith 1981

This book is copyright.
Apart from any fair dealing for the purposes of private study,
research, criticism or review, as permitted under the Copyright Act,
no part may be reproduced by any process without written
permission. Inquiries should be addressed to the publishers.

National Library of Australia
Cataloguing-in-Publication data:
Adam-Smith, Patsy.
  Outback Heroes.
  ISBN 0 7018 1562 0 .
  1. Country life — Australia — Addresses.
  essays, lectures. I. Title.
994

Created by Mead & Beckett Publishing, Sydney
Edited by Jill Kitson
Designed by Barbara Beckett
Typeset in Australia by B&D Modgraphic, Adelaide
Printed in Australia by Griffin Press Limited, Netley, South Australia

5 4 3 2 1
95 94 93 92

CONTENTS

OUTBACK HEROES	8
THE TRAVELLING POST OFFICE	12
ON THE DESERT	22
PRIDE	29
THE WASHAWAY	32
THE DRIVER	34
THE SWAGGIE TEACHER	43
THE GREATEST OF THEM ALL	46
THE OVERLAND TELEGRAPH	47
TOMMY WINDICH	63
A HUNDRED BLACKGUARDS OF THE WEST	70
SPIDER	76
BOB THE DOG	79
BATTLEFRONTS OF OUTBACK	80
BEFORE THE BITUMEN	87
RUSSIAN JACK AND JAMES BALZANO	93
PARAWAY	95
STARLIGHT	102
SINGING THE CATTLE	111
KIMBERLEY MUSTER	117
THE GLORY RIDE	122
DON McLEOD'S MOB	125
THE DALY RIVER O!	133
THE ANTI-HERO	138
THE ENTOMBED MINER	139
THE BUSH-LOST BABIES	146
TOM BARTON AND THE BURDEKIN	163
OPERATION FLOOD	170
FIRE	175
THE VALLEY OF THE SHADOW OF DEATH	189
THE DISASTER	197
THE IRON MAN	202
DORFER'S HONEYMOON	204
MOTHER BUNTINE	207
THE LADY MIT THE VEIL OR 3,000 MILES SIDE-SADDLE	212
HAWKERS	219
PAPA BOUGHT FOUR CARS	221
THE BISHOP WITH 150 WIVES	233
MATTHIAS	236
THE DIARY OF MARY WATSON	237
MAYDAY	243
PUBLISHED SOURCES	252
SOURCES OF ILLUSTRATIONS	253

To the people of the Outback who never know how brave they are; to my grandfather James Adam-Smith and his sons who helped pioneer the tall timber country and lost their houses to 'the Red Bull' and rebuilt each time after the bush-fires went through; to my father who went out in flood and fire and all he ever said about it was, 'Ah well, it's all in a day's work'; to Grandfather Adams who overlanded across the arid wastes and grandmother who waited at home with the children and the terrors and loneliness of the Australian bush; and to all those stoics, the outback men and women who have helped me all these years and whose valour has strengthened my pride of country, I dedicate this book.

Courage

Robert D. Fitzgerald

I have not seen your shadows on the pages
   Of history and legend to gain thence
   Naught of the spirit that moved you to immense
And mad endeavours in forgotten ages:
   O Brave Men, of all times, my every sense
Worships your visions and heroic rages;
Your strength has given me strength, and it assuages
   My anger at my own poor impotence.

Then be beside me always, you who heard
   The call of a moment when the deed was all,
   And life was but a little pleasant thing,
Which, for a dream's sake or a sacred word,
   A man might take in his strong hand and fling
   Joyously into darkness over the wall.

OUTBACK HEROES

With a light hand on the reins, a firm grip on his shotgun, this bushman epitomises the pioneer heroes of the outback.

God bless them for their big soft hearts
And the brave brave grins they wear.
Henry Lawson

Many brave acts have been played on the Australian stage, many a hero honoured and many a hundred heroes forgotten or never recognised. The bones of many a man moulder in hidden valleys and lonely streams, men who died alone with none to witness their valour, none to know if they 'died game'. Some who set off into the brazen, molten, dusty wastes knew the dangers, took every precaution to avoid them, but accepted that 'doing a perish' might be the last entry they would scratch on the sand of the unknown country they traversed. Others, when the 'long necks' of their water bags reminded them that to tarry meant death, took the gamble with no great care for the cost once they had set their course.

There were those 'up north' with the fever that robs a man of his strengths—the dengue or malaria—or the wasting diseases their stout hearts laughingly called the 'Barcoo Rot' or the 'Belyando Spew'. Yet they stuck to the task they had set their hands to as if life, 'a little pleasant thing', was quite happily to be exchanged for a vision, an ideal or a bet. Some, those men who travelled a thousand miles behind a mob of cattle, did not refer to any map, because they were making it up as they went—and yet they would have been embarrassed to have been called explorers.

Many a man has had his spirit, the very soul of him, broken by his attempt on some endeavour that failed, some trial that, had he been successful, laurels would have been his due. There are those men and women who broke the bush and, in turn, were broken by it; there were those who faced flood, fire and drought and fought back.

These people flourished because Australia was the type of country it was—and is. Many played their parts against the backdrop of the nation's settlement and pioneering period: and we must not forget that, in some areas, pioneering was going on until quite recent times—men, women and children living in conditions not much less primitive and dangerous than the first settlers faced. Yet, in spite of all the omens of failure and ruthless opposition from nature and the elements, mankind so often triumphs, sometimes, even in the jaws of death. Others, those reformers who stimulated a nation's conscience, faced ridicule, the most painful of all crosses to bear.

It is often claimed that heroism is found only in martial achievement, in illustrious warriors, the din and turmoil of warfare. The clashing of armed soldiers in battle excite the minds of those who hear a distant drum, see the flags and pennants and faintly sense the trilling of trumpets in the traditional setting fit for heroes. Australia has had her share of these things and heroes have not been found lacking. It is not of these valorous ones that this book is written, but of those who were heroic in the sunlit days of peace, brave in the prosaic times when no drum roll and thunder of cannons and companies of men were there to feed courage and to bear witness: men and women who went in jeopardy of their lives or their reputations, some unknown, unsung, uncelebrated.

'There were heroes in Australia,' Henry Lawson wrote, 'that the world shall never know.'

The Oxford dictionary defines a hero as 'a man who exhibits extraordinary bravery, fortitude, firmness or greatness of soul, in any course of action or in connection with any pursuit, work or enterprise; a man admired or venerated for his achievements and noble qualities'. To be heroic is 'having recourse to bold, daring or extreme measures; boldly experimental, attempting great things . . . of a bravery, virtue or nobleness of character; exalted above that of ordinary men'. The greatest obstacle to being heroic is the doubt whether one may not be going to prove oneself a fool; the truest heroism is to resist the doubt, and the profoundest wisdom, to know when it ought to be resisted, and when to be obeyed.

In a sense, courage is almost a contradiction in terms. It means a strong desire to live taking the form of a readiness to die. 'Perfect courage,' said François, Duc de la Rochefoucauld in 1632, 'is to do without witnesses what one would be capable of doing with the world looking on.' And that is true of so very many of Australia's heroes of that elusive acreage of the mind we call 'the outback'.

The cartography of the outback is not to be found in geographical terms; indeed the term started as slang, but has survived long enough in the Australian language to be accepted today as orthodox. Sidney Baker, describing 'the outback', said, 'From early days we rejected English environmental terms. This was quite logical because our "outback" was not, and never will be, "intimate". Our environmental concepts were different and the terms we use to describe those concepts were a measure of the difference between England and Australia'.

The outback is a thing of the Australian mind. It has been with us as a race since the first men pressed over the coastal mountains expecting to find an inland sea. Instead of oceans and grasslands we found a fierce country that forced us to retreat to the coast. It was as if we had been repelled trying to board a proud ship, whose defenders instilled in us for all generations fear,

Below left: Heading inland into the unknown, a family of South Australian pioneers camp en route with their small flock of goats—providers of milk and meat.

Below: Those who broke the bush were sometimes broken by it, and up north pioneers also had to contend with malaria and dengue, 'the fever that robs a man of his strengths'. This photograph was taken at Pine Creek in the Northern Territory in 1890.

Above: It took courage to raise a family somewhere that was just 'an empty place on the map'.

Above right:
It was no Place for a Woman where the women worked like men;
From the Bush and Jones's Alley come their haunting forms again.
Let this also be recorded when I've answered to the roll,
That I pitied haggard women—wrote for them with all my soul.

admiration, love and curiosity: and a folk-belief that men who conquer the elements in this land are truly Homeric.

This was the last of the continents to be made known and we were the last of the old-type pioneers. When men began to push into the inland in the 1820s it so excited observers that European papers wrote and illustrated with etchings and drawings both the wild, wide, unique land, and the people who were developing as a new race because of their unprecedented challenges.

It was survival of the toughest for men and women settling this land anywhere beyond the crescent of settlement on the southern, eastern and south-western coasts. There were deserts extending 2,000 miles from settlement and impassable terrain that cut off in a practical sense places much closer to cities. Gippsland, Victoria, is one such area; here, in parts only 100 miles from Melbourne, the region was a mountain fastness (some of it is to this day). When Melbourne sent Burke and Wills off on their fatal expedition to northern Australia in 1862, Gippsland was still as challenging as anything the explorers would meet. Few had been able to penetrate the swamps or the thick forested mountains until the 1880s.

The challenges of the inland have never receded. Other nations still see us as a race to whom a sudden challenge, unique experience or disaster can come in everyday life. When Prime Minister Harold Holt disappeared, his death drew headlines in foreign newspapers which in other circumstances would scarcely record the death of a leader of so small a nation. In this case it was news: it was felt that surfing off a sparsely populated coast where sharks cruise and octopus lie in wait is what could be expected of Australia. One is still asked overseas, 'Whatever happened to that Prime Minister of yours?'. An Australian might well say, 'Which Prime Minister?', because people *do* disappear in Australia—they drown in rivers, 'do a perish' in deserts, fall down disused mine-shafts, are bitten by deadly snakes and killed by prettily painted sea creatures; others are swept away by flash floods that spread five miles wide down what was yesterday a dry, dusty creek bed, and men, women and children die every decade in fires that leap from the crown of one tree to the crown of another until thousands of acres are ablaze and families trapped in this harsh, beautiful country. Little children are 'bush-lost' and never seen again, and rogues steal cattle and drive them across dry-stages and lands where none have been before them. And all these tumultuous events call out the reluctant heroes who see their acts as being 'all in the day's work'.

Beyond the outer rim of the comforts and safety of close settlement, the outback is a pulse-point for the national folk-nerve, which reacts to the disasters, the lives, the stories told of the courage needed to survive or to conquer the empty places on the map. In days to come, other acts of heroism will follow, other Australians will show their mettle, 'give it a go' outside the heat of battle in the crystal, limpid light of day, without the pennants and trumpets to quicken their blood and the comfort of comrades watching to record if they 'died game'. There will always be men and women—and, as the records show, children—who have 'hailed the advent of each dangerous day and met the last adventure with a song'.

Left: A team of shearers relax outside the shearers' huts at the end of the day. Travelling from one outback station to the next with his team, the shearer is away from his family for months on end, working hard in tough conditions.

Below left: They come from all the places off the beaten track, the heroes of Australia.

Below: One of the last of the sundowners.

THE TRAVELLING POST OFFICE

No highways or bridges eased the journeys of the early travellers. When rivers flooded, wagons and coaches had to be hauled across with a tow-rope.

The roving breezes come and go, the reed-beds sweep and sway,
The sleepy river murmurs low, and loiters on its way,
It is the land of lots o' time along the Castlereagh.

The old man's son had left the farm, he found it dull and slow,
He drifted to the great North-west, where all the rovers go.
'He's gone so long,' the old man said, 'he's dropped right out of mind,
But if you'd write a line to him I'd take it very kind;
He's shearing here and fencing there, a kind of waif and stray—
He's droving now with Conroy's sheep along the Castlereagh.

The sheep are travelling for the grass, and travelling very slow;
They may be at Mundooran now, or past The Overflow,
Or tramping down the black-soil flats across by Waddiwong;
But all those little country towns would send the letter wrong.
The mailman, if he's extra tired, would pass them in his sleep;
It's safest to address the note to "Care of Conroy's sheep",
For five and twenty thousand head can scarcely go astray,
You write to "Care of Conroy's sheep along the Castlereagh".'

By rock and ridge and riverside the western mail has gone
Across the great Blue Mountain Range to take that letter on.
A moment on the topmost grade, while open fire-doors glare,
She pauses like a living thing to breathe the mountain air,
Then launches down the other side across the plains away
To bear that note to 'Conroy's sheep along the Castlereagh.'

And now by coach and mailman's bag it goes from town to town,
And Conroy's Gap and Conroy's Creek have marked it 'Further down.'

Beneath a sky of deepest blue, where never cloud abides,
A speck upon the waste of plain the lonely mailman rides.
Where fierce hot winds have set the pine and myall boughs asweep
He hails the shearers passing for news of Conroy's sheep.
By big lagoons where wildfowl play and crested pigeons flock,
By camp-fires where the drovers ride around their restless stock,
And past the teamster toiling down to fetch the wool away
My letter chases Conroy's sheep along the Castlereagh.

A. B. Paterson

It has always been a point of honour in the outback to get through with the mail, no matter what the risk. In most states there are stories of mailmen who perished in flooded rivers, creeks or fires, or who were speared or killed by blacks. He was a most important man in the outback, respected even by bushrangers who, although they robbed him of gold, coin or any other valuables he was carrying, rarely tampered with the mail.

'Whether it is good news or bad news you are carrying,' the bushranger Thunderbolt is said to have told a mailman outside Bonshaw, NSW, 'it is your duty to deliver it.'

The inspiration to future mailmen in Australia was John Conway Bourke, who blazed the trail of the overland mail service between Melbourne and Sydney. Melbourne had grown rapidly after its establishment in 1835 and the squatters from New South Wales saw the new colony as an outlet market for their sheep, except that no one had overlanded sheep along the route that had been almost forgotten since Hume and Hovell passed that way.

The new settlement offered a potentially fine market to sheepmen who got in early, and so, in the spring of 1836 the pioneer squatters, Joseph Hawdon and John Gardiner, and sea captain John Hepburn, set off from the Murrumbidgee, down through Gundagai, across the Murray (then called the Hume) and became the first men to overland cattle to Melbourne.

This party got through safely, but by 1837, natives began to attack parties making their way south to the market. The journey became dangerous and men crossing the Murray and Goulburn 'gambled with death': The Woradgery tribe resented the invasion of their hunting grounds and put up a brave and formidable resistance. During 1837, ten squatters attempted to settle on the choice land over the Murray River and the Woradgeries, led by their ferocious leader, Merriman, 'hounded every squatter out of the area'.

Along the 200 miles between Yass and the Murray, there were scarcely any settlers; between the Murray River and forty miles north of Melbourne there were none. In this 160 miles of Woradgery territory white men travelled at their peril.

In the meantime, on 13 April 1837, Melbourne's first post office opened; in charge was the Clerk of Petty Sessions, E. J. Forster. In the eight months until 31 December, the staff had handled 1,056 letters and 1,355 newspapers. But much of this had already been handled in Sydney, and the irregular mail services from that town irritated government and business. It was agreed

Above: Cobb and Co.'s camel mail, with an Afghan driver, leaves The Reefs, near Milparinka (NSW), during the 1882 drought, when the desert journey was too dry for coach-horses.

Top: John Hawdon won the contract to carry H.M. mail between Melbourne and Sydney after he had blazed the way overlanding cattle to Melbourne. En route he found his mailman—John Conway Bourke, a young stockman, who saved one of Hawdon's wagons when the floodwaters of the Murray threatened to sweep it away. Bourke swam the river with a tow rope so the wagon could be hauled to safety. Hawdon's mob of cattle, despite being swept downstream, were also crossed safely.

Above: Cobb and Co. drivers had to be men of some calibre, for they were responsible for the safety of up to twenty passengers (on the large coaches) and for the delivery of H.M. mail — which even bushrangers respected.

that an overland mail service must be established. But no man would submit a tender, not because the track was practically unknown, but because of the Woradgeries.

Joseph Hawdon, the pioneer overlander, believed that 'a good, determined bushman could get the mail through, despite the Woradgeries, floods, bushfires and runaway convicts-turned-bushrangers'. He wished to tender, but first he must find the man. In July of that year, 1837, he set off on his second overland drive with cattle, to set up a property down south, to re-assess the dangers of the route, and to find a man honest enough, and a trustworthy enough bushman, to carry the mail.

He found his man on the way south. This trip, the River Murray was in flood, a turbulent torrent from the wet winter of that year. The crossing was fraught with dangers, but Hawdon had a tow rope taken over the swiftly flowing river and tied to a gumtree, and a tarpaulin-wrapped waggon attached to the other end. Three men on the floating waggon attempted to haul the waggon over the water by taking up the slack on the line, but the current caught the clumsy craft, the line snapped taut and broke, and the waggon was swept away downstream, spinning and rolling. None of the three men clinging to the crazy boat could swim, and none of the watchers would risk their life in such a reckless rescue. On the bank the men shouted and the men whirling away on the flooded river shouted. Out guarding the cattle, a young stockman heard the noise, and guessed the reason for it. He galloped downstream to where the makeshift boat would pass, and before it reached this spot he stripped his clothes off and raised his arms to dive into the water. Hawdon, running along the river bank, shouted to someone to stop him: 'The fool!' But John Conway Bourke had already plunged in, and was swimming strongly. He reached the waggon, the three men aboard helped him, and they edged it over to the New South Wales bank where he climbed out and had it tied firmly to a tree before Hawdon and the other overlanders reached him.

This adventure made the stockmen even more nervous about the crossing, and now they refused to attempt it, even by swimming their horses. So, Bourke went in again, took a line over, hauled another tow-rope over, and fixed it securely. His swim gave the riders courage, and one by one they got their horses into the river and battled over to the opposite bank. The waggon was hauled safely over and the cattle stampeded into the river for their swim across.

Hawdon now knew he had his man, and the brave young stockman, as game as they come, agreed to ride the mail on the lonely route. (Hawdon contracted for a fortnightly service to Sydney and return at £1200 per year. We are not told what young Bourke was given of this.)

On New Year's Day, 1838, the settlers had a champagne luncheon at the Lamb Inn in Collins Street, to toast the success of Hawdon's overland mail, due to set off that day.

When the time came for Bourke to leave, the crowd plunged out of the Inn and gave him a great cheer. With the mail secure in two leather saddle bags, he mounted and rode away—with two long-barrelled 'hair triggered' duelling pistols stuck in his belt. (Hawdon had refused to risk the mail with an unarmed man.) For about four miles out of town a group of young bloods rode with him as a guard of honour. 'Then, with whoops and cheers and cracking whips, the escort drew rein, and with Hawdon, and a stockman, Mick O'Brien, Bourke started on the first stage.'

Bourke's memoir of his pioneer ride is flippant, as he could afford to be, seeing that he was writing it sixty years after the event.

When I first set our, amidst the cheers of the boys who gathered to see me off and wish me luck, some shook their heads in doubt, for there was no definite route, and the natives were hostile. Her Britannic Majesty's Mail (weighing about 15 lbs), myself, my provisions and bedding, my wardrobe, and my armoury (consisting of two old horse-pistols) found ample accommodation on the back of one horse, a sure but by no means a fleet-footed animal. There were no places to put up at. I carried my damper and my billy with me, and when night came, and the horse and I got tired, we pulled up in the scrub, and camped out for the night. The mailbag made a very comfortable pillow ... My last adventure on that trip was more ludicrous than serious. When trying to swim my horse over the Hume, he got stuck a little way out from the bank, his legs sinking into the soft clay. I took off the saddle and mailbag, but he still remained fast, and there was nothing for it but for me to swim the river and get assistance at Howlong, or 'Oolong', which is the original and proper name. When I got across, after a long and desperate swim, I set off for Weatherall's station, almost as naked as when I was born. A pack of 50 dogs caught sight of me, and with a common impulse came on like a tornado of devils. There was not much time to think, and you can't appeal to a flock of hungry dogs upon the sacredness of the person of Her Majesty's Mail. There was a big gumtree just at hand, and I forgot my dignity in the presence of such an acceptable haven of retreat, and boldly ran up as far as I could get while the dogs, disappointed in having lost what no doubt appeared the makings of a satisfactory breakfast, howled round the tree and tried to get up after me. Mr Weatherall came along with a gun, and calmly proceeded to take aim, with the assurance that if I did not come down in 'half a jiffy' he would blow some of the feathers off me. 'Who are you, anyhow, and what do you want?' he demanded. 'Take those dogs away,' I replied, 'I am Her Majesty's Mail from Melbourne.'

That settled him, and he just sat down and laughed, and after he could laugh no more, he looked me over cannily from top to toe and observed, 'So you are the mailman, are you? Well, I don't think much of your uniform. Where have you got the letters?'

Bourke stayed only long enough to borrow clothes and a horse, and he then galloped back to the Murray, but the wounded, bogged horse was too far gone and he put one of his revolvers at its head to put it out of its misery.

Bourke rode the full stage to Yass in six days, but the mail took five weeks to reach Sydney because from Yass the mailbags were often carried on by bullock team. Riding alone on the long and hazardous journey, the young stockman adhered to the timetable until a through coach service replaced him in 1841.

Above: Hardy old-timer Charlie Carter, alongside the remains of his dray in 1887, was one of the earliest carriers between Melbourne and Ballarat during the goldrushes.

Top left: Armed with only a pair of duelling pistols, John Conway Bourke, the first overland mailman, left Melbourne on 1 January 1838 to ride the 200-mile stage to the Murray alone, through dangerous Woradgery country. From there the mail went on to Yass and Sydney. Bourke held the job for three years, until the coach-service took over.

Below: Saddlebags bulging with mail, S.T. Gill's Bush Mailman and horse cautiously broach the flooding creek. From the outset, bush mailmen saw it as their job to get the mail through—come hell or high water.

The Fizzer

In her book, *We of the Never-Never*, Mrs Aeneas Gunn, tells of one of the mailmen of the outback in the early years of this century. Mrs Gunn lived on Elsey Station, 300 miles south of Darwin, in those days, no-man's-land. For months at a time the station people were isolated from the outside world, their loneliness broken only by the coming of the mailman on his long round trip from Katherine.

Her words are prophetic. She was not to know, as she wrote her book, that the Fizzer would in time lose when 'throwing dice with death':

The Fizzer was due at sun-down, and for the Fizzer to be due meant that the Fizzer would arrive; and by six o'clock we had all got cricks in our necks, with trying to go about as usual, and yet keep an expectant eye on the north track.

The Fizzer is unlike every type of man excepting a bush mail-man. Hard, sinewy, dauntless, and enduring, he travels day after day and month after month, practically alone—'on me Pat Malone', he calls it—with or without a black boy, according to circumstances, and five trips out of his yearly eight throwing dice with death along his dry stages, and yet at all times as merry as a grig, and as chirrupy as a young grasshopper.

With a light-hearted 'So long, chaps,' he sets out from the Katherine on his thousand-mile ride, and with a cheery 'What ho, chaps! Here we are again!' rides in again within five weeks with that journey behind him.

A thousand miles on horseback 'on me Pat Malone', into the Australian interior and out again, travelling twice over three long dry stages and several shorter ones, and keeping strictly within the Government time-limit—if it wasn't a death experience. 'Like to see one of 'em doing it 'emselves,' says the Fizzer. Yet never a day late, and rarely an hour, he does it eight times a year, with a 'So long, chaps', and a 'Here we are again'.

The Fizzer was due at sun-down, and at sun-down a puff of dust rose on the track, and as a cry of 'Mail ho!' went up all round the homestead, the Fizzer rode out of the dust.

'Hullo! What ho, boys!' he shouted in welcome, and the next moment we were in the midst of his clattering team of pack-horses.

For five minutes everything was in confusion; horse bells and hobbles jingling and clanging, harness rattling, as horses shook themselves free, and pack-bags, swags, and saddles came to the ground with loud, creaking flops. Everyone was lending a hand, and the Fizzer, moving in and out among the horses, shouted a medley of news and instructions and welcome.

'News? Stacks of it!' he shouted. The Fizzer always shouted. 'The gay time we had at the Katherine! Here, steady with that pack-bag. It's breakables! How's the raisin market? Eh, lads!' with many chuckles. 'Sore back here, fetch along the balsam. What ho, Cheon!' as Cheon appeared and greeted him as an old friend. 'Heard you were here. You're the boy for my money. You *bally* ass! Keep 'em back from the water there.' This last was for the black boy. It took discrimination to fit the Fizzer's remarks on to the right person. Then as a pack-bag dropped at the Maluka's feet, he added: 'That's the station lot, boss. Full bags, missus! Two on 'em. You'll be doing the disappearing trick in half a mo'.'

In 'half a mo'' the seals were broken, the mail-matter shaken out on the ground. A cascade of papers, magazines, and books, with a fat, firm little packet of letters among them: forty letters in all—thirty of them falling to my lot—thirty fat, bursting envelopes, and in another 'half mo'' we had all slipped away in different directions—each with our precious mail matter—doing the 'disappearing trick' even to the Fizzer's satisfaction.

The Fizzer smiled amiably after the retreating figures, and then went to be entertained by Cheon. He expected nothing else. He provided feasts all along his route, and was prepared to stand aside while the bush-folk feasted. Perhaps in the silence that fell over the bush homes, after his mail-bags were opened, his own heart slipped away to dear ones, who were waiting somewhere for news of our Fizzer.

Eight mails *only* in a year is not all disadvantage. Townsfolk who have eight

Above: Mrs Aeneas Gunn at the time of her marriage.

Top: In her classic book, We of the Never-Never, *published in 1908, Mrs Aeneas Gunn described the death-defying 1,000-mile journey undertaken eight times a year by the 'Fizzer' and his team of pack-horses.*

*The mailman with his packhorse was one of the most welcome guests who ever came to the isolated settlers' homesteads. (*The Travelling Post Office*, p. 12)*

hundred tiny doses of mail-matter doled out to them, like men on sick diet, can form little idea of the pleasure of that feast of 'full bags and two on 'em', for like thirsty camels we drank it all in — every drop of it — in long deep, satisfying draughts. It may have been a disadvantage, perhaps, to have been so thirsty; but then only the thirsty soul knows the sweetness of slaking that thirst.

After a full hour's silence the last written sheet was laid down, and I found the Maluka watching and smiling.

'Enjoyed your trip South, little 'un?' he said, and I came back to the bush with a start, to find the supper dead cold. But then supper came every night and the Fizzer once in forty-two.

At the first sound of voices, Cheon bustled in. 'New-fellow tea, I think,' he said, and bustled out again with the teapot (Cheon had had many years' experience of bush mail-days), and in a few minutes the unpalatable supper was taken away, and cold roast beef and tomatoes stood in its place.

After supper, as we went for our evening stroll, we stayed for a little while where the men were lounging, and after a general interchange of news the Fizzer's turn came.

News! He had said he had stacks of it, and he now bubbled over with it. The horse teams were 'just behind', and the 'Macs' almost at the front gate. The Sanguine Scot? Of course he was all right; always was, but reckoned bullock-punching wasn't all it was cracked up to be; thought his troubles were over when he got out of the sandy country, but hadn't reckoned on the black soil flats. 'Wouldn't be surprised if he took to punching something else besides bullocks before he's through with it,' the Fizzer shouted, roaring with delight at the recollection of the Sanguine Scot in a tight place. On and on he went with his news, and for two hours afterwards, as we sat chewing the cud of our mail-matter, we could hear him laughing and shouting and 'chiacking'.

At daybreak he was at it again, shouting among his horses, as he culled his team of 'done-ups', and soon after breakfast was at the head of the south track with all aboard.

'So long, chaps,' he called. 'See you again half past eleven four weeks'; and by 'half past eleven four weeks' he would have carried his precious freight of letters to the yearning, waiting men and women hidden away in the heart of Australia, and be out again, laden with Inside letters for the Outside world.

At all seasons of the year he calls the first two hundred miles of his trip a 'kid's game'. 'Water somewhere nearly every day, and a decent camp most nights.' And although he speaks of the next hundred and fifty as being a 'bit off during the Dry', he faces its seventy-five-mile dry stage, sitting loosely in the saddle, with the same cheery 'So long, chaps'.

Five miles to 'get a pace up'—a drink and then that seventy-five miles of Dry, with any 'temperature they can spare from other parts', and not one drop of water in all its length for the horses. Straight on top of that, with the same horses and the same temperature, a run of twenty miles, mails dropped at Newcastle Waters, and another run of fifty into Powell's Creek, dry or otherwise according to circumstances.

'Takes a bit of fizzing to get into the Powell before the fourth sun-down,' the Fizzer says—for, forgetting that there can be no change of horses, and leaving no time for a 'Spell' after the 'seventy-five-mile dry', the time limit for that one hundred and fifty miles, in a country where four miles an hour is good travelling on good roads, has been fixed at three and a half days. 'Four, they call it,' said the Fizzer, 'forgetting I can't leave the water till midday. Takes a bit of fizzing all right'; and yet at Powell's Creek no one has yet discovered whether the Fizzer comes at sun-down, or the sun goes down when the Fizzer comes.

'A bit off,' he calls that stage, with a school-boy shrug of his shoulders; but at Renner's Springs, twenty miles farther on, the shoulders set square, and the man comes to the surface. The dice-throwing begins there, and the stakes are high—a man's life against a man's judgement.

Some people speak of the Fizzer's luck, and say he'll pull through, if anyone can. It is luck, perhaps—but not in the sense they mean—to have the keen judgement to know to an ounce what a horse has left in him, judgement to know when to stop and when to go on—for that is left to the Fizzer's discretion; and with that judgement the dauntless courage to go on with, and win through, every task attempted.

The Fizzer changes horses at Renner's Springs for the 'Downs trip'; and as his keen eyes run over the mob, his voice raps out their verdict like an auctioneer's hammer. 'He's fit. So is he. Cut that one out. That colt's A1. The chestnut's done. So is the brown. I'll risk that mare. That black's too fat.' No hesitation: horse after horse rejected or approved, until the team is complete; and then driving them before him he faces the Open Downs—the Open Downs, where the last mail-man perished; and only the men who know the Downs in the Dry know what he faces.

For five trips out of the eight, one hundred and thirty miles of sunbaked, crab-holed, practically trackless plains, no sign of human habitation anywhere, cracks that would swallow a man—'hardly enough wood to boil a quart pot', the Fizzer says, and a sun-temperature hovering about 160 degrees (there is no shade-temperature on the Downs); shadeless, trackless, sun-baked, crab-holed plains, and the Fizzer's team a moving speck in the centre of an immensity that, never diminishing and never changing, moves onward with the team; an immensity of

Above: Aeneas J. Gunn.

Top: 'The Fizzer', Henry Ventilius Peckham.

Left: Among the best horsemen in outback Australia are the Aborigines. Many have gone droving with their fathers since childhood.

'So long, chaps!'—and the Fizzer lights his pipe before setting off on his 1,000-mile mail trip from Katherine, though this time he is not 'on me Pat Malone': he has an Aboriginal to help with the horses.

quivering heat and glare, with that one tiny living speck in its centre, and in all that hundred and thirty miles one drink for the horses at the end of the first eighty. That is the Open Downs.

'Fizz!' shouts the Fizzer. 'That's where the real fizzing gets done, and nobody that hasn't tried it knows what it's like.'

He travels its first twenty miles late in the afternoon, then, unpacking his team, 'lets 'em go for a roll and a pick, while he boils a quart pot' (the Fizzer carries a canteen for himself); 'spells' a bare two hours, packs up again and travels all night, keeping to the vague track with a bushman's instinct, 'doing another twenty miles before daylight'; unpacks for another spell, pities the poor brutes 'nosing round too parched to feed', may 'doze a bit with one ear cocked', and then packing up again, 'punches 'em along all day', with or without a spell. Time is precious now. There is a limit to the number of hours a horse can go without water, and the thirst of the team fixes the time limit on the Downs. 'Punches 'em along all day, and into water close up sun-down', at the deserted Eva Downs station.

'Give 'em a drink at the well there,' the Fizzer says as unconcernedly as though he turned on a tap. But the well is old and out of repair, ninety feet deep, with a rickety old wooden windlass; fencing wire for the rope; a bucket that the Fizzer has 'seen fit to plug with rag on account of it leaking a bit', and a trough, stuffed with mud at one end by the resourceful Fizzer. Truly the Government is careful for the safety of its servants. Added to all this, there are eight or ten horses so eager for a drink that the poor brutes have to be tied up, and watered one at a time; and so parched with thirst that it takes three hours' drawing before they are satisfied—three hours' steady drawing, on top of twenty-three hours out of twenty-seven spent in the saddle, and half that time, 'punching' jaded beasts along; and yet they speak of the 'Fizzer's luck'.

'Real fine old water too,' the Fizzer shouts in delight, as he tells his tale. 'Kept in the cellar for our special use. Don't indulge in it much myself. Might spoil my palate for newer stuff, so I carry enough for the whole trip from Renner's.'

If the Downs have left deep lines on the Fizzer's face, they have left none in his heart. Yet at that well the dicethrowing goes on just the same.

Maybe the Fizzer feels 'a bit knocked out with the sun', and the water for his perishing horses ninety feet below the surface; or 'things go wrong' with the old windlass, and everything depends on the Fizzer's ingenuity. The odds are very uneven when this happens—a man's ingenuity against a man's life, and death playing with loaded dice. And every letter the Fizzer carries past that well costs the public just twopence.

A drink at the well, an all-night's spell, another drink, and then away at midday, to face the toughest pinch of all—the pinch where death won with the other mailman. Fifty miles of rough, hard, blistering, scorching, 'going', with worn and jaded horses.

The old programme all over again. Twenty miles more, another spell for the horses (the Fizzer never seems to need a spell for himself), and then the last lap of thirty, the run into Anthony's Lagoon, 'punching the poor beggers along somehow'. 'Keep 'em going all night', the Fizzer says: 'and if you should happen to be at Anthony's on the day I'm due there you can set your watch for eleven in the morning when you see me coming along.' I've heard somewhere of the Pride of Harness.

Sixteen days is the time-limit for those five-hundred miles, and yet the Fizzer is expected because the Fizzer is due, and to a man who loves his harness no praise could be sweeter than that. Perhaps one of the brightest thoughts for the Fizzer as he 'punches' along those desolate Downs is the knowledge that a little before eleven o'clock in the morning Anthony's will come out, and, standing with shaded eyes, will look through the quivering heat, away into the Downs, for that tiny moving speck. When the Fizzer is late there, death will have won at the dice-throwing.

I suppose he got a salary. No one ever troubled to ask. He was expected, and he came, and in our selfishness we did not concern ourselves beyond that.

It is men like the Fizzer who, 'keeping the roads open', lay the foundation-stones of great cities; and yet when cities creep into the Never-Never along the Fizzer's mail route, in all probability they will be called after Members of Parliament and the Prime Ministers of that day, grandsons, perhaps, of the men who forgot to keep the old well in repair, while our Fizzer and the mail-man who perished will be forgotten; for townsfolk are apt to forget the beginnings of things.

Three days' spell at Anthony's, to wait for the Queensland mail-man from the 'other-side' (another Fizzer no doubt, for the bush mail-service soon culls out the unfitted), an exchange of mail-bags, and then the Downs must be faced again with the same team of horses. Even the Fizzer owns that 'tackling the Downs for the return trip's a bit sickening; haven't had time to forget what it feels like, you know', he explains.

Inside to Anthony's, three days' spell, over the Downs again, stopping for another drink at that well, along the stage 'that's a bit off', and back to the 'kid's game', dropping mail-bags in twos and threes as he goes in, and collecting others as he comes out, to say nothing of the weary packing and unpacking of his team. That is what the Fizzer had to do by half past eleven four weeks.

Elsey Station, on the Roper River, 300 miles south of Darwin, was the Gunn's home at the turn of the century. Here the Fizzer would arrive on maildays, 'never a day late, rarely an hour . . . with a cheery, "What ho, chaps! Here we are again!"'

ON THE DESERT

Any family that lives out beyond settlement faces loneliness, and needs the will to be brave against its isolation—especially in 'the centre'.

The loneliness and isolation of the workers on the Nullarbor line was exemplified on 16 October 1915 when a fettler's wife, Mrs Chambers, took her two-year-old child for a walk 'to look for rabbits' and was never seen again. When she didn't return to camp at the 231-mile peg, gangs of fettlers and black trackers set off to search for them; a motor car (a rarity in those times at that place) travelled many miles by day as well as in the dark of night in the hope that the headlamps would attract the missing pair if they were alive, but no trace was ever found of them.

They may have fallen down one of the 'blow holes' in the plain which has many limestone caves, or the woman may have lost her bearings and gone on wandering further and further away from the little outpost at the 231 and joined the skeletons of others who have disappeared without a trace in 'the centre'.

The Pickford family immigrated to Australia in the 1930s Depression. Mrs Charlotte Pickford describes their first Christmas at Quorn, South Australia:

We arrived at Quorn at Christmas, fresh from Wales where the Depression was so bad Joe had walked from one mine to another for three years and hadn't got work. He wanted a decent life for our children so we came here but when we arrived everyone told us there was no work here either.

It was December when we got to Quorn. There had been a drought for seven years. The town seemed to be in a perpetual fog of dust. It blew through to the north in the morning and back through on the way south at night. It covered everything including the food, the butter, everything. I was amazed to find they celebrated Christmas as do the English with a hot dinner with the temperature 104 in the shade.

After our meal this day there was a clap of thunder like an encore and it rained four inches in twenty-four hours. Boxing Day they were calling for men for a washaway at Willochra. 'You'll be up to your waist in water all day,' Joe was warned. Old men, boys who had never had work because of the Depression, were loaded on the train and off went Joe with his miner's gear, hobnailed boots and all. For three weeks' work he got more money than our whole family had had for three years. I saw my first five pound note. I took it to show my parents. Joe was proud. He kept saying, 'Now don't make a mistake and think that one is a one pound note. That's a five pound note.'

But there was no more work going.
Joe remembers:

Things were bad. Out of work fettlers were selling their parrots in the city. You always knew a navvy's cocky. 'You bloody bastard,' that was the extent of their repertoire. I had been brought up Chapel. I'd never heard the like before.

Then three days before the next Christmas I had a chance and took it. I'd never

'The Belle of Beltana' (South Australia) is mentioned in many an overlander's journal, but none thought to record the camel-riding lady's name.

been away from my family for Christmas. I went 600 miles up the track to Abminga. I was the only man that got off the train there. There was nothing left inside me by now. Anyway you like to look at it.

'I suppose you could do with a bit of a feed, boy,' the ganger said. He sent me to the kitchen and they gave me bacon and eggs, a better feed than I'd have at home in a twelvemonth. 'It's a bloody hard country you've come to now, lad,' the ganger said.

'It's a bloody hard country I've come from,' I told him.

On Christmas morning I missed the bells, the cards, the carols, and it was daylight at four in the morning! On Christmas Day! But this day turned me into an Australian railwayman. Our ganger, Mr J. McCourt, told us to wash up ready for Christmas dinner at midday. We went into the hut, men of half-a-dozen nations and none of us that had had it easy for a day, and there we sat down to such a feed, the like of which we'd never seen before. There was duck, turkey, goose, chicken, veal, beef, four vegies, Christmas pudd with holly on top and a bottle of drink at each man's place. When Mr McCourt came in he looked around our faces. Then he spoke to us: 'Well, here we are away out in the Never-Never and I don't suppose another table in Australia has more on it than ours so hop in boys and enjoy yourselves.' That night there was a leg of ham on the table and each man cut his own—as much as he wanted. And that night I lay in bed wondering what my kids were eating.

I never looked back from that day on.

There came a vacancy in the permanent gang at Oodnadatta and the ganger said he'd take me on. I wired my wife. 'Ship sails Thursday. Prepare to move.' This was Monday but I wanted them up in this country by the weekly train. I knew we were here to stay.

My length was from Oodnadatta down to Mt Dutton. When Charlotte arrived with the boys there hadn't been rain in that area for three years. Then it rained an inch and a half—and not only water. It rained fish. Quite big fish. Out there in the desert hundreds of miles from the sea or from a river. Talk about the Australian national dish being fish and chips! We had great feasts.

This phenomenon is, of course, not peculiar to Australia nor is this the only time it has happened inland but logical explanations of the scientists have never made it seem less than a miracle to the fish-starved people of the arid regions.

Joe Pickford, with the poetry of the Welsh valleys in him, speaks about this arid country as if it were the promised land.

When I first saw the sand hills called Big Ben, Loch Lomond, they appeared to be afire. The sun was striking them and they were striking back. And down at Irrapatana where the sand was wavering and shimmering as though on fire I thought what a magnificent land, what a country.

On Sundays Charlotte and I got dressed, dressed the children in their best clothes too, and went for a walk down to where the trees grew along the dry creek bed. We called it 'giving our clothes an airing'. Of course the wives of all railwaymen would get all dolled up to go down to see the train come in each week.

Joe Pickford was a teetotaller:

I hadn't had a drink until I was thirty-nine. In Wales we had made herb beer with nettles, dandelions, wormwood, but that was medicinal. When we came to live in the dusty dry hot inland we changed a lot of our habits. In the end I was making forty-eight bottles of home brew a week and none of non-alcoholic. Legally one must keep the alcoholic content of home brew to less than 2.1 per cent. After a while word of our brew got around—I would always take a cold bottle to the loco driver in his cab where the temperature was often 120 degrees, and all other travellers that came to us had some, even a bishop and his clerk polished off a bottle when Lottie sat them down to a lunch of home-made bread, cheese and pickled onions—and then we had a visit from a police trooper.

Above: The Long Straight—the section of the Desert Railway that stretches 297 miles without a curve, from near Ooldea to Loongana—is the longest stretch of straight railway line in the world.

Top: The gangs of workmen who built the East-West line across the desert had little machinery to make the job any easier.

Right: Christmas in the land of hard work and opportunity. In their 21 December 1889 issue, the Sydney Mail *published this illustration entitled 'The Selector's Dream', showing a selector and his family enjoying the fruits of nine years of hard work in the bush.*

He came in, hot and dusty, and said could we give him a cool drink. I'd made a charcoal cooler, a safe with the walls made of double thickness of hessian with charcoal in between the layers kept damp with water dripping down from a tray on the top. This safe had four shelves and Lottie put her butter and meat and such on three but the bottom one always had twelve bottles of home brew.

I got one out and the trooper drank it and smacked his lips and said it was good and that he'd like his wife to taste such a good brew, so Lottie wrapped a bottle up for him. Next week he returned. Lottie went straight up to him and said, 'And what did the analyst's report show, Trooper?' He grinned. 'Less than 2.1 per cent. I was happy to be able to send a report in to H.Q. and add a note that it was the best beer I've ever tasted and that such refreshment was needed in the country.'

We stored our beer under the bath out in the wash-house and one night a fettler who boarded with us had his bath but forgot the beer and seven bottles blew up under him. Bang, bang, bang, I heard it. 'My beer! He's bust my beer!' I ran out and there was beer running down the steps and out into the sand and the fettler was roaring with laughter. Lucky for him he had the door locked.

Mrs Lottie Pickford always kept goats:

First thing I was told by the old railway hands was that goats were a necessity in the bush. The milk was good and we used the kids for meat. 'Desert lamb and green peas' was a choice dish, but we usually had to hide from our visitors the fact that our lamb was kid. We had a school teacher boarding with us at Oodnadatta and he had three helpings of lamb one Sunday and he'd been drinking milk all week but when I told him it was all from the goats he gasped. I asked him how he thought a cow would survive in the pasture we could provide in the sand hills.

The railways department employed a doctor at Oodnadatta. He was the only medico for 1,400 miles, from Farina to Pine Creek. He was the dentist too. This was in the days before Flynn's Flying Doctor Service was created, and before Tregear's pedal radio was invented to make the service practicable.

Joe Pickford and the other fettlers at Oodnadatta knew the Reverend John Flynn well:

We had other ministers of course but John Flynn was different. He'd sit in the kitchen and tell us his dreams. 'I lie under the stars and wonder what I can do. There's something, I know, that can be done. People at a place a hundred miles in this direction and others two hundred miles in that and you are unable to speak to these, your nearest neighbours. Perhaps some cable—I don't know yet. There must be some way.'

The Australian Inland Mission men were immediately practical. The Reverend Partridge fitted up a utility with leather, nails and a boot-last:

'Here, let me have a look at your boots!' he'd say. He'd go out with these and four pairs of boots and a pair of shoes belonging to Mother and you'd hear him hammering away there and back he'd come and you couldn't have seen better. He taught himself how to do this because he found it was one thing he could most help the bush people with. He had other tools, he mended the leg of our kitchen table once and our gate another time.

When the creeks came down one year he couldn't get through on the track so he took his ute up on the railway line. This was pretty dangerous so the road foreman ordered auger bits put through sleepers so no one could use the bridge. When the fettlers got to the line next day they found he'd got over all right: he'd knocked all the spikes down in the opposite way to that he was travelling and driven over them.

The Commonwealth Railways seems to have had less red tape than other government railways, or perhaps it was that their lines—from Port Augusta, South Australia, across the Nullarbor to Kalgoorlie, Western Australia, and

Xmas 1880

'the Ghan' to Alice Springs—ran the Department. Santa Claus on a full-sized train is something few kids see, but he—and his wife!—were eagerly awaited in the wastelands, and physical cost wasn't counted.

SANTA RIDES THE RAILS
(in temperature of 116 degrees)

There's a group of country children waiting in the heat,
On a country platform with a sleeper for a seat,
They watch the track intently for the first sign of the train
For the railway Father Christmas is on the job again.
(S.A. Railway Institute Magazine)

Bill Crowe, Driver, Trans-Australia Line, Commonwealth Railways, writes:

We were at Wirraminna doing the inaugural run of Santa Claus to children of the railway settlements across the Nullarbor. Rose, my wife, had come to help and to cook for me. Commonwealth Railways had given us a workman's van to live in on the 'Tea and Sugar' train. It nearly rattled the insides out of us, and of course there was no air-conditioning. Rose sat there cutting up five hundredweight slabs of fruit cake into slices and bagging sweets by the hundreds and helping me blow up the thousands of balloons. We had to cook for ourselves in the van, we were kept flat out and I got into the long red cloak and white whiskers at each siding where there were kids. The heat was intense. Birds were planing in off the desert to land on the telegraph wires and falling over in exhaustion. It was 116 degrees at Wirraminna. We'd been working like steam in the van to get things ready for our arrival and when we got there the children were waiting for us at the siding. Rose hung on until the children were occupied with opening their gifts and then she began to slide to the ground. A short time in the refrigerated wagon revived her—but she did look comical packed there among the beef carcasses.

Father Christmas gets a warm welcome when he arrives on the special Christmas 'Tea and Sugar' train on the Trans-Australia line.

We began to take Santa Claus to the kids at the isolated sidings for the same reason men all over Australia on the lines back o' beyond did: these children would never see the old man with white whiskers and red hood if we didn't take him to them and we didn't want them to miss that magic.

And the kids were ready for him—for the real traditional Santa Claus, the benevolent magician. We decided that as the train wouldn't get into Wynbring until 11 pm that night we might as well go to bed as no children would be up at that hour. We gave the butcher three parcels to leave at the siding for the three children who lived there, but when the train pulled into Wynbring the butcher came running up to our wagon, 'Bill! Rose! Quick, they're waiting. The kids are waiting!'

As I dressed in my outfit I called out through the window to the children, 'I'm glad you waited up for me.' There was no reply. Rose was looking out the window and she turned and put her finger to her lips. 'They're puzzled that you should even think they might not wait,' she reprimanded me.

'Gunboat' Smith had a Lord Mayor waiting on the platform to meet him when he arrived at Kalgoorlie after one journey as Santa Claus:

We had the engine all decorated and I was in full regalia, a real dinky-di Father Christmas and a band was playing outside the station and another further down the street and twelve thousand people were up Hannan Street and I had to parade down the streets and they took me to the Railway Institute and gave me a silver cake dish engraved with 'Father Christmas 1921'.

Ron Ryan took a gift for every railway child and scores more for the non-railway and Aboriginal children.

I work on the principle that Santa Claus doesn't know the difference between railway and others and so I hand out gifts to every kid who comes in answer to our train whistle.

Out west from Port Lincoln on Eyre Peninsula it was 117 degrees when I climbed down in my red outfit at Nunjikompita. Waiting for me were seventeen kangaroo dogs and thirty-one children. I had parcels for twenty-three. In that heat and in that costume you don't do your best thinking so I calmly took the parcels my wife had done up for the next stop and handed them out too which left me short of eight gifts which gave the shopkeeper at the next stop a surprise because while the kids were waiting for me to get out one side of the train I flew out the other and galloped over to the store in my white whiskers and red dressing gown and asked him to sell me eight Christmas stockings, quick.

Out on this dry, dusty, always hot and very lonely line I take a middy for every man on the job. The department forbids drinking on the job but I over-ride that. No railwayman in his right mind would knock back a beer in that heat and I get the feeling they get nearly as much pleasure as the kids reaching up for their middy as I pull it out of my sack.

At Karkoo a few years ago, the whole school came to sing carols to me. They sang *White Christmas* and *Sleigh Bells in the Snow* while I perspired under my whiskers in the sun. I felt very benevolent. 'For this reception,' I said, 'I'll give you the day off.' The teacher was speechless but it was too late to do anything. The kids were off and away. When I returned to Port Lincoln I put in a report of the trip to the Commissioner for Railways and in return was advised that it might be as well not to let this matter of my proclaiming a school holiday get to the ears of the Minister of Education.

Yet it's likely that the word of the railway Santa Claus will hold more weight out on this line than any Minister's. I hadn't expected anyone to meet me at Thevenard when I arrived to have my breakfast, lunch and dinner all in one at 11 pm but there was the group of railway children on the platform with their mothers.

'How long have you been waiting?' I asked one woman.

'Twelve months,' was the reply. 'Twelve months, Santa Claus.'

PRIDE

Out in the uninhabited spaces of the arid lands—'out on the prairie'—as rail men say, the railwaymen considered themselves superior to others. No matter how humble his position or tasks in the service he considered himself superior by virtue of being a campaigner in 'the great family of railway workers'. On South Australia's west coast area the Government railway is run as an autonomous enterprise (whether Head Office in Adelaide knows it or not) and the men have an incomparable pride.

Claude Simmons, an old driver recalls:

I had no doubt that I was a part of a great movement that was for the good of my country. Today people laugh about that sort of feeling, but they can't take the knowledge from us that we did have something to be proud of. Peter 'Long Peter' Walsh, the ganger during construction at Minnipa, would give the children sixpence and he'd say, 'Who made the world?' and they'd say, 'God made the world'. And he'd say, 'Who built the railway?' There'd be a silence. 'I'll tell you,' Long Peter would say. 'Peter Walsh built the railway.'

To a man the old drivers, fettlers and rail men of the west coast were proud of their railways and of the service they gave to the community and, as well, of the position they'd won by sweat and toil within the Department.

Claude Simmons has stories galore:

We'd be going along on a night as dark as the inside of a fireman's glove. Our feeble kerosene lanterns had ten glow-worm power. We'd be peering out into the blackness trying to see ahead. If we ran into a sand drift we'd get our shovels out, scoop the sand out till we cleared a way for the engine. Some people today would think we must have been idiots. Were we? We had more satisfaction than any man today gets in a job. We were serving the community and knew it. There'd be a man waiting ahead in the dark at the side of the track for us. He might have come twenty, thirty miles in a buggy. He depended on us. It wasn't the dramatic things like rushing injured settlers to a doctor or bringing a baby into the world on the floor of the van or any of those things that made us feel proud. It was the everyday things.

When the line first went out to Thevenard the land was desert, just as it had been when Eyre journeyed across half a century before. The blacks had speared his mate Baxter, and the ground was so hard that Eyre couldn't bury him but left him wrapped in a blanket on the desert.

The only water here is rare surface catchment in dams. The ships that come to Thevenard for the gypsum freight brought water as ballast and this was pumped into railway tankers and we took it down the line to the settlers battling it out. Twenty-seven farmers had their own storage tanks at the sidings along the line.

We felt very sad for them. I remember one chap who used to take 12,000 gallons. This day when we came he only wanted 1,200. 'What's up?' and he told us. He'd had to cut the throats of 300 sheep. He just couldn't keep the water up to them. He'd killed them yesterday. I asked a German farmer near Penong if he ever tried to conserve water. He walked me half a mile to a huge underground tank he'd dug out five years ago. In those five years it had gathered two and a half inches of water.

Above: The arrival of a water train during the drought of 1882. The railways moved outback with settlement, and in times of drought, flood and fire were a life-line for isolated communities.

Left: The opening of the railway to North Wagga: 1. The arrival of the ministerial train. 2. The town bridge over the Murrumbidgee. 3. The banquet. 4. The Ball. 5. Scene on the line. 6. Loading the first bale of wool. 7. Scene at the Mittagong 'refreshment' station.

Above: The 'water special' to Broken Hill, 1951.

Above centre: Smoke-oh for a fettling gang at Deep Well, South Australia.

Top: A gang of fettlers working a 'quad' — a quadracycle.

Top right: A construction gang laying the track at the start of the East-West line.

Soon after that the railway brought a pipeline over from Port Lincoln. We did that ourselves, railwaymen, no one else, and the desert bloomed like a garden. It was beautiful water, fit to mix with whisky.

The railways on this peninsula opened up the country. The year the railways opened in 1909 the first big clipper ships came into Port Lincoln and the famous grain race to Europe was commenced, all because we were there to bring the barley, wheat and oats to the dockside.

People those days put the railway up on a pedestal. Few people today know what railways did to open up the country and keep the man on the land but the old timers remember.

At the Dog Gate (on the dingo-proof fence stretching down through South Australia) where we stopped to open the gate for the train to go through we'd find Kimbidgina Kate had been there before us. On the gate post she'd leave a billy of tea and a serviette of fresh baked scones. At Drekurmi Crossing where a settler used to pick up mail we'd left in a tin on the way down, there'd be a jar of cream and a bottle of milk for us on the way up.

Clarrie Liddy was a guard on the line:

We developed a lot of hot boxes out on the desert lines. It was nothing to look out of your brake van and see anything up to ten trucks red hot and smoking. Hot boxes were a regular problem on the arid semi-desert lines and on long slow uphill hauls. The signs were a smell of burning or a trail of smoke as the bearings heated through lack of lubrication. Sometimes the truck would have caught fire before the hot box was detected. Cargoes have caught fire this way on many lines and there's a line of commendation in the records on most occasions for the guard who risked his skin to uncouple the truck or rescue its freight. These things happened too far away from civilisation for anyone to know of the heroism and devotion to duty of men on the lonely lines. On the Eyre Peninsula we would try to drag them back to be repaired at Cummins. We've hauled fifteen of them at a time, creeping along dead slow, watching them all the way.

Bill Critchley had a van with brasses in it and he'd go to a siding where we'd left these hot boxes and there he'd camp, miles from anywhere, and repair them. What a lonely life. Who would you get to go out living like that today?

If you got a hot box on a truck you could shunt the truck into a siding but on the engine you could do nothing but wait for it to cool down. Sometimes we could pack it up with oil and go on. There were some good men out on the desert lines. They had to maintain their own locos hundreds of miles from anywhere. There'd be a wheel getting chewed off on their loco and they'd stuff oily waste down it. One driver out on the Eyre Peninsula went to a pub and asked the publican for some dripping. Next trip the publican charged him for it. 'That was good dripping. I wouldn't have given it to you if I'd known you were going to stuff it down your hot box.'

A man knew he had responsibilities. When we left Port Lincoln we headed into the blue and no one heard of us until we steamed back again days later and then they said, 'So, you're back, eh?'

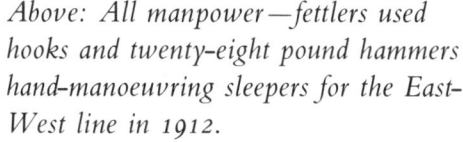

Above: All manpower—fettlers used hooks and twenty-eight pound hammers hand-manoeuvring sleepers for the East-West line in 1912.

Left: A ballasting gang at work south of the Finke River on the Ghan, the line from Port Augusta to Alice Springs.

Below left: Payday. The paymaster still comes once a fortnight to pay the isolated railway gangs.

THE WASHAWAY

George Williams was a driver on the line to Alice Springs:

They were dry years while the line was being constructed from Oodnadatta to Alice Springs. Camels were used to bring water up to the navvies. In the year it went through, 1929, we had Christmas at Alice Springs and there was a thunderstorm and it poured. The Todd River came down. We were floodbound for a week. We got the line patched up and got away but no other train got back in for five months.

We had rounded up all the unemployed we could find at Alice Springs and got to work. The water was moving at a terrible speed. A little kid had got stranded in the middle of the river on a tree and Jack Penglaze, a short little fellow with us, decided to try to swim in and grab the kid. He went in and the current got him and swept him down the river. He got out. Then he got us to tie a rope round him and he went upstream and got swept down and grabbed the kid and we pulled on the rope till we got them to the bank. The kid was all right but Penglaze was nearly skun. The poor cow was down for days, an awful mess.

This patching up was one of the pioneering jobs in rail repair in this area. Flash floods are a hazard that one must expect in this part of the country. Politicians get up in the House and raise Cain every time a train gets stranded by floods here—every several years or so—but they never say where the money would come from to build a track that would withstand such intermittent phenomena. We learnt early that nothing permanent could be done until the water went down but that we could do a safe temporary job in some circumstances.

In 1929 we put in pig-sties at the washaways for nearly a hundred miles down as

Anxious moments for everyone as the Adelaide Express edges its way through floodwaters at Murtoa.

far as Bundoomah. [A pig-sty is a criss-crossing of sleepers beneath the rails to replace temporarily the earthworks or bridges that have been swept away.] On the way back up to Alice Springs to get the train out we had to build the bloody pig-sties again: the floods had come down again and swept them away. The navvies had to struggle downstream and collect the sleepers and set them up again. The track had a top on her like an ocean wave, no ballast under it, but the train crept over; and on down south it went.

For five months gangs worked trying to rebuild the line before they could bring another train over it. The rails were good and the sleepers okay but in one part the original route was not good, so this old ganger broke the road and put a deviation in and started construction and this took more material so he hired camels to drag gear around to him. By this time the water had gone and the desert re-asserted itself. Sand hills made it a terrible tough job.

One of the worst washaways on that line was in 1938. At Margaret Siding they used 3,000 new sleepers and 300 old sleepers packed together for pig-sties with rails spiked to them. The fettlers were brought from gangs north and south. They travelled and slept in cattle trucks. Not that there was much sleep. They rested only while being taken from one washaway to the next. Their cook had a stove set up in one end of a flat top with a tarpaulin over his tucker and a water tank hooked on behind.

We had a passenger train on the line and these navvies built the line up ahead of us. We left the passengers in a camp and we went off to help the navvies by day. The passengers took it well. The stewards and cooks looked after them and the people of the outback were marvellous. There were barbecues and dances at night and sing-songs round a log fire.

Of course the navvies saw none of this. They just went on sweating it out on the washaways. One day one of the passengers made his way up to where we were toiling. We were nearly finished, we had it by the neck. This passenger worked on a Melbourne paper and he took a photo of the men resting. I was pretty mad. I threw a shovel to him. 'Have a go,' I said. He tried but he couldn't shovel salt into a boiled egg. I tried to teach him but he never did learn.

One year between Oodnadatta and Finke there were washaways before and after us. That time we couldn't get supplies up so we had to have food flown out and parachuted down to passengers.

And all the while the navvies toiled on, re-building bridges and tracks with nothing but picks, shovels and their own skill and knowledge. There were no engineers running up and down giving orders in those days. Those old gangers did it all and all anyone ever called them was 'a navvy'.

Above: Checking for a washaway on the flooded North–South line south of Marree, South Australia.

Above middle: Gangers inspect the damage after 1932 floodwaters swept the locomotive off the line at Alice Creek, en route to Alice Springs.

Top: The flood-devastated Briagalong Bridge across the Avon River in East Gippsland, Victoria. The navvy's nightmare—fire—leaves fewer reconstruction problems than floods do.

Left: Navvies on the line to Alice Springs construct a 'pigsty' of sleepers to bridge a washaway after flash floods swept down from the usually dry Finke River.

THE DRIVER

Right: The pioneering spirit is still as strong today as it ever was. A family who remains to run a property in time of drought cannot be less than courageous.

When the Trans-Australia line across the Nullarbor was first broached in the Senate it was jeered at, and the *Argus*, the most powerful newspaper in Victoria, ridiculed the idea and continued for years to refer to the project as the 'Desert Railway'.

While some jeered and others remained indifferent a small tough army of men got on with the job of building one of the world's greatest railways. The terrain, the isolation, climate and conditions in which they worked repelled observers and little has been chronicled of their campaign. Within a few months of their having left, the story of their travail disappeared along with evidence of their having been there. Their memorial, the long line they built, stretches silver and primitive across the red sand for 900 miles and the ribald boozing, gambling, sweating but hardest-working of all Australian navvies have been all but forgotten.

One of the few men, probably the only one, who worked on the construction from the beginning and who later became a loco driver and took many a train over the line he helped to build, is Bill Twilly. He started off on the construction of the East-West line in 1914. 'Shovelling sand for 10s 6d a day on stale bread, oily butter, salt beef and a bit of rice', he wrote in 1968.

It was a tough job. I doubt if we will ever again see men work under the conditions the men on the Trans-Australia did with horses, camels, shovels and picks. Remember that on this 900 miles not one stream of water was crossed, no man lived and the land was so flat no tunnel had to be built, no bridge across gulches. We lived in tent-houses—sometimes wood part way up with a canvas top, sometimes a cutting in the earth with a tent above that. Willy-willies when they came swept in and blew the top off these houses. I saw a man near our tent-house left standing among his furniture with his roof gone in the wind of the willy-willy.

Even as the line was built we had to use sand scoops fastened on to the front of a slow-moving train to clear the sand off the line.

When we couldn't make bread we had damper and brownies. We kept flour, baking powder, pepper, salt on hand in case we were cut off and of course vinegar and onions for turkeys. We used to get about two wild turkeys a week. We'd rub them with vinegar and put an onion inside them and hang them for a bit then cook them in a kerosene tin. They were very good eating. We caught most of them up Wirripa way near where the rocket range is today. We kept our food cool by digging a hole in the ground, lining it with clinkers from the engine around a kerosene tin. We made jellies and icecream in that out there in the above-century temperatures.

Port Augusta just before the beginning of the 1914 war got to be a busy town as the men started to come for the construction jobs. There weren't enough houses and the men who brought their families home-built their own camps out on the sand hills a mile out of town. The single men lived in tents.

There were a few settlers scattered over the Nullarbor near Pimba and they'd come with camels hitched to their buggies to see the railway progress. The ladies

would sit there in long white dresses and big hats. Lots of people thought camels would be more important than the new cars away from the railhead. I saw there an Afghan sell eight camels for £100 each.

Few of the settlers were doing more than live on their overdraft. The railway at Pimba gave work to the men and their horses that had been driven off the land up Quorn way when the sand rolled in and hid their land, fences, houses, everything in the big drought that was all over Australia in 1914.

They'd never known it easy and now they knew it harder still. Some said railway work was better than farming, not so lonely. And it wasn't like working for a hard boss. A good ganger on these lines would overlook a lapse of a day off on the booze or crook with a hangover. When a man turned up next morning he'd say, 'Now let's get a day's work out of you,' and by God you gave it to him.

Prime Minister Andy Fisher came through Pimba on his way across to Perth to go to England. At that time there were only two women there. My wife and Mrs Foley, the wife of the ganger Bob Foley. The men had been celebrating and then brawling and there was skin off and black eyes and the place lived up to the name the men gave it of 'the Dardanelles'. The line hadn't linked up with that being built across from Western Australia and Andy Fisher crossed the gap on a camel. I often wonder what he thought of us. Of course he didn't see the real Pimba.

As the line moved out it got harder to work. Men shifted camp every couple of weeks to keep near the work. A butcher, bread and stores van came out to us once a week with fresh provisions, but we had nowhere to store food, no ice or anything and in that heat, often over 100 degrees in the shade, the bread was a rock in one day and we had to eat the meat the day we got it. If the train was late the men would be grizzling, 'Where's the b— tea and sugar train?' It was often late, particularly after the line got out past the 100-mile post, so there were many calls for the Tea and Sugar train and the name stuck and when later the line was finished and railway people lived beside the track the train that took their supplies just continued to be called the Tea and Sugar and it is to this day.

Later when I began to work on engines I'd be on the Tea and Sugar train and we'd take a long time to get out to the railhead and in the dark we'd come along near where we knew there was a camp and blow the whistle and out they would come with hurricane lamps from their tents, men and women with sugar bags to carry their foodstuffs in.

The butcher's van had a section for live sheep, for slaughtering, a counter as a shop and at one end was the butcher's bed, but as we stopped every half hour or so at a camp I don't think he got much sleep.

We had a few second-hand engines from the New South Wales Railways to build the line and had only bore water to use and this ate away the copper plates and the tubes in the boilers. The tubes would then leak and we would be hours late, steam blowing over our faces and into our fire preventing it from getting up more steam and we'd have to stop to take on more water and when we'd eventually get back to Port Augusta they'd be waiting for our engine to take the next train out. Boilermakers worked around the clock, twenty-four hours a day, shift work and all hard labour. If they had time before the engine went out they'd wait till it cooled down and then wash the boiler out with sea water and get the shale out that the bore water had deposited. This deposit, when we had to work the engine up a steep grade, would cause the engine to prime and we'd get wet steam instead of dry and we'd roll back and make another run at the grade and often as not finish up out of water. We used to carry a long rod to enable us to fit a steel plug in the end of water tubes burst in the boiler and we could get the engine home on this.

The engines were so poor and the bore water so bad for them that loco depots were put along the line, the first at Pimba, 114 miles out. They were staffed by a fitter and mate, a boilermaker and mate and a fuel man to coal the engine. There were loco depots at roughly each 100 miles—Kingoonya, Tarcoola, Barton and Cook. Some of the crews brought their families out to these depots. It was hard living for a woman.

The navvies on the line had a hard life and most of them said, 'A day's work for a day's pay'. If there was a loafer in the gang the rest of them told him off. They lived in tents with an old wire stretcher, water in a kerosene tin, no shower but a 'half-

Left: Drought and long dry stages have been the lot of overlanders in the outback from the beginning.

Jack Wollard, the only ganger who saw out the building of the East-West line from beginning to end, 1913–17.

Right top: The Long Straight stretches for 297 miles across the Nullarbor — 'treeless' — Plain.

Right middle: Horse-drawn sandscoops called 'tumbling Tommies' cleared the way for the rails to be laid for the Trans-Australia line.

Right bottom: East-West line navvies alongside a trench they are excavating with a pipe-trenching plough drawn by a team of donkeys.

and-half' bath each weekend. For this you got a kerosene tin of water. You put a bag on the dirt floor beside it, put your right leg in and washed that side of your body, then stepped out and put your left leg in and washed that side. Then you used the water to wash your clothes. That was Sunday work.

For the other six days of the week the navvy built a mile of railway every day — an unparalleled feat in construction work. He sat for midday dinner in the sun with a billy of tea and a hunk of bread and salt beef for crib. After work he'd wash in a tin dish of water and go over for tea, a kerosene tin of black tea on the end of the table, some poor greasy soup, boiled beef, cabbage and potatoes and rice. The dining room was made of bags sewn together. Getting near Tea and Sugar day most camps were down to damper for food. When the navvy got tired of this life he'd clear off to Port Augusta for a few days' booze and sometimes get run in a few times and then he'd go to the office and get a pass to ride on the train and go back to work.

When my wife and two children came out with me to Wirraminna I put up two tents for us, we had a couple of stretchers, bedding, table, two chairs, frying pan and billycan. I dug a hole in the ground for a fire and hung the billy over it for a cup of tea and said, 'Well Mum, that's home'. There was no other woman there. A mile away was a blacks' camp, about a hundred of them with dogs, and they'd come around our camp to cadge food but they'd be lucky if they got any because we only got ours once a week. We only had bore water and not much of it. I had a camp oven which was handy for roasting meat and cooking damper. There was nothing to do at nights. We'd sit around the fire and bake a couple of potatoes in their cases.

There was no doctor. The men had a bottle of pain killer, 2s a bottle and you took a few drops in water when you got sick in the stomach and you had Epsom salts for the weekend. I had a little flask of brandy, eucalyptus and olive oil and I'd mix them in a bottle for us as embrocation. When the children got a cold I'd warm the bottle in warm water and rub their chests and backs and put them to bed in the tents. When they were a bit sick I would warm a little water over the candle, put it in a spoon with a little sugar and brandy and we didn't trouble the doctor for twenty years.

As the line moved further out we began to run coal and water trains out for the engines. Soon, as the line got well into the desert lands, we were full time trying to keep water and coal up to them. The further the line got out the harder it was on our old engines and we rarely got them out and back without trouble. The stables along the line for the 200 horses that were worked then came in handy. We always carried a bag of horse manure or sawdust and if the tubes started to leak we forced water and manure into the boiler through the injector and it would force the leaks to take up and help get the train home.

Some of the drivers were hard doers. Bob Castling was driving the loco for track-laying out past Wirraminna and he got two weeks' holiday and he went to Sydney. After he had been gone three weeks the driver sent to relieve him went in to Port Augusta and made a fuss about being in the bush too long. 'Sack Castling,' our loco superintendent shouted. 'Sack him.' So out the line we heard Bob was sacked. The night he got back one of our drivers met him. 'You've been sacked, Bob,' he told him. That was the least of his worries. He'd spent all his money in Sydney and now he was broke. But he walked straight in to George Gahn, the loco boss — with the clerk shouting to him that he'd been sacked — and he said, 'Well George, what is it to be? Sydney or the bush?' George Gahn grinned and said, 'Get a pass and get out to Wirraminna. Now!'

I fired for this driver and got to know him well. When he got married he took his wife shopping and told her all she'd need to buy was a washing tub and a scrubbing board. 'I've got White Rose furniture ready for you.' White Rose furniture was kerosene cases nailed together to make cupboards, chairs, tables and beds.

By this time the old engines wouldn't get us back to Port Augusta but had to be repaired at Pimba so we could carry on. This day two engines were in trouble so they made a double-header out of it, two engines on one train, and set off to take the train with the pay car out to the camps. Arthur Jones, one of the Pom drivers — there were five of them brought out from England and India — he was driving one and Barney McBride the other. At Wirrappa they had to pick up a truck. The guard got off to shunt and he needed a little bump to get his truck to couple up but the

Above: Joyce's camel team and most of the township of Kalgoorlie gathered to meet the first train from Port Augusta.

Top: The Trans-Australia line brought water to the dry wastes en route. Camel teams wait at the rail head to fill up.

foreman saw the green light and said, 'Right away, Arthur!' He whistled the second engine 'Right away!' and off they went, leaving the guard and the trucks behind them at Wirrappa. There's a bit of a rise out from there and Arthur Jones said to his fireman, 'By jove we're going well. Old Barney's putting in well.' On the engine behind, Barney was saying to his fireman, 'Arthur's doing a good job tonight.' When they got to Birthday Siding Arthur was oiling his engine and one of the men from the gang came up and said, 'Where's the pay van?' 'On the other end of the train,' Arthur said. 'No, it's not. I've been there.' Arthur said, 'It's a long train. You didn't walk far enough.' When the Station Master came up and told him he'd lost half his train Arthur said in his Pom accent, "Aye, there's allus summat happening aht here."

Another hard doer on the construction was Ginger Heffernan, ganger or a plate-laying gang. He was at Wynbring putting in a loop line when the train came along, with a truck that had a hot box. They shunted it off into a siding. This truck was loaded with chaff for the horses at the works at the head of the road. When the train arrived at the head the horse drivers came looking for the feed for their horses—so they said. But it was something else in the truck they wanted. When they found it had been shunted off they refused to work and they encouraged the navvies to stop work too. They said they couldn't work horses that were not being fed. Captain Saunders, the civil engineer, got busy and found the chaff was at Wynbring and when he found Ginger Heffernan had his gang there he got in touch with Ginger and asked him if he would get his gang to transfer the chaff into another truck and have it sent on. Ginger got his gang into the truck working and half way down the chaff they came on a case of whisky and they told Heffernan. 'Well,' said Ginger, 'you know what to do with it.' A little while later Captain Saunders came through on a section car to attend to the strike and he stopped to see how the transfer was going. He took one look at the gang and came back to Ginger and said, 'Heffernan! Your men are drunk!' 'Captain,' said Heffernan, 'you're a bloody observant man.' Next day Ginger said to his men, 'Come on. You had a spell yesterday. We'll do some work today.' And they worked all the harder for having had a spell.

Another day a surveyor came along to look at the pegs and his car stopped near where Ginger's gang were plate-laying and the driver filled his petrol tank from a tin he carried and he put the tin down and as these tins are very handy for a water tin one of the gang took it. When the surveyor came back the driver said, 'One of the gang stole our petrol tin'. So the surveyor went to Ginger and said, 'One of your gang has stolen our empty petrol tin'. Ginger goes back to the gang and says, 'Line up, all you men'. So they lined up there on the sand beside the track, some leaning on picks, some leaning on shovels. 'Now,' said Ginger Heffernan. 'This man has lost a petrol tin and I am going to search each one of you.' The surveyor was so annoyed he got in his car and drove off.

In construction days there was always someone sly-grogging and before the train left Port Augusta for the head of the line they would hide their grog in with the goods in the trucks and get it out when they reached the gang. There was only one old carriage on the construction train and some would have to travel in the trucks. There was often trouble that way. The worst trouble though was to make it go farther. That was really bad stuff. At the 125-mile camp a chap used to make beer with hops and used to put a few pennies in it to make it work.

This 125-mile camp was the worst of all. It was in a hollow, 300 men were camped there, there was no hygiene or sanitation. The butcher killed his sheep there beside the tent boarding houses and flies in the thousands were there. We could smell it as we crept down the slope into the hollow with our hand brakes hard on. There was a long camp made of bags. That was the gambling school. On pay day men would start with two-up; when it came dark they went into the bag camp and there was a long table down the centre and kerosene lamps and they'd play dice all night and go on until they were broke and then they'd go back to work again. Those that won would catch the train and go away for a few days' holiday; some would get on the drink and the next day they'd be desperate for a bottle and the sly-grog chaps would come out. They'd sell grog for 20s a bottle, a lot of money when the pay was about 12s a day. Most times sly-grog was 15s a bottle: a mixture of whisky, metho and water.

Living was rough as well as tough. Any camp without women is bad but this was a worse loneliness than most because of the country these men had to live and work in. Some went mad. Sammy Morgan cut his throat and his wrists in the DTs, another man came into a tent and said the loneliness was killing him and someone said, 'Oh go and cut your throat,' and he went out and when he returned he said, 'Look, I've done it'. And he had. They wrapped rags around it and took him in to Port Augusta next day and he lived.

The horse stables were opposite the camp and they attracted the flies too. Fever broke out and each day men were going down with it. We took them to Port Augusta and when the hospital was full up we put them in an old carriage shed and a little room in the main street and this was used as a hospital for fever chaps as they came down from the line. Sometimes they lay out in the paddock on their stretchers. When they got too bad they took them to the hospital. A few died.

Above: The Trans-Australia . . . 'on this 900 miles not one stream of water was crossed, no man lived and the land was so flat no tunnel had to be built . . .'

Top: Construction material follows the Trans-Australia line out west.

There was a policeman stationed at each of the big camps to keep law and order, but like an old mining town these camps had a law of their own. If one of the men was no good the others got on to him. They were used to the bush, work and sleep and talking to the flies. All the same, day in, day out. Some of the men had been most of their lives like this, working on building railways with contractors, in other states. A lot of them had worked in Western Australia. They didn't need a policeman to keep order in their camps and most of the policemen knew it and got on well with the navvies but one policeman stationed at the head of the road tried to alter their ways by stopping the two-up. He was warned to get away from the school. But he would interfere. Next time they moved camp to keep up with the railhead they loaded all the tents except his. The ganger told them they must load the police tent. They said he could load his own. The ganger talked them into loading it but the train had only gone a couple of miles along the way when a fire broke out: the policeman's tent was in flames.

They were hard years yet even while you were battling through you felt you were in the middle of history. I had forty-four years on the railways and mostly saw only the hard years but I did get a few of the years of comforts before I left—rest houses with refrigerators and beds made up with sheets ready for you and flywire doors—everything.

Above: The navvy wields his twenty-eight pound hammer to drive the spikes into the final rail on the East-West railway, 17 October 1917.

Above right: Women and children joined the men in camp settlements on the building of the world's greatest engineering feat of its time—the East-West railway.

Right: Midway between Kalgoorlie and Port Augusta on the old Trans-Australia was the Tivoli Boarding House, where passengers could get hot pies, a cuppa and even a 'half-and-half' bath in a tin tub.

THE SWAGGIE TEACHER

There are parts of this continent that remained primitive and called for a pioneering spirit long after the city dwellers lost interest in the outback. In 1964 when the Queen pinned the MBE on Ernest Tambling, it was for being 'the Swaggie Teacher'.

This man was unique. He was an itinerant school teacher whose students were the children of railway workers down the length of the Northern Australia line of the Commonwealth Railways—from Darwin to Larrimah, 'Tammie' taught the kids, European, Chinese and Aboriginal.

I was only twenty-five when I came to the Territory from Queensland. A very young twenty-five. I went down the railway to find children who would need my teaching and I saw a way of life I'd never seen or heard of before. A friend back in Queensland had asked me to let him know what life was like in the Territory so I wrote and told him. Everything. And that was a lot. A month later I opened the *North Queensland Register*, the paper that used to come to Darwin in those days and there was my letter, under my name. They hadn't left out anything.

I didn't know what to do. I knew the locals would all have seen it. I thought of those tough fettlers down the line. I set off down towards them in the train. Not out of bravery. I just couldn't think clearly and it was the day to go anyway.

The first family, at the fifty-seven mile peg, were the Flynns. Nellie, a coloured woman, was married to Tom, an Irish fettler, and I was to teach three of their children. When I jumped off the moving train Tom was there to steady me. He shook my hand. 'You're the first ___ that had the courage to write about us as we are while you're still with us,' he said.

So I began my work. I travelled in the guard's van. I had my books packed in one kerosene tin, my change of clothes in another. When I got near my destination I'd throw them out, then my bike, then I'd jump.

My job was to go from house to house, teach the kids, set lessons at night which I'd correct when I'd return on my way back up the line. Most parents welcomed the chance to have their kids taught, but at Stapleton one father wouldn't let me in the door. 'I don't want any bloody school teacher hanging round my place. My wife can teach my children all they need.' I later found out he had seven daughters and wasn't going to trust no rattler-jumping foot-loose school teacher with them.

I went 280 miles down the line. Short distances I rode my bike along the clearing under the telegraph wires. Otherwise I climbed on board the train. I had a special permit to pull up any train at any time, even the pay train.

I got to know the crew well, I got to know every bump on the track. I even got to know the train well. I learnt to drive the engine, act as guard. I'd do the shunting while the guard got his meal and often signed the ticket for the staff (the 'safe working' staff without which the train could not proceed).

If I was camping overnight with the train I'd doze off at the side of the track with the crew. The lepers would be chained to the wheels of the truck further up. I'd have a yarn with them. I was never afraid to work among the lepers. I later taught many lepers. Seven children in one week were taken from my class at Bagot to go to a lazaret. Every time I got a brown spot I took particular notice of it, but that's only taking precautions.

The old Travelling School of the NSW Department of Public Instruction was funded by two well-known English public schools, Eton and Harrow.

Once I was camped under the fig tree at fettler George Close's place about a mile from the line. The Closes were camped under two big banyans and were building a cottage. I knew Maude was looking after black Paddy Bradshaw who had a sore leg. 'Properly sore, Missus,' he told her and she washed and dressed it. This day Paddy came at daylight, usually he came at night. Maude stared at him in the light. Before he set off for the track George said to her, 'What made you go white?' 'Paddy's got leprosy.' She'd seen the leonine brows some believe you can recognize a leper by. They sent for a doctor. He had come by the time I was next down the track to teach the children. 'He's riddled with leprosy.' He wouldn't last long. Nothing would stop it. 'Burn all his clothes when he goes.'

'You tell him, George,' I could hear Maude in the night.

'No, Maude. I couldn't do that.'

'I can't either.'

So George took him down to Brock's Creek on the quad and the doctor took him on the train to the leprosarium. He died three weeks later.

It was a scourge in those days but I always thought malaria was worse. You saw people sitting all over down the line with a rag dipped in vinegar over their forehead, vague with fever. It came with 'the fever winds' in April. Len Scott the guard was good to these people—he'd rustle up some quinine for them.

None of my young pupils seemed to get it. They were a tough bush-bred lot and I had to become a part of the life that was lived wherever I threw my swag off. They come up to me now in the street in Darwin, grown men and women that I taught down the permanent way when they were children. I was proud of most of them.

One boy I taught, Harry Chan, became Lord Mayor of Darwin, the first Chinese to have this position in Australia.

Fettler George Close and his wife Maude remember the young Queenslander Ernest Tambling, when he first arrived in the Territory:

George got his first good job in 1924, painting the railway bridge at Adelaide River. We lived in the big shed then with our three children. It had been a refreshment room until then with sly-grog on the side.

Then we rode out to have a look at seventy-four square miles of land for lease. Tambling, the teacher, came with us to have a look. He was camped in the old station house at Burrindie to teach our children. 'What are you going to call it?' 'The Banyans,' I said. George asked why and I said, 'You would have called it Railway Rest or Points Place or something.' I ran the property while George went off on the railway each day and we worked together at the weekend. Tammy would come over and camp under the tree while he was teaching the kids from then on.

He'd run the mile to the railway line and sprint up and down waiting for the train. 'What's the silly b___ doing?' the ganger asked George one day. 'He calls it his Constitutional,' said George. 'Ah! He'll get over that.'

He did. The Territory and the railway life changed Tammy so Queensland would never know him again.

Other states had travelling teachers, usually 'self-reliant, single men' able to 'ride and drive and doctor a horse, mend a wheel . . . and, if threatened by fire or flood . . . able to extricate himself and his boy and save His Majesty's property.' Queensland had seventeen travelling teachers by 1916, all travelling in buggies and visiting each isolated family four times a year. Figures for 1913 show that 846 families with 1,893 children were visited by the travelling teachers, who covered 60,000 miles in Queensland for that year.

Off to school. Sometimes teachers travelled to outback children; sometimes the children travelled to them.

45

THE GREATEST OF THEM ALL

Nellie Flynn of Rum Jungle, 'the greatest of them all', as the *News* of Darwin called her, has a spirit that set her off on the *News* Walkabout of 1969, when she was aged eighty-seven. Number 66 in the field of 595 walkers, she was game to try the fifteen-and-a-half mile walk in the heat.

Nellie is the widow of Tom Flynn, a railway ganger half a century ago (see p. 46). The couple and their family were used as characters in Xavier Herbert's book, *Capricornia*. Herbert, then known as Fred, was a fettler in Flynn's gang and Flynn became the 'Mick O'Pick' in the novel.

The annual Walkabout—which was started in 1961 by 'walking Jimmy Wadsworth'—has been Nellie's big day out since that year. The start is from the old Fourteen Mile Peg out from Darwin, 25,000 metres (about fifteen-and-a-half miles by the time they get through Darwin to the Oval).

The rules are:

6.30 am: boys and girls under 12 years of age start off as do pioneer men and women; 6.40: veteran men, and boys and girls 12–15; 6.50 am: senior women, girls 15–18; 7.30 am: senior men.
Competitors must WALK and not RUN or LOPE at any stage of the race.
Competitors may take refreshments *en route*, also receive 'wipe downs', but pacing is out.
To qualify for certificates walkers must reach the finishing line by 11.30 am.

These happy, game and determined people set off 'along the bitumen' in a walk that was once 'just a stroll' to Nelly.

Fabulous walking grandmother Nellie Flynn scored a great cheer when she left the starting line at 6.30 am and at 87 she was still going along steadi.y at the RAAF base (a few miles out of town) when she was persuaded to ride in so that she could be at the presentation ceremony.

Nellie had been in the first walk in 1961. She had bought a new dress and hat for the second walk in 1962 when she read that she 'was ill and would not be walking'. Nellie bounced up to Darwin and into the newspaper office. 'What's this about me being sick?' she asked. This voluble bundle of warm energy said, 'I won the married ladies' race at the picnic last week. My third year in a row. Fifty yards.' She had decided that for this year's marathon she would carry something lighter. 'In 1961 they say my bag of water and a few biscuits was too heavy.' That year a special award was introduced for pioneer walkers, the Nellie Award. 'Fabulous Nellie Flynn plodded doggedly on to wipe half an hour off her time last year. She finished in well under five hours, an extraordinary 3 mph walk for an 82-year-old pioneer.

After the race Nellie is usually invited to the Residence (the 'Government House') of Darwin where she sips tea and nibbles biscuits while other invited walkers down a cold beer.

Above: Nellie, aged 87, in the finery she wore at the presentation ceremony in 1969 for Darwin's annual fifteen-and-a-half mile Walkabout.

Top: Nellie Flynn and her husband Tom, back in the days when Ganger Flynn became the 'Mick O'Pick' of Xavier Herbert's novel, Capricornia.

THE OVERLAND TELEGRAPH

Building the Overland Telegraph from Port Augusta, South Australia to Darwin was one of the greatest events in Australian history—an epic of pioneering adventure and a triumph of tenacity. Completed in 1872, this arduous undertaking combined the hardships, trials and fatalities that were inevitable in any great work of that age. Men, working in extremely adverse conditions, combined their endeavours in a way that was an inspiration to their countrymen. Their surveying gave birth to new towns: Darwin and Alice Springs, Rum Jungle and Charlotte Waters. The strand of wire they attached to 36,000 poles for 1,973 miles, made it possible to send or receive messages from Europe in a matter of minutes as compared with the months taken by steamship.

The Franco-Prussian war of July 1870–January 1871 had been fought and ended before the small garrison at Darwin knew it had begun. Closer to Asia than they were to any settlement in Australia, they had been ten months without mail. This may not have mattered—apart from the added burden to the great isolation—because Darwin had in those years little to communicate in return. What was truly a disadvantage was that no part of Australia was connected at any point with a telegraph or cable system to any other nation in the world. The country was in the outer darkness; news sent by ship was two months old when it arrived. This was certainly an improvement on the five or six months that a passage from England had been in sailing ships, but it was still a sorry state of affairs for a land whose gold and pastoral sales, for the past twenty years, had been of importance on the European market. Thirteen thousand miles isolated the new land from the old. As ships dropped anchor in Australian ports newsmen hurried on board to learn the news—already two months old. Other countries, by the 1860s, had telegraph and knew of world events minutes after they happened, and Australia wanted this swift communication herself.

The Suez Canal had opened in September 1868, and a telegraph cable was laid from Suez to Aden and from there to Bombay. Darwin was founded as a permanent town on 5 February 1869 and it was seen as only a hop, skip and a jump across islands to link the new northern town with the land cable in India—which meant being 'linked with the world!' as newspaper headlines screamed.

The London-based British-Australian Telegraph company (companies involved with the manufacture of the cable stood to make immense profit) wrote offering to bring the cable ashore at Port Darwin. But the greatest task would be to string a line from Port Augusta over much unexplored land to the northern post.

It could be said that a whole state was heroic in deciding to perform this most remarkable task: South Australia, with a population of only 184,546 and no goldfields wealth, decided to bridge the unknown. Six men lost their lives, and hundreds of men suffered before the work was done. The

Left: The planting of the first pole of the OT at Port Darwin was an historic occasion for the entire population of newly-founded Port Darwin who attended in tropical white.

Left top: The Gulnare *photographed at the OT camp at Southport, Port Darwin.*

Left below: *Captain Sweet's photograph of the original telegraph station at Port Darwin.*

Northern Territory was under the jurisdiction of South Australia; communication was by ship as much of the inland was unknown and thought to be impregnable. A voyage from Adelaide to Darwin around the coast took six to eight weeks. Four months could elapse before a reply to correspondence in either direction could be received.

When talk of the impending work began, the government schooner *Gulnare* set off from Adelaide in April 1870 with the first resident and his family for the Territory and arrived in Port Darwin at the end of June. They were welcomed by a handful of men with their wives and children who had taken up land a short time before. At 4 pm on 15 September of that year, the entire population gathered to watch 'the planting of the first pole'. All dressed in tropical whites, they witnessed the shiny, peeled ironwood pole hoisted, 'In the name of her most gracious Majesty, Queen Victoria'. The next day work began.

It was a stupendous endeavour for the times. The British Australian Telegraph Company (London) agreed to lay a submarine cable from Java on condition that a land-line be completed from Port Augusta to Port Darwin by 1 January 1872, with heavy penalty rates for failure. That left just over fifteen months to cross the 'perilous and virtually uninhabited' expanse that until 1862 had been considered uncrossable. (In 1859–62 John McDouall Stuart had disproved the theories of 'an inland sea', but no track north had been blazed by 1870.)

South Australia undertook the challenge for two reasons: to earn the transit revenue on all cable messages to the eastern colonies, and to open overland communication with the Northern Territory, her colony.

The task was divided into three sections. The southern section was through semi-arid but pastoral country and gave no great trouble. The central section through arid, unimproved country caused great hardship but was done in time, but the northern section presented problems that called for superhuman effort. An enthusiastic worker, Alfred Giles, kept a journal and recorded 'their heroic struggles against told and untold difficulties in exploring unknown lands and in beating a track for generations to follow, expand and extend.'

Young Giles had rushed to enlist in the expedition:

... my ambition stimulated by having read John McKinlay's diary of his search for Burke and Wills, and again of his marvellous escape with his party from the Alligator River, where he was surrounded by floodwaters, and escaped by killing his horses and drying the flesh, and using the hides to cover the frame of a frail boat, or raft, that he had constructed, and which actually conveyed his party to safety at Escape Cliffs, just in time before the rotting hides collapsed. And the great Stuart! I had read of his first attempt to cross Australia with only two men, and his retreat from hostile savages at Attack Creek. But not before he had planted the Union Jack on Central Mount Sturt. When starting upon his second expedition, had I not jumped upon my pony and followed his party to North Adelaide, where someone called 'Go forth again, ye brave little band, Explore the wonders of an unknown land'.

Giles had lost no time and was soon being interviewed and warned of the difficulties that might occur on the journey. They might often be short of water and provisions. 'Can you,' he was asked, 'live on bandicoot and goanna?' He said he already had done so and was then taken on at £1 a week and found.

My kit consisted of extra clothing in the way of three pairs of white moleskin trousers, several shirts, socks, and handkerchiefs, three pairs of boots, two hats, seven yards of calico and mosquito netting, belts, pouches, knives, pipes, a nightcap, and so on. All stores were to be sent to Beltana Station, but we were to go on to Umberatana Station to select the horses.

There the horses were shod and equipment handed out, and here they got an idea of some of the problems. The men were given 'wretched equipment' that would not withstand the terrible terrain and climate. Instead of leather, 'poor canvas' was used for their water bags with nothing to prevent the sweat of the pack horse seeping through and so badly made that:

often when full it was our horror when longing for a drink, to see a packhorse bump in between trees, squash the bag, and throw up a jet of the precious fluid that we expected to have on reaching camp. Our cooking utensils were also of the most scanty and primitive kind, and consisted of five quart pots with pannikin to fit, one billycan, a damper dish, and a three-gallon bucket to boil beef in, a knife, fork, and spoon each, and a small frying-pan. We had no tents, but a couple of small calico flys and strip of oilcloth six feet long was supplied to each of us to lay our blankets on at night or to put over us if the rain fell. We had one shovel (as a fire shovel) to use

The Overland Telegraph camp at Packard's, Port Darwin, photographed by Captain Sweet, master of the 200-ton government schooner, Gulnare, *which brought supplies for the northern camps from Adelaide.*

when making dampers. We had, however, several tomahawks, chiefly to present to chiefs of wild tribes we might meet, and also some beads and trinkets. We had hobble-chains and spare leather for making hobble-straps, but no horsebells; no baking-powder of any sort, and our dampers consisted only of flour, salt, and water—and perspiration. We had eye lotions, Holloway's pills and ointment, castor oil and other oil for the rifles, saddles, and so on. We had no blackboys or trackers, and how we came to start without horsebells has been a marvel and mystery to me ever since. Perhaps they thought they would attract—or more probably frighten—the savages; but we were all good trackers, and did not miss the bells very much.

But the horses were 'splendid': 'Two saddle horses each, mine were Warlock and Elinga; Mr Ross [the leader of Giles' party] had three, Stanley, Chester and Rambler. "On Stanley! On!" we heard Ross call often'.

They had scarcely begun the great trek before he was writing, 'Dug for water'. Then, '. . . large numbers of savages armed with spears and other weapons, shouting and gesticulating in a decidedly hostile attitude. As there were only three of us, we retreated, and at night slept with one eye open.'

Wire, insulators and other equipment, as well as supplies, had to negotiate the long overland trail of semi-desert for 1,200 miles and more from Port Augusta, while those working on the northern end had to have their equipment and supplies sent through the jungle-like growth from the tiny and new settlement at Port Darwin, where the ships from Adelaide would land their goods for them.

The work went well in the dry months but no thought had been given to 'the Wet'. No one from contractor to overseer or the men had realised the problems of the damp, humid, enervating months that recur each year in the northern latitudes. The rains came and the wet season began. Creeks that were almost dry in October became raging torrents in December. What had been a dry route became swamplands. The draught horses were too big for the heat and the mud and unable to forage for themselves as lighter horses do. In the steamy, muggy heat and rain, flour and biscuits became weevily and were almost inedible.

'I had a lovely pair of boils on the back of my neck,' wrote eighteen-year-old S. W. Herbert, 'with prickly heat as well being tormented by flies and mosquitoes made life almost unbearable. The climate was hot and muggy. Blowflies were a perfect nuisance, . . . moist woollen shirts became fly-blown, and live objects would soon appear.' Teamsters bringing supplies were held up at the flooded East Finness River, and broached the cargo, and

A three-man maintenance team prepares to replace a rotten telegraph pole in the OT line, one of 36,000 planted across the 1,973 miles between Port Augusta and Darwin.

Right: The overlanders, whether drovers or explorers, had constantly to dig soaks to water their horses in desert lands.

Below right: In the outback the camel is known as the 'Desert Schooner'. With a heavy load of food, camp gear and eighteen-gallon water kegs, camels enabled many a brave party of explorers or surveyors to survive the long dry stretches. (Spider, p. 76)

Overleaf: One of the consolations for the hard work and loneliness of outback life is the timeless beauty of the landscape.

drank the rum, unwittingly christening what later became Rum Jungle. Supplies were low, and what there was was bad. Men were ill with dysentery, all had prickly heat.

Young linesman Herbert wrote, 'The flour was dirty and full of weevils. The bread looked like currant cake when it was baked. The weevils swelled and burst in the dough in the camp oven heat, and discoloured the bread but we were obliged to eat it despite its smell and flavour. No one would touch the rice as it was alive with tiny grubs.'

The teamsters who managed to get through reported that many wagons were hopelessly bogged along the track. The wet season was at its worst, the food position acute. For weeks they had been without tea, sugar, soap, salt, tobacco or grog. 'We have nothing to fill our guts,' a delegation told the foreman. He foolishly replied 'sugar is a luxury, not a necessity to fill your guts'. The men met and fifty-six voted in favour of a strike—the first strike in the Northern Territory. It was 7 March 1871.

Because of the distances and now 'the Wet', communication with the authorities, or even with their own parties was difficult and at times impossible. Ships were sent to Adelaide from Darwin with requests only a day or so before parties made their appearance to tell that the situation was completely reversed. At one time communiques were sent on an astonishingly roundabout route by a passing vessel, the Dutch corvette *Curaçao*, on her way to Batavia. An appeal sent by her for extra supplies, men and transport animals to be sent from Adelaide, went to Batavia, then to Singapore, Rangoon, Calcutta, Bombay, and then to Ceylon, where it was put on a mail steamer bound for Adelaide.

In the midst of one of the worst times for the men and the overseers a surprising delight befell them. A man unconnected with the new enterprise, but himself a most enterprising fellow arrived. It was Ralph Milner. With his brother, John, and some stockmen, Milner, at his own expense and initiative had started northwards from Port Augusta in September 1870 with 4,300 sheep, 150 goats, 160 horses and two bullock-wagons to cross the continent. This was an epic droving feat, surely one of the greatest the world has known. The men had to find their own way across the continent from water to water; their ewes lambed on the way and they continued with a now increased flock. But north of what is now Alice Springs, at the Devils Marbles, they lost 3,000 sheep and lambs and 100 goats from eating poison plants.

On 30 August 1871, after twelve months' droving they reached Attack Creek. The natives here 'lived up to their reputation', and one crept up behind John Milner and crushed his head with a club, killing him instantly.

Ralph Milner and the drovers went on and by the end of November reached the Roper River. They had been on the track for 14 months and had 3,000 sheep in their mob.

The construction crews were hungry. But the rain kept pouring down, 'It is raining pitilessly,' Engineer Robert Patterson wrote. 'Every drop falls on my head like lead. It means ruin if it lasts, as the teams will not get through until too late. The lives of 200 men are imperilled for want of supplies.' Patterson was himself riding along the route to the Katherine River where the line had been completed through to Darwin. But a fault had developed (the wire in these early days still had much research and work to be done on it to make it satisfactory). Patterson and crews were now cut off from the outside world, 'without news, without hope'. Returning along the boggy track he passed team after team of horses and supply wagons bogged. He learnt that bullock teams attempting to get to the construction camp further up the Roper were in trouble. Those moving made only three miles a day.

On Christmas Eve he set off for the Roper River hoping a vessel had

arrived. His horses travelled seven miles in nine hours. Then he came on Ralph Milner's camp. He bought 1,000 sheep at 25s per head and arranged for them to be delivered to his various camps. This would avert famine—if the sheep could be got there without being drowned.

At the Roper River landing the construction crews awaited rescue. They had three days' supply of weevily flour left. It was still raining, when New Year's Day 1872 dawned: the stipulated period for the construction of the Line had elapsed. There were still 394 miles of line not completed. Communication was established between Port Augusta and Tennant Creek, 1,134 miles. They had put only ten poles to the mile in some sections to speed the work, but messages could be sent and that was what the contract demanded. The northern end was also open for messages. (The submarine cable from Banjoewanji, Java, had reached Darwin on 24 November 1871.)

As each section finished its work the men rode northwards to assist those ahead, not knowing what they would find when they crossed the gap. One party found tragedy.

The officer in charge of Telegraph Operators, Benjamin Clarke, wrote in his diary of 25 December 1871. 'Christmas Day. Spelling here today. The following inscription has been punctured on a tin nailed to a board and placed at the head of the grave which has been fenced in by a railing filled up with brush.'

In memory of C. W. I. Kraegen aged 40 who perished here for want of water
about 20.12.71
buried 21.12.71

The body was enclosed in a blanket and decently buried. Clark and his men found three empty water bags.

Further north the rain still pelted down. Alfred Giles was now with the northern party. He had experienced much since that day he ran into the recruiting room to join this great endeavour. 'Stanley, the horse that had carried Mr Ross 3,000 miles across the continent died after a severe attack of spasms, caused by eating some poisonous bush or weed. He was a grand old faithful servant, and I who had been associated with him from our beginning at Umberatana felt my loss keenly.' The mishap left them short of horses. 'Mr King had to ride the pack-horse Gentle Annie; Old Wombat, the other pack-horse, had to carry both packs.'

Giles helped Surveyor Packard to cross the Elsey River and watched him set off down the Roper River with six men to meet the schooner *Gulnare* which was to bring supplies from Darwin. Later he learned that only a day later this party was attacked by natives. 'A large body of savages appeared from the banks of the river, fully armed with spears, waddies, nulla nullas, and so on, and with so many hostile accompaniments as to compel the party to defend itself. Spears were thrown and shots exchanged. The wagon formed a good break against the spears, and enabled the whites to entrench themselves behind it.'

Among the provisions was a large cask, or hogshead, filled with corned beef, which upon reaching camp was generally emptied and the beef spread out to dry. Among the party was a man, who was of very low stature, and when the shots were being fired and the spears flying he sprang into the meatcask and fired his revolver through the bunghole. He popped up his head now and again to see how the battle was going—a real, live Jack-in-the-box. The attack was short and sharp, but none of the party were injured, and the sound of the guns probably frightened the savages more than the bullets. Possibly they were some of the same tribe who attempted an attack on our—Ross's—party earlier in the year on the Stangways River, 20 miles further east.

Left: Beyond the rim of settlement in Australia, the great variety of terrain has been a constant trial for travellers. Near these great stony outcrops are the desert lands of the centre that have turned back many a brave explorer.

Pack horses stampede alongside a Northern Territory river—one of the many hazards that confronted the men working on the OT line. But their worst problem was the Wet season.

The strange anomaly of this northern region was that while water flooded some areas in some months, there was no water at other times. Giles and others did 'flying' trips searching for water. 'We generally went some thirty miles, returned the next day to water our horses, and then set off in a different direction, but we never found any water in any instance.' Later near the Roper they discovered a large sheet of water, 'which we named the Warlock Ponds after my favourite old saddle horse, Warlock, which was lost, and never found'.

Well-sinkers dug for water and lined the well 'with trees called gutta-percha, which exudes a strong and bitter gum. As the water rose up it absorbed this taste and turned the water quite black and bitter and nothing would drink it'.

When young Alfred heard of Milner's sheep 'not more than sixty miles away!' he wrote 'Fancy!' It was a journey packed with surprises. And with valour.

Near Daly Waters, Alfred swam the 100 yards across the flooded creek and swam back to state that it was unsafe for swimming horses across because of the dead timber and submerged trees and the swift current. He attempted to get his own horse over by leading him with a rope but the current swept him downstream. So, he recrossed the stream, and pulled the horse ashore. His wet clothes were at the other side of the river as 'the rain came down in torrents and the wind blew a hurricane. Being without clothes I found the warmest place was in the water, where I remained until the storm passed.' He then retrieved the wet clothes, and trudged off leading his horse.

The small party of five were 'bogging down to the horses' bellies' and now 'had only some tea, sugar and a small tin of preserved meat' left between five men. 'Ian Knuckey proposed we should kill one of our horses and suggested that my pack horse Gentle Annie was the fattest. I agreed that she was, but added that I would have to be fairly starving before I would agree to sacrifice Annie.' The following day they struck the northern line and heard a horse bell. Police-trooper Keppler met them and told of parties retreating where they could and others very short of provisions. But he, the policeman, was also very short and could give Giles and his party only one good meal. 'Taking off the camp oven-lid he said, "Look at that for a feed!" There, coiled round the camp oven was an immense goanna, beautifully cooked. We enjoyed it immensely with johnny cakes and tea.'

Further on through the sticky, boggy land they came on a camp where men, beset by humidity, dampness, heat, sandflies, mosquitoes and flies, with no books to read, nothing to do while imprisoned by the Wet, were succumbing to disease, malaria, rheumatism and fever.

Milner got his sheep through to the men by mid-February, and after shearing their eighteen-month-old growth of wool the men roasted the first fresh meat for months. Men had been attempting to work, but 'the country was in such a state of bog that when lifting the poles into position they sank to their knees in the soft soil, and the holes for the poles were full of water and could not be jammed securely.' Later the boy wrote, 'we began to wonder when we would get out of this, the whole country was inundated and heavy rain falling.'

A 'boat' was made to go down the river to look for the expected supply ship. They took the wheels off a wagon, lashed a tarpaulin around it to make it watertight and then lashed ten empty kegs underneath for buoyancy. In pouring rain five men set off, including one Jim Burton, 'an old sailor'. They had oars of bush timber for the 100-mile row to the mouth of the Roper River. When they met the ship they found it could make no headway against the floodwaters and high wind, so they arranged for two long boats to be rowed upstream to the hungry men. From the Roper landing food was sent by pack horses to the other groups of men trapped in the bog areas. Later, schooners were able to reach the beleaguered camp and by the time the Wet ended there was not only food but great quantities of construction material landed.

The schooner *Gulnare* arrived at the Roper landing with supplies as did two other vessels, quite a feat in itself to navigate 100 miles inland up an unexplored river. But already many men had decided to leave. The whole scheme appeared to be as bogged down as the weather had bogged the men, wagons and horses.

In April the rains ended, the Wet was over. While the men began again to plant poles and thread the wire the penalty clause was still in force and the South Australian government was in severe disputes. The directors in London not only threatened, in precise terms, to refuse to honour the contract and, instead, take their cable to Burketown, Queensland, but they laid a £100-a-day penalty on the state for every day over the contracted date. To help ease the burden it was decided to run a pony express, an estafette service, to carry messages for transmission across the gap between the ends of the north and south wires. In this way they could transmit messages between England and Australia within a week—or less if the dispatch-riders had a clear run. Revenue carried from this traffic would be set off against the penalty that the failure of the completion of the line was costing the government.

One of the gamest men working on the whole project, R. R. Knuckey, first rode the gap to establish a route. A dispatch was sent from Darwin to the telegraph station on the Elsey terminal; from there Knuckey rode the 262 miles to the Tennant Creek terminal where it was wired to Adelaide on 20 June 1872, the first transcontinental telegram.

Camps were formed along the estafette route and John Lewis and his brother Jim with Ray Parkin Boucout, six other riders, and sixty horses established the unique service. On one trip Boucout covered 262 miles in 131

OT officers at the Roper River camp.

hours, of which 101 hours were spent in the saddle, and only thirty hours resting.

In the meantime, the parsimonious British-Australian Company had been embarrassed and then held to ridicule: their submarine cable across the Timor Sea from Banjoewanji to Darwin had gone dead! Eighteen days later it was still dead, the fault lying somewhere at the bottom of the sea. The Hon. John H. Barrow, Treasurer of South Australia, joyously sent a telegram to London. 'At present we are without means of telegraphing to London via Port Darwin in consequence, we believe, of the continued interruption in the working of the Company's Submarine Cable.' By the terms of the contract the London-based company now had to pay South Australia a penalty of five per cent per annum or the capital cost of building the land line. And the poles were being erected and the gap closing while the difficulty of finding the break in the cable went on.

The poling was finished on 9 August and by 22 August 1872, the two wires lay a few feet apart, near a depot camp of men and horses. Patterson completed the job.

Half the party seized hold of one end of the wire and the other half the other end, and stretched with might and main to bring the two ends together. All our force could not do this. I then attached some binding wire to one end. The moment I brought it to the other end the current passed through my body from all the batteries on the line. I had to yell and let go. Next time I used my handkerchief to seize the wire with and in five minutes Adelaide was in communication with Port Darwin. It would have been with England had the cable not broken down.

At twelve noon, Patterson sent a message that the great task was done. They had over-run their contract by six months, but Charles Todd, officer in charge, wrote of the 1,973 miles of line, 'No line passing through a similar extent of uninhabited country, where the materials had to be carried over such long distances, no line of equal length and presenting similar natural obstacles, had been constructed in the same short space of time.' On 21 October the fault in the submarine cable was found and service restored. Todd commented grandiloquently, 'The Australian colonies are now connected with the grand electric chain which unites all the nations of the earth.'

Wine and rhetoric flowed as celebrations were held in Adelaide, Sydney and London to mark the end of Australia's news isolation from the rest of the world, and men who had faced and endured danger, disease, hunger and loneliness drifted off in the way many brave people do.

Left top: OT workers at the Roper River jetty.

Left below: OT workers holed up at the Roper River camp over the Wet season.

Left: The demonstration held in Adelaide on 15 November 1872 to celebrate the successful connection of the Overland Telegraph and the end of Australia's news isolation from the rest of the world.

Where The Dead Men Lie

Barcroft Boake

Out on the wastes of the Never Never—
   That's where the dead men lie!
There where the heat-waves dance for ever—
   That's where the Earth's loved sons are keeping
Endless tryst: not the west wind sweeping
Feverish pinions can wake their sleeping—
   Out where the dead men lie!

Where brown Summer and Death have mated—
   That's where the dead men lie!
Loving with fiery lust unsated—
   That's where the dead men lie!
Out where the grinning skulls bleach whitely
Under the saltbush sparkling brightly;
Out where the wild dogs chorus nightly—
   That's where the dead men lie!

Deep in the yellow, flowing river—
   That's where the dead men lie!
Under the banks where the shadows quiver—
   That's where the dead men lie!
Where the platypus twists and doubles,
Leaving a train of tiny bubbles;
Rid at last of their earthly troubles—
   That's where the dead men lie!

East and backward pale faces turning—
   That's how the dead men lie!
Gaunt arms stretched with a voiceless yearning—
   That's how the dead men lie!
Oft in the fragrant hush of nooning
Hearing again their mother's crooning,
Wrapt for aye in a dreamful swooning—
   That's how the dead men lie!

Only the hand of Night can free them—
   That's when the dead men fly!
Only the frightened cattle see them—
   See the dead men go by!
Cloven hoofs beating out one measure,
Bidding the stockmen know no leisure—
That's when the dead men take their pleasure!
   That's when the dead men fly!

Ask, too, the never-sleeping drover:
   He sees the dead pass by;
Hearing them call to their friends—the plover,
   Hearing the dead men cry;
Seeing their faces stealing, stealing,
Hearing their laughter, pealing, pealing,
Watching the grey forms wheeling, wheeling
   Round where the cattle lie!

Strangled by thirst and fierce privation—
   That's how the dead men die!
Out on Moneygrub's farthest station—
   That's how the dead men die!
Hard-faced greybeards, youngsters callow;
Some mounds cared for, some left fallow;
Some deep down, yet others shallow;
   Some having but the sky.

Moneygrub, as he sips his claret,
   Looks with complacent eye
Down at his watch-chain, eighteen carat—
   There, in his club, hard by:
Recks not that every link is stamped with
Names of the men whose limbs are cramped with
Too long lying in grave-mould, cramped with
   Death where the dead men lie.

TOMMY WINDICH

'Two well-known and reliable natives, Tommy Windich and Jemmy, who have already acquired considerable experience under former explorers,' were two of the five persons appointed to make up John Forrest's party in 1869 when he was sent off in search of the missing explorer, Leichardt. Of the two, Tommy Windich was to become the most brilliant bushman and peerless travelling companion, and Forrest shared his company on other journeys and always set him apart for praise.

Jemmy Mungara had reported seeing the spot where the remains of the missing white man lay, believed murdered. While Jemmy and his information was found to be unreliable, Tommy Windich from the beginning proved to be invaluable, and when death from thirst threatened, he calmly continued to seek water and saved the party. When their food ran low, Forrest's journal records, 'Tommy shot a fine emu which was a great treat to us all'. Four days later, 'Tommy shot a red kangaroo which we carried to camp'. On this whole journey Forrest's party had been led a merry dance by the 'wild' natives; Jemmy's story was a farrago of near and bent almost-truths—for instance, the bones he had reported were those of horses, and this he seems to have known all along.

But as he turned to head the long trail back to Perth because the men and horses had been without food or water for forty-eight hours, Forrest made for a brook he had seen on the way out. 'I named it Windich Brook after my companion Windich', he wrote in his journal.

Later, Windich accompanied the explorer on a journey across the lower part of western and southern Australia, a reverse journey from that taken by Eyre who had crossed in the opposite direction. Immediately the expedition got into dangerous country the name of Windich is firmly in Forrest's diary.

30 May—Recruiting ourselves and horses until 30th. We took a flying trip to the northward. ['Flying trips' are short-period explorations in a different direction from the laid-down route, in Forrest's case to search for water for the main party.] We found a little water for our horses in rock holes. Tommy Windich found the shoulder blade of a horse . . . no doubt the remains of the horse Mr Eyre was obliged to kill for food at this spot.

24 June—Started for Eucla, carrying 30 gallons of water, and walking in turns. Since leaving Cape Arid have not seen a gully or watercourse of any description—a distance of 400 miles.'

But the most difficult, arduous journey was yet to come. In 1874 Western Australia's Governor Weld had determined that the unconquerable must be conquered. 'An expedition to ascertain the nature of the vast region separating Western Australia and the other colonies and determining the possibility of opening up direct overland communication.' There were 1,000 miles of no-man's-land; solitary, isolated, Western Australia lay cut off from the rest of the continent. The spirit of adventure for which the west had been noted had been crushed by the burning, arid, tree-less wastelands that had driven back, killed or swallowed without trace every man who had attempted to cross it. (Eyre had followed the coast from east to west, an 'indescribable journey', but had not ventured inland.)

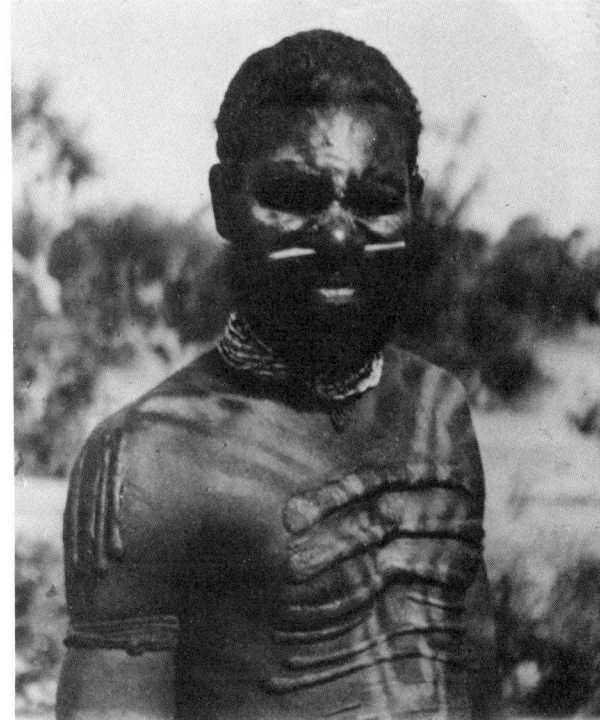

Above: A portrait of John Forrest, the Western Australian explorer.

Top: The tribalised Tommy Pierre who, with Tommy Windich, was one of the two Aboriginals who accompanied explorer John Forrest on his 1874 expedition.

Who would take up this challenge? Who would walk the barren wastes where Baxter's body still lay wrapped in a blanket as it had for the past thirty years on the ground that was too hard to dig; where Eyre and Wylie, his Aboriginal companion, had journeyed 'attended by almost unexampled demands upon human endurance', in a land where nothing moved but the sun, that ball of fire that rolled and broiled in the sky that shed no rain?

'There is,' said the *Argus*, 'no country in the world that has so tried the endurance and perseverance of men on exploring expeditions as South Australia has done.'

Threading its way up from Port Augusta to Darwin the Overland Telegraph that was completed in 1872 drew a dividing line through the centre of the continent from north to south. To the east of the Telegraph the country was known; to the west was an enigmatic land mass bordered, 1,000 miles away, by the few scattered settlements near the Swan River in Western Australia.

It was this 'no-man's-land' that isolated his state from the rest of Australia that sent the young Western Australian, John Forrest, off on the journey that has caused his name to be linked with those of the other men who conquered the unknown—John Franklin, Stanley, Dr Livingstone and Grant.

'Should he succeed in this journey,' the Governor wrote of Forrest's trek, 'his name will fitly go down to posterity as that of the man who solved the last remaining problem in the Australian continent, and whatever may come after him, he will have been the last (and certainly when the means at his disposal and the difficulties of the undertakings are considered, by no means the least) of the great Australian explorers.' Forrest was to attempt to cross the continent from Geraldton, Western Australia, until he met up with the Overland Telegraph. Sturt had crossed the continent from south to north and others had followed. 'The last remaining problem' was to be tackled by Forrest. He fitted out his expedition for the remarkably small sum of £330 for this gigantic, hazardous, long journey, 'the finishing stroke of Australian discovery'.

John Forrest left Geraldton on 1 April 1874 with six men who included his brother Alex and Aboriginal Tommy Windich, both of whom had been on treks before with him, as well as Tommy Pierre, another native much admired by Forrest—a tribalised man with cicatrices scored across his chest and upper arms and a bone through his nose. They had twenty horses, most of them pack horses; three men rode, three walked every day. By 1 May they began to keep night watches; they were entering country where the natives were reputedly cannibal as well as hostile. On 3 May John wrote in his journal, 'Tomorrow we enter on country entirely unknown'.

Almost immediately the hostility of the desert surrounded them. They pressed on searching for water, mirages encircled them, their eyes reddened and wept from the glare of the molten sun striking the sand through which they struggled leading their horses; forty Aborigines attacked. At 4 pm on that day John wrote an account of the attack in his journal. 'The natives seem determined to take our lives', he wrote. Forrest's men had ridden out for fifty miles and found no water. Their present camp held water for no more than a few days and the Aborigines showed no signs of retreating. Forrest built a store hut and from this the men could defend themselves against a spear and waddy attack.

John and Windich had made four 'flying trips' from the fort to look for water without success. Now they set off determined to pass the point last reached fifty miles out. Seventy miles away they found water and set off back to bring up the others, but their horses knocked up. For the last twenty miles they had to drag the winded animals along behind them.

They brought the rest of the party forward over the seventy miles of arid

Members of Forrest's 1874 Central Australian exploration party were (back): Tommy Pierre, Tommy Windich, James Kennedy and James Sweeney; (front): Alexander and John Forrest.

land where there was no feed at all and with only the little water they had been able to gather at 'Weld's Springs' where the natives had attacked. So it went on. From one seeming disaster they moved to temporary relief over and over again. They came on a single native who appeared to have been following them and asked if he had intended to eat them. He replied that he was trying to escape his tribe who had just eaten his brother.

This land was amongst the worst—if not the worst—in the world, yet beyond this fact Forrest recognised a dire sign. His party was attempting to cross one of the world's most inhospitable regions when that region was in the grip of a drought. It seems impossible that such an arid area could be worse at any one time than another, but all the signs proved this to be so. Windich showed him where natives had dug soaks for clear water to a few feet in other years, where now they must dig fifteen feet for a handful of brackish water. 'It is certainly a wretched country we are travelling through', Forrest noted in his diary.

There had been no rain in the two years since Giles came this way to wash away the foot prints of his animals. Windich and John went on alone, 'flying' ahead searching for water. Their horses broke down and the men dragged ahead on foot pulling the horses after them. If they halted for a moment the poor beasts lay down and it was difficult to get them up.

13 July—Over the most miserable spinifex country. Windich shot an emu.
14 July—Eating emu was our chief occupation today I think.

He and Windich go off again 'flying', searching for water. When they found a little, 'We had a pannikin of tea and gave our horses an hour and a half's rest, then continued over spinifex'. Next day, 'searching every spinifex rise for water. My horse, Brick, knocked up. About one o'clock we found enough water to give our horses a drink and to make some tea for ourselves.' They must move on, the lives of the rest of the party depended on them. 'I had to walk and drive my horse before me, and then we had hard work to get him to move.' The next day his horse gave in again and Forrest went on without him. When they found water they brought the horse up, hobbled him, hid Forrest's saddle and gear in a bush, and set off back to bring up the party.

By 22 July, with horses well watered and fed, 'started in company of Pierre to look for water ahead' but travelled fifty miles on that day and found none. Forrest would have liked to go on and see what the land was like, 'but the horses would have enough to do to carry us back'. They reached the camp with neither of the men or their horses having had a drink of water for thirty-six hours.

Forrest sets off again with Windich, 'taking a packhorse and ten gallons of water [a horse will drink six gallons of water a day on ordinary work] and two small tins for our own use'. The following night it rained a little, so Forrest left the water at the place he had camped, thinking the rain had been widespread. Forty miles further on he camped without water for the horses. Afraid the rest of the party would be following on the strength of the light rain he went on. The next night was again without water. The third day, 'Little Brown our packhorse so knocked up we had difficulty in getting him to walk.' They returned to where they had left the water drums and watered their horses.

'Little Brown completely gave in and we were obliged to leave him. Pushed on, and reached the party a little after dark, having been absent five days, in which we travelled about 200 miles.'

Alexander and Pierre went on a flying trip looking for water, 'Kennedy and self went back and brought Little Brown and pack saddle, etc., back to camp. Windich shot an emu. Thermometer 95 degrees today'. In two days time Alexander and Pierre returned. They had not found water.

That night Forrest wrote:

I now began to be much troubled about our position, although I did not communicate my fears to any but my brother. We felt confident we could return if the worst came, although we were over 1,000 miles from the settled districts of Western Australia. The water at our camp was fast drying up and would not last more than a fortnight. The next water was 60 miles back and there seemed no probability of getting eastward. I knew we were in the very country that had driven Mr Gosse back [and Mr Giles]. No time was to be lost. I was determined to make the best use of it if only the water would last, and to keep on searching. I gave instructions to allowance the party, so that the stores should last four months, and made every preparation for a last desperate struggle.

To get to the glistening wires of the Overland Telegraph line in South Australia, Forrest and his party had to cross 'the most miserable sandy hills and plains of spinifex'.

Windich and Forrest went off searching for water,

instructing my brother to follow on the seventh [August]; before leaving to bury some flour and everything that could be dispensed with, and to carry all the drums

full of water. (He has since informed me that he buried on left bank of brook, seven yards north of a small tree with a tin plate nailed on it, on which is written, 'DIG 7 yds. N.', two pack-bags, containing 135 lbs flour, six leather water-bottles, two tomahawks, one pick, one water canteen, one broken telescope, three emu eggs, some girths and straps, one shoeing hammer, one pound of candles, and left a lantern hanging on a tree. A bottle was also buried, with a letter in it, giving the latitude and longitude of the camp, and a brief outline of our former and future intended movements.)

All their tea, sugar and bacon had gone.

The two men rode out, 'camped for the night without water for ourselves or horses'. The following day they walked, 'as our horses were knocked up for want of water'. Later, 'our horses scarcely moving and ourselves parched with thirst. The sun was very hot.'

At about noon we found some water in a gully by scratching a hole, but it was quite salt. As our horses would not drink it, it can be imagined how salt it was. We drank about a pint of it and Windich said it was the first time he ever had to drink salt water. I washed myself.

But he knew that as the surface water ahead dried up progress would be impossible.

We are three days in advance of the party, and if we can get enough water for our riding horses we shall be able to stop them before there is any great danger, although we may lose some of the horses. We camp for the night without water for the horses or ourselves.

On 17 August, while climbing a hill, Forrest heard three shots. Windich had gone to try to shoot a kangaroo and now he heard the Aboriginal coo-ee—and looking round saw a native running away. 'Fearing that Windich had been attacked by the natives I descended towards him as quickly as possible.' But Windich was coming along with a big kangaroo on his back — 'he had fired at three'.

They went on 'over the most miserable sandy hills and plains of spinifex'. After thirty-five miles:

Hope to find water, our horses too poor to go long without it. Was obliged to abandon police-horse, Brick, today as he is completely done up. Nothing but downright poverty is the cause of his giving in; and the same in the case of Fame and little Padbury, which we abandoned over a month ago. It is a wonder to me they do not all give in, as many are mere skeletons, having had only very dry grass ever since we left. Poor old Brick held up as long as he could, but was forced to give in and we had to leave him to his solitary fate. He will probably go back to the spring.

By now the party had come up. They got a little water for the horses by digging out a soak in a gully. Next day: 'Windich's horse completely knocked up, and we had to walk and drive him before us this afternoon. The day was excessively hot, and the horses are very thirsty. We have only about a quart ourselves.' Next day: 'Windich's horse scarcely able to walk. About noon it could go no farther and mine not much better. What is to be done?' He and Windich once again set off on a flying trip, this time on foot. 'The sun's heat was excessive. Windich saw emu tracks, but they did not lead to water. We returned unsuccessful. No time was to be lost.' The two sipped water and set off again. 'Windich shot a wurrung which he said had lately drunk water.' They followed emu tracks until they found a spring. 'After having a good drink we went back and got our horses, reaching the spring with them after dark; they were very thirsty and completely done up.'

23 August—Shot an emu. Awaited the arrival of the party. Heard gun-shot, and saw Kennedy coming on, walking. Found that the party were only half a mile off. They had been very distressed for water, and had left 120 lbs of flour and a pack-saddle five miles back, Taylor's mare about three miles back, and Burges and his saddle two miles back. When they saw my note, directing them to the water, they had gone back and got Burges, and with great difficulty got him close to camp, when he lay down and they left him. Windich and I started back on foot at once with two buckets of water, and met Burges within a quarter of a mile of camp, crawling along; we gave him the water and he then went on to the spring. We went back and found Taylor's mare, and brought her slowly to camp. We are now safe again, and I must give the horses a few days rest. The weather has been hot, and if we had not found this spring, not more than five horses would have lasted out the day. I will send back and get the flour, as it is only five miles off. The party were all very glad to see such a fine spring, as their position was very dangerous, having only three gallons of water with them altogether.

27 August—Left camp with Tommy Windich to look for water ahead.

Again they found water and brought the rest of the party on. And so it continued, for two months until Sunday 27 October: 'Long and continued cheering'. Ahead, the sun glistened on the wires of the Overland Telegraph. The 'awful desert' had been bridged, they had vanquished 'an unknown country, a wilderness, a long line of travel'.

We have not much to refresh the inner man with, only damper and water, but we have been used to it now more than a month, and do not much feel it. The horses are all very tired.

28 October—We travelled down the telegraph 21 miles.

29 October—When we were nearly ready to start, police-horse Butcher lay down and died in a few seconds; he appeared alright when we brought him in and was saddled as usual. We took off his shoes and left him where he died. I was sorry for the poor old horse, he had been rather weak for a good while but had borne up well to the very last.

They now had three horses left between five men, and travelled 35 miles that day before they camped. 'Damper and water as usual'.

But next night: 'Dinner: roast beef and plum pudding!' They had reached Peake Downs cattle station and here they rested for four days before facing the welcome awaiting them. At this time Forrest wrote, 'To Tommy Windich I am much indebted for his services as a bushman, and his experience generally. Accompanying me on many occasions, often in circumstances of difficulty and privation, I ever found him a good, honest companion.' He recorded well of the other members of the party but had singled Windich out for special mention.

Now followed a time almost as arduous as the terrible crossing. 'The last of the greatest is coming in', newspaper headlines read, referring to the explorers who had attempted the 'awful, arid, spinifex desert'. All the way to Adelaide they were fêted and speeches made. As they reached Adelaide all the explorers of the arid lands still living rode out to meet them, one man riding the horse of explorer, Burke, another that of Sturt. By 3 November thousands had flocked to Adelaide to see them ride in. 'Balconies and housetops were thronged, all along the route were flags, flowers, decorations, evergreens, streamers and arches of welcome adorned with large pictures of bush life.' The bells rang peals and there was a general holiday. Mayors and Town Clerks of Adelaide and surrounding cities drove out in their carriages to meet them. Forrest was moved by the 'presence of members of various exploring expeditions who, from their own experience could best estimate the value of the results we achieved and the difficulties encountered. Riders carried standards with the dates of various

Land that was parched by a two-year drought when Forrest and his party crossed it, could become a quagmire after rain. These overlanders on Forrest's route are crossing Lake Barlee.

The demonstration that greeted Forrest and his party on their arrival in Adelaide on 3 November 1874.

expeditions—1860, January 1862, July 1862'. Forrest had his men wear 'the rough, weather-beaten, shockingly dilapidated garments in which we had been clothed, and were mounted on the horses which had served us so well. We each carried our rifles and each led a packhorse carrying the kegs for our water.' It was all wonderful to the men of the party, but arrival at their home state was even more so. A champagne breakfast, and the band playing 'When Johnny Comes Marching Home Again' was followed by a procession through Perth 'in a carriage and six with Tommy Windich and Pierre riding on gaily-decked horses immediately behind us'.

At the mayoral reception Forrest thanked his 'brave and faithful companions' and Pierre happily spoke. (Windich had been asked to speak but 'could not summon courage to say a word'.) Tommy Pierre, with the tribal markings and a bone through his nose was splendid.

Tommy said,

Well, gentlemen, I an very thankful to come back. I thought we was never to get back. (Laughter.) Many a time I go into camp in the morning, going through desert place, and swear and curse and say, 'Master, where the deuce are you going to take us?' I say to him, 'I'll give you a pound to take us back'. (Cheers and laughter.) Master say, 'Hush! what are you talking about? I will take you all right through Adelaide'; and I always obey him. Gentlemen, I am thankful to you that I am in the Town Hall. That's all I got to say. (Cheers.)

But for brave, shy Tommy Windich, the journey itself was the thing.

A HUNDRED BLACKGUARDS OF THE WEST

Above: Rev. George Halford (later Bishop of Longreach Diocese) began the Bush Brotherhood in Longreach on 14 September 1897.

The Queensland navvies were not reputed to be any less rough than any others in the days when only the toughest men could hold a job in the big railway construction gangs. Into one of these camps of navvies out from Longreach, early this century, there came a small, very English parson. He was the Reverend Frederick Hulton Sams.

The young parson stepped up to the men—they had just knocked off work—and asked them if they were weary. Weary? Who did he think he was having on! They didn't reply.

'Oh, well then,' said the parson, 'if you're not weary perhaps you'd like to have a round or two with me,' and pulled two pairs of boxing gloves from his bag, put on one pair and handed the other to a man nearby. 'You look as though you'd be handy with your fists.' In this way the toughest men of the tracks met 'the Fighting Parson'.

The Reverend Hulton Sams had come direct from London to Longreach as the newest recruit for the Bush Brotherhood, the small band of Church of England clergy who renounced the comforts of conventional parishes and devoted their lives to bush people. None of these Bush Brothers was in any way an ordinary man—their founder was a bishop who renounced his position to go out and live in a tent with the railway workers—and Sams was truly one of the most individual of them.

Sams' background does not at first lead us to think of his becoming this truly Christ-like man. His father, Reverend C. F. Sams, was the rector and rural dean of Emberton, Buckinghamshire, England. He was educated at Harrow and Trinity College, Cambridge. He was trained for the ministry and ordained priest in 1908 and served one year in Birmingham. In the same year he volunteered for service in St Andrew's Bush Brotherhood in Queensland, and for five and a half years worked as a Bush Brother in central and western Queensland, with headquarters at Longreach.

Bishop Halford, who was in Longreach when Sams arrived, wrote that the clergy who gathered to meet him thought he was 'elevated with liquor' and after having shown him to his room retired to discuss 'the problem'.

The poor clergy hadn't seen anything yet. One wonders if they didn't wish Bishop Halford would collect his Bush Brothers and disappear down the railway track, leaving them to get on with their respectable business of having tea with the Mothers' Union. One night Bishop Halford wrote in his diary, 'There was a terrific din in the lane outside and I couldn't make out what was happening—a buggy and two ponies were clattering about and the driver yelling out at the top of his voice. It was only Sams coming home after a western trip.' Another man writing of his first meeting with 'the Fighting Parson' said, 'His nose had been well skinned a few days previously boxing in Windorah and one eye was partially black but that didn't trouble him at all.' Sams himself wrote about 'the slow, hard-hitting John May whose awful right hand raised that egg on my cheek'.

Sams came to be known as one of the best fighters in the west. A lightweight, St Frederick of Betoota, as he jestingly described himself, often took on men two stone heavier than himself. 'Win or lose,' another wrote of him, 'it made no difference to him. He just loved boxing for the sport of it.' Little wonder the tough navvies admired him.

Among the stories told of him is the one about his epic journey to be with a man he had heard was dying at Aramac. At that time Sams was fifty miles away at Jericho. A fettler volunteered and together they pulled a trolley in steady rain for seven hours over the fifty-mile track. He would not allow anyone to see his hands for some time after this: 'Hard though his hands were,' wrote Halford, 'they were in a frightful state from this unaccustomed work.'

When World War I broke out Sams applied to enlist as a chaplain but the Church did not accept him. He then enlisted in the army, became a lieutenant, and was killed in France on 31 July 1915 when he crawled out from cover to try and get water for three wounded men. He was then aged thirty-three. One of the men who had known him in the west of Queensland wrote a poem as a memorial to him; its concluding lines are among the most moving ever written about an Australian:

> And could a call for aid have come
>   'Ere his last parting breath,
> A hundred blackguards of the West
>   Would have hedged him in from death.

The little Anglican church at Jundah, western Queensland, is dedicated to his memory.

When Bishop Halford arrived in Australia and went to Longreach in 1897, it was at the beginning of a severe drought that lasted without a break for four years. At this settlement, 500 miles west of Rockhampton, there was 'a severe spiritual drought also', recorded the new leader of the Bush Brothers. At his 'welcome' only one man, three women and a few children were present. He worked there until the drought broke in 1902 . . . 'they had

Above: Four Bush Brothers, including Rev. Hulton Sams (far left) and Rev. Guy Maude-Roxby (far right), who died during his service at Aramac, Queensland, where he is buried.

Above left: Brother Fred Hulton Sams, the fighting parson (left), who carried two pairs of boxing gloves into the bush with his Bible.

just struck water in the bore but it was undrinkable; however, it promised baths'.

In 1909 he was appointed Bishop of Rockhampton, a comfortable, highly esteemed position which would have delighted most clergymen, but in 1920, 'to the surprise and embarrassment of the Church', he resigned his office and his goods (the 'vow of poverty') in order to devote himself as a poor friar to the isolated railway navvies and settlers. He wrote, 'The Church does not go to these mobs of men on construction work,' and he believed they would welcome any comfort or help he could give them.

A friend who was returning to England gave him an old T-model Ford and he set off on the roads to the west. 'At the Burnett Settlement I lived in a tent by a lagoon for two and a half happy years. I did my cooking and washing on an oil drum and lived among the best fellows I have met in this land.'

For nine months while the railway was being built at Dawson, he lived in a humpy made of saplings covered by bags, with a dirt floor, to be near the navvies as they worked from section to section. 'From the start the men have been most friendly. They let me go into their tents, sit on their bunks and talk of the Lord, or around their camp fires where we talked freely. My heart went right out to these fellows. I longed to help them.' No other man in any part of the world would have written so tenderly of the navvy. The Bishop wore shirt and trousers only and for all this period left off his clerical collar.

The vow of poverty and celibacy seemed to attract only the mightiest of men. They all had memorable personalities.

The Reverend James Robertson Maxwell Hall was 'the boss' of the Bush Brotherhood in the early 1920s at Cunnamulla in Queensland's far south-western corner which stretches to the South Australian border and takes in the outer Barcoo and thousands of square miles of shifting sandhills in 'the Kidman country'.

Although he was a university man and 'spoke in cultured accents', he was a fair-dinkum, bush-born Australian from Taroom, in the Dawson River country. He took his BA at Queensland University as well as the Heavyweight Boxing Championship, and he was a first-class rugby player.

He was also a first-class outback joker. Joe Murphy told the story of meeting him in 1924 when Murphy was 'a very callow seventeen-year-old'. At the Cunnamulla boarding house where he was lodging, Murphy was called to the phone:

After introducing himself the clergyman demanded to know why I had not attended his early morning service that day, seeing that I must have heard the bell. The church was only a stone's throw from the boarding house.

I explained that, as I did not belong to his flock, some mistake must have been made. Jimmy said that he did not care to which denomination I belonged and that I would have to attend regularly all his services. If I did not, he would promptly kick my backside.

The threat of violence stung me into a declaration that it would take a better man than he to kick my stern. Up to then I had not seen Jimmy in the flesh, and I did not know that he had been heavyweight champion of his university.

My brash declaration brought a suggestion from Jimmy that I should meet him immediately in front of the local court house, where he would be pleased to accept my challenge. I hurried to the venue only to find it deserted. I paced up and down for several minutes before loud guffaws drew my attention to two men seated outside the hotel, diagonally opposite.

I recognised one of the two as my new boss. He had just given me a job to start next day. The other was a burly stranger wearing Blucher boots, khaki shirt and trousers, a floppy, dust-stained hat and a little black bib and clerical collar.

Murphy got even with the clergyman later:

Above: Bush Missionary (to selector's hopeful heir): 'My little boy, can you tell me what the good shepherd does with strange sheep when he finds them going astray?'
Little Boy (scorning the B.M.'s ignorance): 'Why, he fakes their ear-marks, and boxes 'em up with his own mob, of course.'

Right: The man who best symbolises the wide outback country of Australia is the swaggie. Sometimes called sundowners or travellers, these men roamed the whole continent, from north to south, east to west. To a man they were battlers, and of each it could be said that he was as game as Ned Kelly to take on the lonely stretches that he trod, owning no more than he could carry on his back.

Above: Today the road trains are a familiar sight outback, but their progenitor was the 130 hp AEC motor that the Army took through the desert in 1934. (Before the Bitumen, p. 87)

Right: Camels were the major form of transport over two-thirds of the continent for three generations of men. Foreign to this land, they nevertheless settled to it immediately on arrival in 1864.

Hearing a jackaroo say that he was on his way to call on Jimmy at the rectory, I told him, quite untruthfully, that he was wasting his time because Jimmy had resigned from the ministry and was shearing out at Dynever Downs.

I nearly got the sack as a result of the speed with which my story spread over the bush telegraph before it was exploded. I dodged the bullet which I richly deserved through the intercession of Jimmy. He claimed it was the best joke which had come under his notice for some time.

Jimmy's stipend as a Bush Brother—if he received a regular one at all—must have been very small. Yet there was always a handout at the rectory for anybody seeking it. And, whenever Jimmy shrewdly saw that a nip of rum would be beneficial rather than harmful, it always went with the handout.

Jimmy, who was then the only resident clergyman in Cunnamulla, was responsible for a bit of information which circulated among the floating population of bagmen who camped under the Warrego River bridge on the outskirts of the town. As a result of the information the bagmen knew that the matter of religious persuasion was mentioned or not mentioned, according to the caller's own choice, on visits to the rectory, which were always welcomed.

As Jimmy was a palpably sincere parson, a man of culture and a forceful though simple speaker, his services were always well attended. But the knowledge that his charity sometimes left him on short commons himself, was not confined to practising members of his own flock. Whether it was a 'dry quid-in' during squatters' festivities in race week, a tarpaulin muster before cutout at a big shearing shed, or a sling suggested by the ringkeeper at the two-up school, there was never a shortage of contributors. It was well known that the proceeds were earmarked for the charity dispensed by Jimmy to all and sundry among the genuinely and sometimes not-so-genuinely needy folk, no matter what their religion.

On Sunday mornings Jimmy was fully occupied with services and Sunday school. In the afternoon he played for one of the local teams in the regular football competition. He also represented the town in inter-district matches.

After Evensong he regularly took his choristers to the silent-picture show. (Screening never started until after the end of all church services. Radio and television had not then arrived.)

When a group of locals began to have genuine doubts whether it was right to hold regular picture shows on Sunday nights, Jimmy naturally was called in as adviser.

Jimmy said he believed that the Sunday night pictures were a big factor in maintaining the town's good moral record. The pictures continued.

Towards the end of 1929, with the expiration of his vow of celibacy which he had taken as a Bush Brother, Jimmy married Topsy Warner, a daughter of Bobbie Warner, one of the district's pioneer squatters.

I wrote Jimmy's obituary for the old Sydney *Bulletin*. As I typed it, I thought of the time he threatened to kick my rear if I did not attend his service a quarter of a century earlier.

If I am lucky enough to make the final grade, I look forward to kicking off the same celestial football as the Reverend Jimmy Hall, who is a certainty to be a big noise Up There.

Above: Brother Erskine of the Brotherhood of the Good Shepherd ready for the track. The Brothers were the mavericks of the Anglican clergy who camped with the construction gangs and pastoral workers throughout the outback.

Left: The bush evangelists turned up in the most unlikely places—such as the rowdy gambling camps along the construction of the East-West line.

'SPIDER'

Above: Three Desert Railway identities: Joe Pickford, Spider Willard, and Lottie Pickford.

Right top: Spider's pack camel with a full load aboard, photographed in the spinifex.

Right below: Surveying for the desert railways was a long and lonely job. This is the surveyor for the Trans-Australia line, photographed in 1908 at the border of South Australia and Western Australia. When Spider left Marree, South Australia, with a railway surveyor, he didn't get back for two and a half years.

'Riding the Desert Schooner' was tough at any time, but heading off for two and a half years as Harold 'Spider' Willard did in 1926 took courage.

Near the end of his days, when he was living in a pioneers' settlement at Marree, South Australia, he told his story:

I've been a bit of everything, scoop driving with horses, camel driving, spiker (driving dogs into rails), rock cutting with hammer and drill. Most of the time I worked with camels. My father and three brothers worked on construction of the East–West line, but I say I helped keep the railway going.

There was a camel depot at Frome Creek, thirty-five miles nor'-east from Marree out near Lake Eyre. There were 300 to 400 camels there all the time being handled, yarded, branded and broken in to pack, saddle and team work. We had 200 camels and calves, fifty bulls and the rest were working camels. Our boss was Charlie Kunoth, 'Bumblefoot' we called him. All the men working for him loading camels for the railheads had nicknames. There was 'Pandy Jack' Gerard from Pandy Pandy Station near Birdsville; Bill "——" James who was noted for his swearing; 'Cleanskin' Billy, a kid; 'Stuttering' Bob Hughes; Jackie 'Nuisance' Nauson; Jackie 'the Rambler'; 'Scandalous' Jack Scanlon; 'Dungaree' Tom; 'Pyjama' Jack, and I was called 'Spider' but I can't remember why.

Some of the men were Afghans, some of us not. The Afghans mostly went with pack camels, the white men with teams, they seemed to handle teams better. In between droving, us men headed back to camp.

We met the train at Marree, later at Oodnadatta, and our teams did almost all the carting away from the rail until the line went on to Alice Springs in 1929. At one time we took the parts of a huge reinforced concrete tank from the rail at William Creek across to Coober Pedy where the opal miners were living in caverns they had dug under the ground to escape the heat.

We used five teams with fourteen camels to a wagon for this trip and each wagon had four to five tons. This was over very heavy sand—on a good track we could have put on six to seven tons. At one stretch on this 110-mile trek we had to 'double-bank' the teams to get through and at times I saw the lead camel actually crawling over the top of the sand hills.

When we were carting sleepers for the East–West railway we put five to six hundredweight of sleepers on a camel. I have carried eight to nine hundredweight on a lead camel to weigh him down, but only in an emergency would I do that. Practically speaking, if a camel can get up on his feet with a load he will carry it.

We never worried so much about getting a kick from a camel as we did from a horse. Camels have got very small hindquarters, but if they struck up with the front leg the knuckle could split your head open. Always when we were hobbling them we kept behind their front legs.

My longest job with camels was in 1926 when I crossed the great Nullarbor Plain from north to south. I was driver for a surveyor. There was talk at the time—and intermittently ever since—that a north-south railway should cut up north from the Trans, the East–West line, and he was doing a survey for the government. We took two riding camels and five pack camels with food and water, an eighteen-gallon keg of water on each side of a pack animal—that water was for Mr Mahoney and

me. We got water for the camels on the way by digging a soak at the few places we could find.

We started from Marree and went north 200 miles to Oodnadatta, then 200 to the Musgrave Ranges where Mr Mahoney needed to trig and map an area. The first day we got into the ranges we were attacked by the blacks. I felt it coming. We couldn't see anything but I knew they were there by my camels. I rode up beside Mr Mahoney.

'I think there are blackfellows here.'

'Oh, I shouldn't think so,' he said. He was from the south part of Western Australia. There were no wild tribes left down there.

'Our camels are giving me the sign,' I told him. 'They're frightened.'

Within two minutes whirra whirra whirra, the spears and boomerangs were coming over our heads. Mr Mahoney knew that distance was better than cover. 'Get out of it!' So I turned the string (of camels) and hustled them. They were so frightened they wouldn't speed. The blacks followed us.

'What will we do?' I said.

'Fire a few volleys over their heads,' said Mr Mahoney.

That slowed them up and though they followed, the spears fell short of us.

'Let's get out of these hills,' Mr Mahoney said.

When we got into camp we circled, made a stockade with our pack saddles through the night. But we knew the danger was more likely to be in daytime so we travelled fast for two days due south before re-entering the ranges and we didn't see any more of them.

(They were a wild mob out in the ranges. Not long after our brush with them there was a murder there and a police trooper went out with a black tracker but the tracker left him outside the ranges. I never knew a tracker willingly to enter the Musgraves.)

Water was a problem all the way. Between the Musgrave Ranges and Ooldea we were seven days between water. The camels were near to done in. We were pretty worried, but when we were coming into that country near Ooldea I said to Mr Mahoney, 'I've been into this country before and I think we're close to a rock hole. A big rock hole.' The little budgie birds were flying by. I climbed a sand hill and there were the Ooldea Wells in front of us. I swung the glasses round and there was the railway line and the Ooldea siding.

'What did you find?' said Mr Mahoney when I got back to him.

'The Ooldea Wells,' I told him.

'That's the salvation of us,' he said.

We stopped at Ooldea for three days and filled up with water. Daisy Bates was there with her blacks, all civilised people after the Musgrave mob.

Then we went across the plains to Eucla, Fowlers Bay, Ceduna and back to Ooldea. We were to part here. Mr Mahoney said they'd probably call the new railway the 'Irish Spider' after him and me — but it's been a long time coming. Then he said 'Hooroo' and I left to take the seven camels back the 350 miles by myself.

Wherever I found water I camped for a couple of days to recuperate the camels and myself. We had some very severe sand hills to cross as well as the Stuart Range twenty miles north of Coober Pedy.

I was away for two and a half years on this trip and in that time I never slept under an iron roof and the first fence or road I saw on the way back was forty-five miles from Oodnadatta.

And then it was back to Muloorina and the camels and ropes every day on real railways business.

Before his epic journey with a railways surveyor in 1926, 'Spider' Willard worked as a camel teamster carrying goods from the rail heads to the cattle stations of the interior. This camel team is carrying horse feed to a railway construction camp.

BOB THE DOG

There is a saying that the outback would not have been settled at all had it not been for the horse and camel. Most men would add the dog to that memorial. The companion and only friend of many a lonely man in a lonely place, there are dogs in bush paintings and photographs from the earliest times, as well as stories of their loyalty and courage.

One of the most loyal and most loved was 'Bob, the Driver's Dog'. Where he came from no one knew, but it was believed he had been the pet of a railway engine driver who had died. He turned up in the Adelaide railway yards in the early 1890s and leapt up on the footplate of a locomotive. He obviously knew his way around and waited for the driver to open his crib tin for him. But he wouldn't go home with any man, he waited and watched for some driver who never did turn up. He travelled all over South Australian railways and was famous for his sudden leap onto the footplate when the engine whistle sounded. Such a whistle once caused him great embarrassment: following the sound, he ran up a gang plank and made a sea voyage on a ship from Port Augusta to Port Pirie.

His loyalty to a lost master gained him much love. So well known was he that an Adelaide newspaper seventy years later reported that a recent questionnaire directed to a number of men over thirty years of age with the name of Robert revealed that most of them had been at some stage or other in their life jocularly addressed as 'Bob the railway dog'.

In 1889 a commercial traveller had presented him with a collar inscribed with the couplet:

> Stop me not, but let me jog,
> I am Bob, the driver's dog.

An 'obituary' of the railway dog appeared in the *Adelaide Observer* in 1895 when he died at the age of about seventeen.

Kind Friend While On This Card You Gaze
   With Wonder and Surprise
Your Old Friend Bob, The Railway Dog
   I Hope You'll Recognise
G.H.   Terowie Dec, 1892

Home-keeping dogs have homely wits,
   Their notions tame and poor;
I scorn the dog who humbly sits
   Before the cottage door;
Or those who weary vigils keep,
   Or follow lowly kine.
A dreary life midst stupid sheep
   Shall ne'er be lot of mine.

For free from thrall I travel far,
   No 'fixed abode' I own;
I leap aboard a railway car,
   By everyone I'm known.
Today I'm here, tomorrow brings
   Scenes miles and miles away.
Born swiftly on steam's rushing wings
   I see fresh friends each day.

Each driver from the footplate hails
   My coming with delight;
I gain from all upon the rails
   A welcome ever bright.
I share the perils of the line
   With mates from end to end,
Who would not for a silver mine
   Have harm befall their friend.

Then other dogs may snarl and fight,
   Round city purlieus prowl;
Or render hideous the night
   With unmelodious howl.
I have a cheery bark for all,
   No ties my travels clog,
I hear the whistle—that's the call
   For Bob, the Driver's Dog.

BATTLEFRONTS OF OUTBACK

The trans-continental motorists, H. H. Dutton and H. M. Aunger, set out from King William Street, Adelaide, complete with water-bag, en route for Darwin. The motorists abandoned their first attempt south of Tennant Creek on Christmas Day 1907. The following year they came north again in another car—met Frank Birtles thirty-five miles north of Alice Springs—recovered the 1907 car and were successful in the south-north crossing.

Frank Birtles, the bravest of the brave wheelmen who criss-crossed Australia in the twenty years after the 'safety' bicycle arrived, crossed all the 'battlefronts of the outback'. By 1911 he had cycled seven times across the continent and twice around it—taking a new route on each trip.

In 1908 he rode from 'Sydney to Sydney', via Port Darwin, Adelaide and Melbourne, a ride of over 8,000 miles. On his cycle Birtles carried not only food and water but 'photographic apparatus' and took splendid photographs of the country known as 'the Never-Never'.

From Sydney he went north to Brisbane, Rockhampton and across to Brunetha Creek where he was laid up with fever (most likely malaria) as the rainy season had begun. As he biked on across the Northern Territory he photographed a deserted cattle station from where the owners had been driven away 'by fever and ague'. Between Oodnadatta and Alice Springs he photographed camel teams that were carrying the mails 340 miles because of the Depot Sandhills, which defied any other form of transport at that time. When thirty-five miles north of Alice Springs, he met the overlanding motorists, Dutton and Aunger, on their way from Adelaide to Darwin across the road-less continent.

Yet, for all its dangers and distance, this, of his many famous rides, makes Birtles appear to be travelling on a much-used country road. In Birtles' day the journeys he took were across Tom Tiddler's Ground—no-man's land. Today multi-lane highways span the land, but Frank Birtles must take bearings to find his way.

In 1909 he followed camel pad and cattle track to cross from Fremantle, Western Australia, to Sydney via Eucla, Port Augusta and Broken Hill. The distance recorded on his cyclometer was $3,056\frac{1}{2}$ miles on the forty-four day ride across the continent; he left Fremantle on 30 September 1909, and reached Sydney 12 November. His diary gave some indication of the hardships on the way:

October 6—Cut my heel badly; sand making it fester. When crossing Lake Lefroy (dry salt lake) rain came on; took three hours to travel half a mile to its sandy banks. Heavy night's rain. Came across an empty case left by the survey party; crawled inside and turned it upside down; of creeping things in plenty. A various assortment of insects kept me awake all night.

October 12—Had a bad day. After travelling in blazing heat through heavy sands arrived at an old well near some rocks; drew some water; the smell that came up was dreadful; worse than any sewer. It was half full of dead rabbits. Could not drink it. Rank poison. Hunted around, and on top of the rocks found some rock-hole water; stray camels had been there. Had to choose between 'stewed rabbit' water or the evil smelling 'muss' that the camels had been wading in. I took the latter; filled up my water tank, and, without drinking any, went on. For sixty miles I desperately drove the 'bike', not knowing whether I was heading up right for the next waters. I followed long undulating ridges, but no sign could I see of granite. Just as it was

Frank Birtles poses with his camera alongside the bicycle he rode for his 1908 trip from Sydney to Sydney via Darwin, Adelaide and Melbourne.

getting dark I saw open country through between the trees; a few minutes later and big granite rocks loomed up in the distance. Taking the bearings I kept on as straight as I could. After several 'spills' in the dark I landed there. With a 40 hp thirst on me I scrambled eagerly over the boulders and found a little pot-hole; drank very slowly, filled up the tank, went back to camp, and went to sleep straight away. Woke up in the morning with a badly swollen ankle; cut the back out of my shoe, put a damper poultice on my heel, and started out again. Here there was some good grass country. The rabbits were about in thousands. 'Bunny' is a good explorer; he finds the pastoral lands first.

October 15—Made seventy miles against strong head wind; country very dry; even bushes are dead; knocked up; flies bad; dingo walked up to camp; greeted him with a bullet. Lonely camp; 400-stage before me without seeing a soul; have to live on what I shoot; travelling over dreary, monotonous limestone plains; howling head winds with dust storms; shot a turkey; had a hot bath in artesian bore; weather very cold.

October 19—Heavy rain; bogged; had to camp two days. Prospected surrounding country on foot.

October 23—Turned south; arrived on beach along the Bight. Went out that night with a piece of lighted bark, and walked slowly around in the shallow water. With a sharp-pointed stick I speared several flounder; had grilled fish for supper and breakfast. This beach is one of the finest in Australia; fine, firm sands, sixty miles long; an ideal place for motor-car races. Fresh water can be got in places a few yards above high-water mark by scooping down two or three feet. Wild grapes and wild peaches grow—the former at the foot and latter at the top of the limestone cliffs, which run around the southern parts of the coast.

On this trip Birtles carried 280 pounds of equipment and, at the time of this photograph, four extra gallons of water to help him across the desert—as well as a bundle of firewood for boiling his quart-pot.

October 24—Got a big westerly gale behind me. Decided to drive 'her' (the machine). Rode 170 miles that day, which brought me to the big Bight Sandhills. Camped on top of a rabbit burrow; wood handy; rabbits rumbling and scratching underneath me all night. Heel still festering.

October 25—Walking; hard work in sun; March flies cruel. Saw spiralling mirage for nearly all day; it kept coming and going. Travelled all night; moon shining brightly. Snakes lying out; several scares. Adders are same color as sand. Got through seventy miles of sandhills next day. Decided to cut south for telegraph line. Heard parrots in the afternoon; investigated, and found a rock hole; camped. The water made me cramped in stomach; started vomiting. Filled up water-bag and continued southerly course; would not drink; no water that night or following day. Bad headache; could not eat; worried about the right way; had not got out to the limestone plains; all mallee scrubs; walking most of the time. Began to wonder in a dull kind of way as to whether I had been transferred to Hades. Weather cooled off in the afternoon; sea breeze came up that reassured me. Poured water over my head and wrists. Next morning out into open country. Followed up a fence, then a track; away in the distance I could see, in a dancing haze, the gleam of a white-washed roof—a telegraph station at Bookabie (South Australia). (The dingo poisoners must have poisoned the rock water. Afterwards on the return journey the scalps are collected.)

At noon on the next day I reached my looked-for goal. Heel and ankle dressed by chemist at Port Augusta.

Frank's use of his camera on his trips preserved some rare photographs of the time. There is one with his Universal Bicycle—'manufactured in Australia by Anthony Hordern from BSA parts'—with its front wheel in the Northern Territory and back wheel in Queensland. This happened at the vermin-proof, wire-netted, barbed-wired fence between Queensland, the Territory and New South Wales, its 3,000 miles making it the world's longest fence.

He carried nearly 300 pounds of equipment with him and at the time this photograph was taken he had four extra gallons of water on board to help him across the dry, dreary run of 600 miles of treeless plains, as well as a little bundle of firewood to boil the billy or 'quart-pot' as the Northern Australians call it. His menu consisted of 'salt beef and flour with "gohanna" and cockatoo' to vary the courses. 'On an average I consumed one pound of food and twelve ounces of water for every ten miles of travel.' That was when things were going well. 'Sometimes I am forced to go without a drink all day, and at other times, such as when I felt fever coming on, I drank four gallons of water a day. For fuel and "steam" I must have consumed some ten times my weight on this trip.'

As usual, he met or passed other overlanders, including two Chinese who had walked 800 miles from Pine Creek across into Queensland when he met them. 'One was shod with sugar bags instead of boots.' The two Asians carried their goods, including two large canvas water bags, on the usual bamboos poles as they ambled steadily over the blue bush plains.

Wood had to be carted many miles in some places on the dreary plain. Frank often mentions the dreariness of the outback in that area. 'The mental and physical strain makes one talk to himself—not softly either!'

In Western Queensland he lined up for water being carted by 'the small boys of the town who earn good money by contracting to supply water by the hundred gallons to householders in the dry season. They use goat teams to haul their tanks. The animals understand all the torrid terms that are used in the language of the teamster. A team of ten goats will pull a four hundred gallon tank and, (in the language of the goat-teamster), "scratch gravel going tphill with any crack team of the west".'

Like other overlanders, he had landmarks to watch for, 'the Hawks Nest', a tree on the Murrangi Track, one of the most important of all. 'It is most important that this tree be found, as bearings have here to be taken for the Murrangi Waterhole, fifty miles away. Miss this, and there are hundreds of miles of unexplored "desert" country ahead, waterless as far as is known.'

On 13 May 1911, he left Sydney for Queensland, on to Pine Creek, then across to Broome and down to Perth, tackling the overland record. He returned to Sydney via Coolgardie, Port Augusta and Melbourne, reaching Sydney on 1 February 1912. The overland route was covered in thirty-one days, two hours, a record for the distance of 3,175 miles. He travelled 100 miles per day but in fact the actual miles would be about 10,000, zig-zagging from water hole to patches clear of sand dunes, and around rocky outcrops. At the end of this epic Birtles had completed 70,000 miles of overland cycling in Australia during six years. Again his diary should tell the story:

5 August—Left Pine Creek (Northern Territory) on overland cycle journey to Broome (Western Australia).

8 August—Camped on Katherine River. Crocodile crawled out onto a sandbank in the middle of the stream; barramundi in his jaws. Fired a bullet at him; he dropped the fish and dived into the water. I swam across, towed my future meal to the camp; grilled about eight pounds of it for tea, salted the rest. Sweet dreams.

August 9—Mosquitoes in myriads; the red flannel shirt a great attraction. Hot night; buffalo 'squawking' softly in the stagnant, scrubby swamp.

August 11—Shot iguana for lunch. Strange reptile; can climb a tree, dig a burrow,

Above: A welcome break for a drover on the road during the 1882 drought—he gets a quart-pot of water from a water-tank. Frank Birtles on his bicycle in the outback in the 1900s was rarely so lucky. His diaries, like those of earlier explorers, refer constantly to his search for fresh water.

Above left: Frank Birtles' bicycle at the 3,000-mile rabbit-proof fence between Queensland, NSW and the Northern Territory—the world's longest fence.

swim a creek, dive like a fish, sprint his hundred in six and a half, swallow anything—from an unopened tin of jam to a discarded sock—lays eggs in the hot sand (which the dingo promptly unearths), and fights like a demon.

August 12—Arrived Willeroo Station. Blacks coming in for a big corroboree. Started to show fight; various tribes standing behind trees, shaking spears and jabbering wildly. Manager of station fired repeating rifle over their camps as a hint to behave themselves.

August 16—Riding fast along a cattle track overtook wild bull going down to water. He kept running ahead. I could not get past. Suddenly he stopped short, dropped his head and charged. I sprinted off the track, got past onto my course. Did not have time to look behind. I beat him easily on the 'straight'.

August 20—Having a bad time. Big rocky mountain ranges, cannot get out; everywhere I go ends up in a narrow gorge surrounded by spinifex-covered cliffs. Water supply running short. Waterbag leaking.

August 21—No water. Raising 'smokes' to try and call niggers up. Got a reply in afternoon; tried to make across to it; stopped by big wall of rock. Camped without water.

August 22—Been dreaming of Sydney surf, and a beautiful rain falling. Dingoes howling woke me up. Must be water about. Got up without 'breakfast' and travelled in the early morning by moonlight. Decided to make back along my tracks. Saw several big 'smokes' (signal fires made by natives) over the ranges; replied to them. Met a party of niggers, who accompanied me to the nearest water—*the same place I had camped at four days ago.*

August 23—Camped on top of a big rock in case of surprise by blacks. In morning tried to get an old buck and gin to pilot me out of the maze of gorges; they could not or would not 'savvy'. Made another start in blazing heat. Soles of my light shoes cut to pieces. Basalt rocks burn my feet; keep stumbling over prickly spinifex.

By 28 August he had stumbled out of the 'maze'.

August 29—Still travelling along the freshly made cattle-track, which would take me down to the Kimberley foothills. Track very dusty and worn down to a foot-deep channel. Run over a small spinifex snake, which bit me on the front of the right leg. Pinched the flesh, cut piece out. Leg black and blue; not hurting much; let blood run freely; feel very thirsty.

August 30—Put poultice of damp black clay and permanganate on wound.

He rested up at a hot spring where game and fish were plentiful.

September 2—Do not like to leave. Still camping. Shot some pink cockatoos (galahs) very tough. Mended my shoes with calico; made a pair of cycling knickers out of a tucker bag, so as to save my good ones on reaching civilisation.

September 5—Just left hot springs. All clothes, etc., nice and clean. Would like good George-street feed. Voted 'bush tucker no good'. Beef and plum pudding better.

September 27—One thousand miles from Pine Creek.

And so the distance cyclist continues his lonesome circuit.

'The bike' may have been the latest fad in Australia as in most other countries, but the pioneer overlanders could expect no special favours. In 1898 Tom Coleman was served with writs to pay £150 for severing the wires of the Overland Telegraph. When he cut the wires, Coleman had thought himself about to die: '. . . a sleepless night, memorable with the helpless agony, the intermittent hot flushes and shivering fits of the dread malarial fever, the terror of every resident in the Territory'. The sudden attack of malaria had caused him to halt between Katherine Station and Daly Waters. To save himself, he cut the wire, hoping to attract the attention of linesmen.

The following day the attack had lessened and still sick and trembling Coleman mounted and tried to pedal southwards on his way to Adelaide, his goal. His cycling partner seems to have been little comfort or help to the sick man.

Noon with its fierce, intolerable glare found us a bare fourteen miles from the well... struggled ahead over the yielding sandy soil. Five miles an hour was our speed, yet every sinew was at its highest tension as we rode, in the merciless heat, bathed in perspiration. The water in our cans was now hot and nauseating yet how we longed for more than the bare mouthful we occasionally indulged in. What if the next waterhole were dry?

He came on footprints in the sand of a solitary pedestrian,

... backwards and forwards, now here, now there, in meaningless wanderings, the footprints continued. In one spot there was the imprint of a man's body. From thence a trail as if something heavy had been dragged along some distance into the spinifex, apparently by another human being.

He followed the trail to where it led to 'a small mound of freshly dug sand surmounted by a crude cross.'

The tracks were those of an unfortunate young fellow who had strayed away from the wells under the delirium of an old wound on the head, inflicted by a native some years ago in revenge for some wrong, real or fancied. Probably a touch of sunstroke had completed the partial derangement and he had wandered farther away into the grim fortress of the sand king.

He rode on, thirst now troubling him greatly.

Presently riding became impossible. Sand, sand everywhere . . . its dust made the throat and nostrils feel on fire. An old linesman had told us 'Wait till you cross the McDonnell Ranges before ye start swearing at the sand'. We didn't wait.

They met two drovers with a flock of sheep.

They stared in wonder at our cycles. They had come from the 'Never-Never' country and had never seen the likes. Two black boys laughed in derision . . . we couldn't even get a hundred yards of solid ground on which to demonstrate the speed of the ship on which our lives depended.

The drovers told them of two water holes in a creek ten miles further on. They toiled on, carrying the bikes much of the way and then saw the holes: '. . . embedded in the slimy ooze lay the carcass of a bullock in an advanced state of decay, the hind quarters just touching the water'. The next waterhole marked on their rough maps was eighteen miles on—and would that be any better? They sat and stared at the dead bullock. 'Our mouths were parched and our tongues were swollen, yet our loathing of that slimy liquid was greater . . .' Finally, they decided they would boil the water before drinking it. But then another difficulty arose. How to reach it? There was only one way if they did not want to be drowned in the oozing mud that was impossible to walk on. 'The only way to reach the water was along the back of the dead bullock.' Further waiting was out of the question, so Coleman took one of the quart pots and gingerly stepped along the carcass, 'with my flesh creeping, and half suffocated by the dreadful stench.'

He had to make four trips to get enough water; this they strained through

Tom Coleman, photographed for Austral Wheel *in 1898, the year he nearly died of malaria in the Never-Never and cut the Overland Telegraph line in the hope of being rescued. Instead he was served with a writ to pay £150 costs.*

a handkerchief, skimmed the scum off the top with gum leaves when the water boiled, and used twice the usual quantity of tea in an attempt to kill 'any foreign tastes'. Even then 'we waited for complete darkness before quenching our thirst with that horrible stuff . . . I shiver even now as I think of it'.

Following an accident on the journey Coleman spent considerable time in hospital after a painful operation which left him crippled—and then came the writs for cutting the wire. Poor Tom Coleman.

From the arid lands north of Kalgoorlie, Western Australia, William Snell set off in 1897: he travelled from Menzies to Adelaide, cycling for much of the way south of the Nullarbor. He covered the 1,700 miles in twenty days, averaging about eighty-five miles a day.

Leaving Menzies on 7 May, he reached Coolgardie (100 miles) next morning. Frequently doing 100 miles per day, toiling through scrub, suffering from want of water, he arrived at Eyre's Sandpatch, thirty miles of loose sand. He had such difficulty in finding his way through that eventually he had to camp. Striking the beach on 13 May, he came across a wreck that was lying there, and had a look through it. Racing along the beach, a shell punctured his tyre, the only puncture that he sustained through the journey. During the day he passed a tank on which was written 'Arthur Richardson, first cyclist from Coolgardie to Adelaide; 3rd December, 1896.' Snell added his name as second cyclist, and the next morning, assisted by a strong rear wind, he raced along at seventeen or eighteen miles an hour, doing seventy-five miles before noon. From Eucla, a telegraph operator accompanied him for some miles, and he reached Nullarbor Station that night, a distance of 120 miles. At Denial Bay the water was so bad that the people were scooping on the beach for some kind of soak. Snell could not swallow what was obtained and had to travel another thirty miles for a drink.

After he left Port Augusta on 26 May it rained so heavily that he covered only five miles. On 28 May, his last day, he rode from Clare to Adelaide, 100 miles. He carried neither lamp nor bell on the journey, and his baggage weighed thirty-five pounds, including a gallon of water and provisions.

After resting a day, he left Adelaide and pedalled to Melbourne. From Coleraine he put 185 miles behind him in one day, and at the Werribee had his only fall, through his chain breaking. He lay for two hours unconscious before being found; then another wheelman lent him a machine to finish his journey. He had cut ten days off Richardson's time.

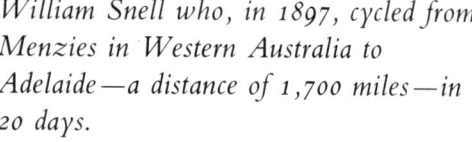

William Snell who, in 1897, cycled from Menzies in Western Australia to Adelaide—a distance of 1,700 miles—in 20 days.

BEFORE THE BITUMEN

Men who have undertaken admirable tasks often live quietly, far from the scene of their endeavours. Brigadier Dollery, who performed two enduring tasks, was a captain in the Regular Army stationed in Melbourne when he had his first trip to the Northern Territory in 1934. At that time the man who, in a few months, was going to take a journey that 'revolutionised transport in the outback', was in charge of the development of motor transport in the army. He had channelled his career in this direction and he became the recognised expert in motor transport.

When a revolutionary new vehicle was brought to Australia for testing in April 1934, it was naturally to him that the Government turned. And when his long and arduous 'test' had been completed, the 'road train' was launched in the sandy wastes and the gibber deserts. A new phase of development for the pastoral and mining industries of outback-South Australia and the Northern Territory began.

What has now become known as the 'road train' in Australia had its beginnings in 1929 when the British Overseas Mechanical Transport Committee and the British and South African Governments pooled their resources to build a transport unit for use within the Empire on roadless tracts of country. Kenya was one country such a vehicle would help. At that time there were very few roads and railways there. Later, Australia and New Zealand joined in the planning, and, after trials of a unit in South Africa, a diesel was produced that was to play a great role in the development of the outback of Australia for the next ten years.

Brigadier Dollery.

This giant (for those times) 130 hp AEC prime-mover was a multi-wheeled tractor with four trailers, and was articulated so that all the wheels tracked in the one spot, enabling a right-turn to be made through a ten-foot gate, an entirely new concept of locomotion. Two Cockney drivers came with the unit under the charge of Captain E. C. Roscoe, RASC, and a 'bush cook' was picked up in Adelaide. The path-finders set off to Oodnadatta. This part of the trip was the easiest because they could travel all the way to the dusty desert town on a road. 'It was from there on that the real ordeal began':

North of Oodnadatta we crossed over trackless wastes of sandhills. Some days we progressed only two or three miles. The maximum speed of the unit was about twenty miles per hour but we at no time reached this. We drove a car ahead of the unit to reconnoitre the best practicable routes; sometimes we were on a track of sorts, but mostly these were obliterated by sand, and we had to make our own tracks. It was tough work. When we got in a too-sticky place, we took the tractor over first and backed it back over its exact tracks, thus consolidating the sand; then we hauled the trailers over one by one. And off we'd crawl again, low gear all the way.

It was a tedious and hard trip, but exciting too. This was a completely new development in motor transport, and all its innovations were novel to us. The unit

Above: The rusting cab of the AEC truck that pioneered the great road trains of the outback.

Top: The remains of the pioneer overlanding truck rots away in a junk yard outside Darwin.

was so beautifully designed that we tried it out going round and round in circles on full lock, and the two trailers behind tracked in exactly the same track as the prime-mover. It was the first time too that we had ever had a vehicle driven on all eight wheels, with a braking system that acted on the rear trailer first and so on down through the trailers until it reached the prime-mover itself. But of course the most striking part of its design in regard to Australian conditions was its ability to negotiate sharp turns.

Often we had to go ahead on foot, particularly over the salt pans. These were very dangerous. What seemed to be solid surface might turn out to be no more than a thin crust on top of treacherous bog.

We saw a surprising number of people considering that there was such a tiny population scattered over this vast land with an area the size of England. Wherever we stopped at a settlement, people gathered to inspect the vehicle and question us about its performance.

We saw a lot of wildlife too, but it was terribly dry and whenever we stopped at a waterhole or bore, animals and birds would flock over for the water we'd release into the troughs. All round Erldunda Station the waterholes had dried up in the drought, and wildlife had come to the station for water. They were as tame as cats. It was nothing to see the homestead kitchen full of birds—goldfinches, galahs, budgerigars, everything as well as kangaroos and wallabies. Further on we saw the most amazing sight when millions of birds came to us at every bore we drew water from. They'd flock to us until the sky was dark with them and then they'd roost on the bore, on the stay wires, on the trough, on our vehicles, everywhere, waiting for us to release water, and once the water began to flow they'd swoop down on it. And when they'd done we'd find many little ones pushed under and drowned by the press of numbers above them struggling for water.

The Cockney drivers, Captain Roscoe, and the then Captain Dollery slept out under the stars at night and for most of the way lived off the land. 'The cook was a good bushman and shot plenty of game but none of us cared for it much. I never liked kangaroo and here in the sand and dust I liked it less.' But there wasn't much grumbling about the cooking.

We had plenty else to grumble about. We carried long rolls of matting to place under the wheels to get us out when we were bogged—sometimes we spent the whole day just driving over the matting to its end, then rolling it up to the front wheels, rolling it out and driving over it again, and repeating the process over and over again. And soon these mats became clogged with barbs from spinifex which made their handling difficult and painful, even with gloves. Our hands were cut and often bleeding.

We rushed at sandhills, and if we gathered enough momentum we rolled over the top and tried to use our speed to rush the next dune, but if we missed we backed on our tracks and rushed again, gaining a little more each rush. We carried all our petrol with us and water as well, because we couldn't rely on getting water in a land so desperately parched itself. We reconnoitred creek beds carefully; these were always danger spots. We cut boughs and stumps out to make a track through the mulga. After we left the little settlement at Finke, we reached the Hugh River, and this we had to cross eleven times in twenty-two miles, each crossing involving a different tactic.

The pioneer transport men reached Alice Springs on 19 May 1934, more than three weeks after leaving Adelaide 1,100 miles away. Nearly everyone in the town turned out to have a look at the new vehicle—stockmen and storekeepers with a view to its future for them, and Afghans with the sad knowledge that this was the end for them. With their camels and donkey teams the Afghans had been the original pioneers of transport in this vast harsh land. Now their era was ended.

At the Alice the trailers were loaded with timber and corrugated-iron for the first building to be erected at Tennant Creek, 300 miles north. It was, not unexpectedly, a pub. The team set off again, following the unmade road north, adjacent to the telegraph line. In this part of the country they met a different hazard—ant hills. Because their wheel base was much wider than any vehicle which had previously passed this way, their wheels straddled the track and many concrete-hard ant-hills had to be chopped down.

When we got to Tennant Creek, we really saw the outback of the Australia of the time. The miners were living in holes in the ground, a few feet deep, with a tent pegged out over the top. They had rough beds of hessian, and boxes for tables. The settlement had all the appearance of an American wild west town in the days of Jesse James. Bearded miners, dressed in moleskins and wide-brimmed hats, many carrying fire-arms, slouched over to us and surrounded the vehicles. Roscoe, the Englishman, said, 'God, I don't like the look of this much'. The rest of us didn't either, so we got their pub unloaded pretty quick and moved five miles further north before we camped for the night.

When the vehicles returned to Adelaide at the end of that historic journey, they were inspected to enable a report to be sent back to the makers in England. All components were found to be in perfect condition. There had been no mechanical troubles, and it had been proved that the cost of operating was less than half the cost of hauling on the railways at that time. Later it was possible to cut freight costs by one cent a ton-mile. Ordinary freight was carried for five cents a ton-mile, but developmental materials were carried at one cent a ton-mile. This original prime-mover was kept on the run for ten years, and one of its last big jobs was to haul 126 bales of wool from MacDonald Downs Station to the railhead at Alice Springs, 156 miles away. Old-timers pointed out that previously that load would have taken a string of sixty to seventy camels to move it. In ten years the unit had covered more than 800,000 ton-miles. It had been bought for $6,000, surely one of the best investments this country has ever made.

When he first knew he was going up this way with the road train, Brigadier Dollery was thrilled to be travelling through the country of *We of the Never-Never*, Mrs Aeneas Gunn's wonderful book:

Later, during the second World War, when I was stationed in Darwin, I conceived the idea of bringing the bodies of the characters of her book all together around the grave of their boss, 'the Maluka', Aeneas Gunn himself. These bodies were buried far and wide over the Territory, and I had a great amount of correspondence with Mrs Gunn and with many others to locate all these characters and get permission to transport their remains to the Elsey.

Below left: The entrance to the Elsey Cemetery on the Bitumen.

Below: The grave of Mr Aeneas Gunn, 'the Maluka' of Mrs Gunn's book, We of the Never-Never, *alongside the Bitumen (the Stuart Highway) on the Elsey. During World War II, Brigadier Dollery arranged to have the bodies of other characters of the book re-buried in the same graveyard as the Maluka.*

The real-life characters of Mrs Aeneas Gunn's We of the Never-Never *(left to right): 'The Dandy' (H. H. Bryant), 'Mine Host' (Tom Pearce), 'Cheon' (Ah Cheon), 'Irish Mac' (Jack McCarthy), 'The Quiet Stockman' (Jack McLeod), 'The Sanguine Scot' (Jock MacLennon), 'The Head Stockman' (Dave Suttee). 'The Fizzer' (Henry Peckham) is shown on pp. 19 and 20.*

Far right: The fire, the quart-pot, the man and his dog at sundown — the epitome of the outback.

Using the services of the Australian War Graves unit stationed at Darwin, the Brigadier removed the bodies to the graveyard. The body of 'the Fizzer' of Mrs Gunn's book, Harry Peckham (see p. 19), was located near the creek towards the Western Australian border where he had been drowned on 17 August 1911 — getting the mail through as might be expected of this man. The bronze headstone over his grave is carved with the figures of pack horses and a mailman. The body of 'the Wag', Constable Kingston, was found after much searching in the Katherine cemetery. There was some doubt as to whether this was the body they were looking for, so Dollery wrote to a South Australian whom he knew had been at Kingston's funeral. The witness wrote back:

We had no coffin, and in those latitudes we must bury a man quickly, so a box was knocked up for the constable from whisky cases nailed on to saplings. However, when they tried to lower the 'coffin' it was found that the box was too big for the hole they had dug — the Wag was a very big man, so two men jumped down on the box but with all their jumping they couldn't make it go down in a horizontal position, so if the body you have found is in a reclining position, then it is that of Constable Kingston.

Dollery was able to verify this.

The ten acres contain the graves of the well-known characters of *We of the Never-Never* as well as those of 'Unknown Travellers' whose graves Dollery found scattered in the bush where they had died. Scarcely a traveller passes this spot beside the Stuart Highway, the Bitumen, without stopping to view the graves of some of Australia's best-known and loved characters. It seems to be one of the few good things that came about because of the war.

RUSSIAN JACK AND JAMES BALZANO

They gambled with death and knew it, these men of the west, the barrowmen who pushed their clumsy make-shift structures over the deserts, past the graves of men who had died on the track. It was a peculiarly Western Australian trait and in that state scarcely a 'rush' began without a few 'barrowmen' turning up—if you could call pushing a heavily laden wheelbarrow across a hundred miles of bush 'turning up'.

A few of their constructions have been brought from the bush into museums. There can be no mistaking a genuine miner's barrow. They knocked them up with anything that came to hand. In the end, they were so proud of their primitive constructions they wouldn't have used more refined materials had they been available.

Some barrows would take an effort by an ordinary man to push them unladen, though with some the going was easier, because odd strips of solid rubber and bits of leather were nailed on the rim of the wooden wheel and secured with ribbons cut from tobacco tins. Other patches of tin and rough-hewn boards were used to mend fractures in the wheel.

Some barrowmen cut down trees and sawed planks to make the body and sawed through tree trunks to create solid wheels two inches thick. In Coolgardie there is an example of the average barrowman's burden. Made of a forked sapling, it has straps for the shoulders and 'double' handles to protect the pusher's hands when thrusting through the prickly bush. These outer handles can also be used as uprights to support a rough cover over the load in the rainy season 'up north'. Its load includes a small saw with an old horseshoe for the handle, a shovel, a tomahawk with a sapling for the handle, a quart pot, a frying pan, a camp oven, a miner's dish, a sugar-bag, and a battered felt hat.

In 1895, James Balzano, one of the legendary barrowmen, was doing poorly at Darlot Diggings in the far north from Kalgoorlie, so he built a wheelbarrow and trundled off to look for gold elsewhere. For the body and the shafts of the barrow he cut down saplings and bound them together with strips of green hide; the wheel he shaped with a tomahawk from a meat case. On this he loaded his gear and headed south.

Darlot had been a hard living—water cost 8d a gallon and food was equally expensive—so doubtless Balzano felt he could do no worse elsewhere. But, like all the other barrowmen, there was a touch of macho-man in the individuality of his rough, unwieldy contraption. This man trudged over sand hills and stony plains, stopping to dig where he believed the rocks looked like a 'show' but luck was out for him. He trundled down the dust to Hannans (now Kalgoorlie) in time for Christmas with the miners at the new find. The next day he was off again to IOU (known also as Bulong), Kurnalpi and, by January 1896, was across at Kurnowna, 560 miles from where he had originally set off. Unlike most bushmen, Balzano kept a journal and noted in it the new goldfields he visited and the men he met.

Above: These men going from one rush to another carried their goods in a makeshift 'four-hander' wheelbarrow. The greatest of the barrowmen were Russian Jack and James Balzano.

Left: The little paddymelon grows everywhere in the driest of country—but is inedible.

Another truly legendary man among the barrowmen was 'Russian Jack'. He was a giant in frame and constitution, and a generous mate to anyone he met. He pushed his barrow from one end of the state to the other, to the Kimberleys, the Murchison, and the eastern gold fields. His great strength and humanity was revealed on one occasion when he overtook two men, too exhausted to carry their swags further. They were thirty miles from the nearest waterhole. Russian Jack loaded the two swags on top of his own on his barrow and set off to the distant water with the two men hobbling behind him.

At Halls Creek in the Kimberleys he came on a man collapsed, near to death, and loaded both the man and his swag on his barrow and wheeled them off to the settlement.

When the railways pushed out to the mines the rough barrows were left abandoned in the arid lands, the ludicrous chariots of many a bush trek, many a marathon journey. Some were upended over the graves of men who had pushed the contraption where men seldom go; rough affairs, that seem a suitable memorial to the heroes of the waterless miles, those miners who cocked a snook at the odds stacked against them, and when they faced death, took that in their stride in the way they had taken life.

'PARAWAY'

> And if it be that you would know
> The tracks he used to ride,
> Then you must saddle up and go
> Beyond the Queensland side
> Beyond the reach of rule and law
> To ride the long day through . . .
>
> *A. B. Paterson*

In common with many of the pioneers who trekked across the Never-Never with packhorse or camel, Nathaniel 'Nat' Buchanan kept no record of his achievements. This enterprising, dauntless man blazed tracks and left paths for others to settle in comfort in the inland; he suffered hardships and faced dangers with fortitude and courage and modestly went to his grave unheralded.

Some overlanding family sagas are apt to boast that their subject 'never travelled without a book to read or one to write on'. For men like Nat Buchanan, such an extra weight in his equipment might have meant the difference between success or failure, life or death. Nat was a true pioneer: he knew the dangers, took every possible precaution to avoid them, but accepted that 'doing a perish' might be the last entry he would scratch on the sand of the unknown country he traversed. He became a legend well before his death for his droving feats, bushcraft and his skill at observation.

Nat was born in Dublin in 1826 and came to Australia when he was aged six. Later, he did the things that many adventurous Australian young men did in those days—worked on a cattle station, became part-owner of Bald Blair Station with two of his brothers, then, with his brothers, joined the great gold rush to California: he became a 'forty-niner'. It is a commentary on his lack of success as a miner that he had to work his passage home to Australia in a windjammer.

On return he went droving, and this is where his true vocation lay. At first he drove stock from New South Wales to the Victorian gold fields. By 1859 he was setting off from Rockhampton, Queensland, with the explorer William Landsborough to search for grazing country near the tributaries of the Fitzroy and Belyando rivers. Nat suggested that the party attempt to penetrate the so-called desert that lies in a westerly direction and find out what lay beyond. They were the first white men to go west.

As Nat left no diary, no notes, we can only conjecture the travail he endured. Through reading the reports of men who followed later to take up the land he discovered, we know he faced, almost daily, fatigue and fever, hardships and hunger, danger and death. He crossed the desert-like land, and reached 'the immense tract of downs and magnificent plains, that fertile territory' of west and north-west Queensland. Gaunt and spent, the sight of

The tiny townships of Rockhampton and Gladstone (above) on the Queensland coast provided a life-line to pioneers like Nat and Katherine Buchanan living on cattle stations in the interior.

Above left: James Balzano, the slightly built barrowman whose epic journeys are legendary amongst outback miners.

Below left: Russian Jack's wheelbarrow and gear are on display in the Pioneer Museum, Coolgardie, Western Australia.

Above and right: Nat Buchanan and his wife, Katherine, 'a thorough bush woman', when they lived at Bowen Downs station.

the pasture lands justified their labour, fatigue, danger, and most of all, their faith. But the 'long necks' of their empty tucker bags warned them that to tarry was death.

There was little game, and muzzle-loading guns were too slow for certainty, but hunger had been their companion, and starvation their unacknowledged fear. Faint with hunger they boiled their green-hide hobble straps: this tough, unsavory, jelly-like thing to chew was not too unsavory for starving men. They had penetrated into unknown country far beyond the point where man could hope for any other than a slow death. They must go back—or perish. Meanwhile, a party of men back in Rockhampton had become desperately anxious about them. They were long overdue, they were an adventurous pair, reckless in the pursuit of new horizons: it was assumed that this time they had gone too far. They must be rescued; and so a party brought them back to the coast.

The following year they returned and found the Promised Land, 1,500 square miles on the Thompson River. Nat led a group of men to blaze a stock route from Bowen to the runs, three hundred miles inland. In 1863 he married, and took Katherine Gordon over part of the same track in a buggy to the crude building on Bowen Downs station where he was to be the first manager and she the only white woman in the district.

Nat had the homing instinct of a plains pigeon, a sense of locality that made his journeys successful; Katherine had her qualities too. Her father, the pioneer John Gordon, used to say, 'My boy Kitty is the most intelligent worker on my station'. C. Fetherstonhaugh, the bushman of the west wrote, 'She was a thorough bush woman, and a good mate for Nat who was the best bushman I ever met'. To get to Bowen Station one must take ship to what is now Bowen. The passengers at Bowen were landed in small boats and the horses were swum ashore through the mangroves. Then began the 300-mile drive inland to Bowen Downs, a trackless journey full of perils and hardship. When Katherine's first baby was almost due the pair set off on the return journey—this time to Rockhampton. The rains had begun, the Belyando River was running a banker. Katherine wanted to swim across but Nat made a small canoe for her from two pack saddles, some yards of canvas and a few saplings. On this she had to sit, prepared for shipwreck. This ferry was towed by a bridle rein, one end of which Nat held in his mouth as he swam in front. Getting the rest of their gear and the buggy floated over took most of the day and during this time Katherine mounted guard, with a pistol, over the goods that were ferried over, as marauding natives set fire to the bush about her.

For a time Nat settled down, doing only short exploratory journeys. His companion for these trips was a native, Jimmy, and between them they completed hazardous voyages piloting mobs of stock up unmarked routes to new stations.

The country west of the Georgina is particularly dry and subject to drought. In Buchanan's time men were defeated by the barren *terra incognita*, others, striving to see what lay on the other side of the sunset, died, and Buchanan had known some of these men. Yet, in 1877 he set off with 'Greenhide Sam', Sam Croker, to discover what lay between the known regions around the Rankine, and the Overland Telegraph line 500 miles distant. Between the two were blank spaces to be filled on the map. Their success was to find a large part of what we now know as the Barkly Tableland.

Buchanan was never successful financially. After having discovered this rich tract of land he was unable to stake a claim: other men sitting in city offices had applied for country showing blank on the map. This land that he explored is now occupied by the well-known cattle stations, Brunette, Alexandria, Alroy and Avon Downs.

Early in 1878 Nat set off to drove 1,200 head of cattle from Aramac Station in Queensland to Glencoe Station in the Northern Territory, a distance of 1,400 miles. They had three drays and sixty saddle and draught horses. Supplies for twelve months had to be carted with them—Burketown en route which would ordinarily have supplied food had been temporarily deserted because of fever and a then unidentified disease which had earlier that year killed one of Buchanan's party.

There were no tracks, no white habitation. They were delayed by sickness and by the daily necessity of finding water. They moved their cattle five to twelve miles each day, and each travelling day Buchanan rode from twenty to thirty-five miles out searching for water for the next stage.

Beef, damper, preserved potatoes, rice and dried apples were their diet. The only open plain in all the distance they travelled was near the present settlement of Borroloola, 350 miles after leaving Aramac. The mob moved on, but food now became a problem because of bushfires raging around the dry areas. Buchanan and another rider went ahead with packhorses to Katherine—300 miles away—for supplies, and reached the telegraph store on 15 November 1878.

In his absence tragedy had fallen on the expedition. Travers, the cook, alone in camp at midday, had been bending over his dish mixing a damper. There was a flash in the glaring noon-time air—and the severed head of Travers fell into his dish. The dough was swimming in blood—the bloodstained axe beside his body had been stolen from the camp. His mates returned to find his head-less body, dough on his hands, and his fully loaded revolver in his belt.

He was a popular man, 'a good mate', and the camp was desolate. Most of the meagre supply of flour and some of the tools and contents of boxes had been carried off. His mates buried poor Travers and cut his name and the date on a tree close by. A day later the natives returned and attempted to rob the grave but were disturbed and escaped the long-range shots fired at them.

When the relief party of Buchanan and his assistant returned, the now hungry, anxious men moved on the long trail again, down through Roper River country. They struck boggy land in which animals sank to their bellies and the drays to their axle beds: the 'Wet' had begun. Ninety-six inches of rain fell in three months. There was only one joy to be got from all this: instead of killing the newly born calves which must be done on the track, all born here were nurtured and thus a much greater number of cattle were delivered at Glencoe than had set off from Aramac.

By now his family were seeing very little of Nathaniel Buchanan. The vagabonding love of change had captured him. In 1881 he retraced his steps to Glencoe with 20,000 head of cattle, as well as a delivery to Daly River Station. Sixteen thousand head were driven from St George, Queensland, and met up with the mob from Richmond Downs in the Gulf Country near Normanton.

The planning for such an endeavour was huge and complicated. The organisation had to buy horses—some members of the party were sent to ride over 100 miles to select suitable mounts; the plant must be bought, wagons, drays, equipment, and tools, repairs material, saddlery and harness; tucker for the seventy men who would travel in ten separate parties for five months, and medicine chests. Flour was tested at Normanton and Burketown before being accepted (age and weevils turned flour sour in these humid regions), dried vegetables, dried fruit, pure lime juice and Epsom salts and quinine were taken to maintain health and avert scurvy and fever.

When all was well, the long caravan set off, each mob a one or two days' stage apart. Fever struck, one man had to be carried in a dray for a considerable time; George Hedley was attacked by a black at night while half asleep, crocodiles terrified the cattle, one man died from an unknown cause, and in the poor country both cattle and horses got weaker and poorer. But again Nat Buchanan's leadership got the huge mob safely through.

The following year, 1883, he set off again, this time with 4,000 head for the Ord River Station, Western Australia, 800 miles away. A drover was killed by blacks during this trip, and for much of the way constant guard had to be maintained until they reached the Ord on 15 June 1884.

Buchanan was the first to stock the Queensland country which he and Landsborough discovered, first to take cattle on the Barkly Tableland, first to take stock on the northern part of the Territory (Glencoe), first on the Victoria River, and now first on the Ord River: Nathaniel Buchanan had put up a droving and pioneering record which, for its continental scope, has never been equalled in Australia.

Gold-seekers flocked to the Kimberley fields in 1886 using Nat's tracks, and the land-boomers had their stock driven over after he had opened the way. In the rush for land many leases were taken up in 1881 with forfeiture if they were not stocked in three years. The rent was one shilling per square mile. In Western Australia the rent, with immediate stocking, was 5s per 1,000 acres, or 10s unstocked. One area of 12,000 square miles was taken up by Messrs Osmond and Panton. Good drovers were in demand and extraordinary drovers such as Nat Buchanan were priceless.

The country between the Upper Victoria and the Overland Telegraph line had not been penetrated by 1886, 150 miles of dry country, that tried the best explorers. Victoria Valley was said to be splendid country and two men, G. R. Hedley (who had been attacked by the black during Buchanan's earlier trip) and Sam Croker, had each made a trip through part of it, Hedley negotiating a dry stage of eighty miles before he reached the Victoria just in time to save himself and his party from perishing.

Croker was at Powells Creek on his way to Wave Hill when Buchanan arrived with 100 horses for Queensland bound for Wave Hill. It was July 1886 and a little rain had fallen. Wave Hill was 200 miles or more by the way the crow flies, but 600 miles or more via the only known track (through Katherine).

The two old friends of many a night camp decided to explore the shorter route. Friendly blacks took them fifty miles out to the Murrinji waterhole, the first time a white man had been there; for twenty-one days and nights the cattle and horses staged over the dry ground to the waterhole, the leaders then went on with black guides to Yellow Waterhole, another fifty miles away, and again the stock were brought up. They were the first stock through this very dry belt, and they opened up the Murrinji route, from then on known to every Territory drover.

(In 1919 a great feat of skilful handling of cattle was done on the Murrinji track by the Farquharson brothers. They covered the longest dry stage ever recorded, 110 dry miles without loss. Smaller and more mobile mobs, or mobs helped by the thirst-quenching parakeelia plant may have approached this record but the Farquharson brothers were forced to travel this stage without such advantage.)

Of the six white men who opened up this track they all followed droving for many years until in the end, Sam Croker was shot by a half-caste, Archie Ferguson was killed by blacks in Queensland, Mick Barry died of fever in West Kimberley, and Willie Glass and Nat Buchanan died in their beds back home in New South Wales.

In 1892 the Kimberley goldfields market had failed and cattlemen therefore needed another market for their stock. Nat Buchanan and his two brothers-in-law Hugh and Wattie Gordon were engaged to attempt to open an overland route to the Murchison goldfields—1,800 miles away.

They set off in March with 1,000 bullocks from the Elvire over slate, quartz and diorite, with steep hills and spinifex—and government wells from which the troughs and buckets were usually missing: the tired drovers at the end of the day must haul up enough water by hand to satisfy 1,000 thirsty bullocks as well as the horse plant. At first it was difficult to coax the bullocks over to the troughs, they having never seen one before. One very timid bullock went without water for twelve days and then took in a load 'that nearly ended him'.

One night there was a break—the cattle stampeded, several hundreds of them galloping due east. Hugh Gordon followed their tracks for over forty miles and all this time saw no water and was forced to turn back, the return journey by him and his horse being remarkable in such an arid area. (The bullocks were later collected along the de Grey River near Coppin's station.)

Such a journey as these men were undertaking has such a multitude of problems and variables it is hard today to imagine them. When he reached the little town of Nullagine, Jim Boyd with his wagon and horses left the party: the drovers were now facing the unknown inland country between the headwaters of the Fortesque and Ashburton Rivers and needed a more mobile and quickly moving plant; pack horses only would be used for transport.

Before setting out on this stage they repaired canvas troughs, buckets and waterbags. They were now entering a totally uninhabited dry stretch of country. The first long march was fifty miles and the whole of that night was spent in watering the bullocks from a small soak that 'made' slowly. When the animals became too crowded in their eagerness and threatened to trample the troughs Buchanan rushed at them with an umbrella and opened it suddenly in their faces. (This was so successful that he carried a large

Like other explorers and drovers of the time, Nat Buchanan—known to the Aborigines as 'Paraway'—and his fellow-drovers were moving into regions familiar only to the blacks when they overlanded their herds across the Never-Never.

Above: The movement of settlers inland was beset by conflict and danger.

umbrella in the future whether on horse or camel, and 'it became rather knocked about because of its many falls from horses new to such unusual equipment'.) The blacks in these areas knew Nat as 'Paraway' because whenever they asked him 'which way old man boss go this time?' Buchanan answered, 'far, far away', pointing with his umbrella. The name suited the man. He was incapable of staying in one place. For him, fortune was always farther out, far, far away, and so he became known as 'Paraway'. While on the Ord he had a very severe fall from a horse on 'breakaway' ground, and being no longer young he was a long time recovering. But a new stock route needed to be found . . .

The rapid rise of the goldfields in Coolgardie and Kalgoorlie were a great market for fat cattle; if a stock route could be found from the Barkly Tableland straight across to Sturt Creek in Western Australia, it would be an outlet for Northern Territory and Queensland cattle. But most of it was thought to be dry country, it was quite unexplored, believed to be a desert—as Nat later found much of it was. Nat proposed attempting to blaze a direct stock route through this country, and he was provided with seven camels and equipment at Oodnadatta. He set off with one man and six horses and his camels for Tennant Creek where he got an Aboriginal but could not get a white man to come with him. The black he got was not highly recommended, he was a bit of a *munjung*, as wild blacks were called in the Territory: but he could ride a camel, speak pidgin English and knew the country for seventy miles ahead and said he was willing to go to the Sturt with Nat. The other whites now left, so only the two men, Buchanan and Camel Jack the native were cheered off on their hazardous journey by the few people at Tennant Creek.

The telegraph officer and others had tried to dissuade him. The prospect would have appalled most men, but he knew what to expect from the bush. He had always pulled through in his encounters with the Never-Never, and he was not going to pull out from the challenge thrown to him now.

They went well, with Jack on the leading camel and Nat following with the horses, for the seventy miles nor'-west that Jack knew. But when they reached the water and then turned west Jack refused to move. He would go no farther. This was fatal to the expedition. The camels were needed to carry the water and supplies for the six horses and the men: Jack was indispensable as the camel rider. But neither threats nor promises would move him. Things were at an impasse. Jack was a man over six feet tall, and big and active, and Nat was now nearly seventy, part crippled from the fall he had recently had. Jack was too strong for him to tackle. It seemed that all the efforts to conquer this unexplored stretch of country had been in vain; it was impossible in the conditions to make the search for water that was necessary each day.

Sitting by the fire, the old drover of many a dangerous desert trek stared across at the native sleeping with his camel saddle at his head. This saddle weighed sixty-five pounds. And it suggested a bold plan to Nat Buchanan. Quietly he crossed over, attached handcuffs to a chain on the saddle, and then, a ticklish operation this, clasped the other handcuff onto the ankle of the sleeping man.

'He was a very surly prisoner next morning', but all he could do was saddle and pack his camel and ride it in the lead every day. And he rode this way for 300 miles. Only once in that time were they able to get surface water; the camels travelled 150 miles between drinks and carried enough water for the seven horses. After five days' riding Nat decided to release Jack and to go on ahead alone with the horses as water could not be far away now—but Jack refused to leave and went on to Halls Creek over what turned out to be waterless land that killed one of the camels. They met up with Laurence Wells searching for two missing members of his exploring expedition and Nat went with him, taking Jack and the camels to help in the search. Eventually the bodies were discovered, both men dead from thirst.

Nat's final long journey, with the camels he had brought up from Oodnadatta, proved only that a direct stock route was impracticable. Much had been added to the knowledge of the interior, but it was stock routes Nat loved. Camel Jack stayed with him and went on a shorter journey searching for mining or pastoral land east of Tanami and Hookers Creek but without camels. Jack, having never ridden a horse, preferred to walk and at their farthest point east he said he 'wished to go longa my country'. So, with spear, tucker, water-bag, and tobacco he set off alone for Tennant Creek, 200 miles away—and arrived safely. Nat always claimed he was one of the most faithful men he had travelled with.

'Paraway' became a legend long before he died, his feats of droving, his bushcraft and his keen observation of all things seen on his journeys from top-knot pigeons to unusual grasses made him a memorable man in a region of great men. In 1881 the *Bulletin* claimed that he perhaps helped settle more new country than any other man in Australia. Yet he died owning less than thirty acres himself.

West and ever west the insistent call of the Never-Never lured him. Nothing could stop this bushman, nor discourage his ardour. 'Can we look for instances of greater bravery in the exploration of any other part of the globe?' Ernest Favenc wrote.

If spirits move, then Nat Buchanan's still rides away to the west in search of better tracks to better country, far, far away.

Oh he rides hard to race the pain
Who rides from love, who rides from home,
But he rides slowly home again,
Whose heart has learnt to love and roam.
                                    Henry Lawson

STARLIGHT

The term 'duffing' was first used by early convicts to describe faking the brand of an animal—for nefarious purposes, of course. Later the meaning of the word was extended to apply to cattle-stealing, and was used constantly, because 'duffing' was a way of life for many men for many years. The squatters were enraged by the activities of duffers, after all the cattle being duffed were usually theirs, but selectors, or 'cocky-farmers' found it a lucrative and exciting occupation. They would go duffing horses, cattle sheep, anything, as this song that one of them ('Anon') wrote in the 1890s.

Eumerella

There's a happy little valley by the Eumerella shore
Where I've lingered many happy hours away.
On my little free selection I have acres by the score,
And when I unyoke the bullocks from my dray—

Chorus
To my bullocks I will say, 'It don't matter where you stray,
For you'll never be impounded any more.
You'll be running, running, running on the duffer's piece
  of ground,
Free-selected on the Eumerella shore.'

When the moon has climbed the mountains and the stars are
  shining bright
We will saddle up our horses and away,
And we'll yard the squatter's cattle in the darkness of the
  night
And have the calves all branded by the day.

Chorus
Oh, my pretty little calf, at the squatter we will laugh,
For he'll never be your owner any more.
You'll be running, running, running on the duffer's piece
  of ground,
Free-selected on the Eumerella shore.

When we find a mob of horses and the paddock rails are down,
Though before that they were never known to stray,
How quickly we will drive them to some distant inland town
And we'll sell them into slavery far away.

Chorus
To Jack Robertson we'll say, 'Now we're on a better lay,
And we'll never go off droving any more.
For it's easier duffing cattle from the squatters round
  about,
Free selecting by the Eumerella shore!'

With only two stockmen, the greatest cattle duffer of them all drove the stolen herd to market.

Few countries can have paid homage to a man in the way his peers honoured Harry Redford in 1873. On 17 April of that year, when he was brought before the court on a charge that ordinarily would have gained for a man ten years with hard labour, he was found not guilty by the jury: they did not acquit him because they found him innocent—his guilt was far too obvious for that—but the western stockmen on the panel thought it was their duty to pay tribute to the greatest droving feat of all time.

Redford was up on a charge of cattle stealing, 'duffing' to cattlemen. The up-country feeling was that bushrangers were the true representatives of the Australian spirit.

Come all ye lads of loyalty, and listen to my tale;
A story of bushranging days, I will to you unveil,
Tis of those gallant heroes, God bless them one and all,
And we'll sit and sing "God Save the King, Dunn Gilbert and Ben Hall".

It was a strange mixture of a toast, but it was the loyalties of the day. And never were these loyalties displayed more openly than when the populace were discussing what they believed to be the heroic epic of the man known as 'Starlight'. The correct spelling was Readford, but in true Australian fashion the simple spelling began to creep into reports of his trial and so remained.

Redford was no small time 'poddy-dodger'. He went for the big money. But it was not only the vast enterprising coup that gained him laurels, but the fact that he carried it off as though it were the most natural thing in the world to do. And of course it was natural for him, and for the men who freed him after the police had diligently followed his trail for three years. Much of the country that he and his peers were working in those years are the acres that today still demand the highest standards of outback skills. What earned Redford the admiration of his countrymen was that he stole 1,000 head of

Right: The greatest trek of stolen cattle in Australia's history was not too difficult for the men who achieved it. After all, it was the work they were doing every day of their lives.

cattle and overlanded them almost 1,000 miles to market through an area, parts of which had scarcely been explored and some of which had never been explored before, and all of which was harsh country that took massive skill to bring animals—and men—through alive.

Redford had known the lower part of Coopers Creek, that strange, arid area of dust and seeming desolation that can swiftly turn into a flash flood that spreads over hundreds of miles from a 'creek' that for much of its time is without water. Henry Redford, when charged at Roma, Queensland, in 1873 was listed as 'grazier', the occupation he had before he took to duffing. He had Wombundery Station, fifty-four square miles, thirty miles southwest of what is now the little town of Windorah, Queensland, and from there he would have moved cattle or at least prospected for grazing areas round the lower Coopers Creek, the first to do so.

This man, who later was to be identified with Starlight, the hero of Rolf Boldrewood's *Robbery Under Arms*, was a magnificent bushman and drover and became known in western Queensland in the late 1860s when he 'squatted' on Wombundery. One of his neighbours—some hundreds of miles to the north to be sure, but such is the outback of Australia—was a friend, William Forrester. Forrester had a property named 'Forrester', but his main occupation (apart from the odd, dubious 'duffing' of other people's goods, which was endemic of the west) was as a teamster. He had horses and drays and transported stores to outlying properties. On occasions Redford worked for him as head teamster and in this way came to visit many runs. One of these properties was Bowen Downs, which took in twenty-six pastoral runs of almost one and three-quarter million acres, stretched from fifty miles north of what is now Muttaburra, down the Thompson River, past present-day Longreach to where Arrilulah township grew to serve the vast Bowen Downs empire.

On his journeys to Bowen Downs, Redford had used his bushman's wits and seen that the north-western part of the vast property was a difficult area to be serviced by the management or men. Small selectors were constantly driving cattle down south along the Thompson River and, once in their own yards, the brands were quickly altered and just as quickly the duffed stock was sold in Roma or Blackall. He would know that some of the stockmen on Bowen Downs could easily be bribed to tell of stock movements and the whereabouts of station employees. The finding of a safe market was the simplest of all the steps in duffing: so many were in this racket that buyers and butchers were happy to buy without asking questions. (These points were later to be proven—in court.)

Two of Redford's neighbours, Forrester of the property named after himself, and John McKenzie of 'Ernestina', lived near Forest Grove, strategically splendid for thieving. Both these men had been thieving cattle for some years, in a small way. But, after driving over Bowen Downs, Redford had no interest in petty schemes. He would muster a whole herd and have them clear of the Downs before their owners missed them.

He decided against taking cattle eastwards towards the coast, or westwards to the towns growing around the large properties then. It would be safer to overland the large herd to South Australia through uninhabited lands, some of which he knew, and trust that this greater distance may mean that the brands on the cattle would be unknown to buyers down south. He was encouraged in the decision to go south by heavy rains which fell during the first months of that year, ensuring that there would be water for stock almost the whole distance. These same rains had held up the property muster, giving him time to gather cattle together in the makeshift stockyards he and six assistants built near the mud hut which gave its name to the area later called Mount Cornish.

Each of the stockmen was an expert—and needed to be, as the whole herd they had stolen was made up of wild cattle.

Among these men were John McKenzie and James McPherson, one of Forrester's stockmen. As they cut out each few hundred head of cattle they drove them down to Forrester's property, about twenty-eight miles to the south. Redford, knowing that the tracks of so many animals would alert any stockmen seeing them, posted a look-out on a hill north-east of the Long Reach up the river. (This hill is now known as Starlight's Lookout.)

No stockmen disturbed the clandestine muster and the cattle duffers were ready to move their mob by the beginning of April. Redford now told the men of the route south, and described the uninhabited country.

McPherson and McKenzie felt they could not go on with the scheme: the route was more fearful than any yet envisaged. By the time they were finished branding at yards built on 'Forrester', the two men declared they would not travel on to Coopers Creek. This was scarcely ten years after the death of Burke and Wills, and the route the cattle would take would pass those miles where men, much better fitted out than this rough outfit, had diced with death and lost. Their decision meant Redford must go the 1,000 miles with only two men, Rooke and Dowdney, to help drove the cattle.

Stories told up until the present time at Longreach suggest that Redford split the herd into three mobs to avoid the huge dust cloud that would cause suspicion, and headed off down the Barcoo River. At its junction with the Thompson River he moved off down Coopers Creek, past Windorah, on to Wombundery Billabong where he had lived for some years. The rain had done as he had predicted, filled the waterholes and coaxed grasses to sprout for feed. With the herd now travelling together, they passed over the border where Burke and Wills had their depot only a decade before. They went on to the Callamurra Waterhole and Innamincka and turned sou'-sou'-west to cut along Strzelecki Creek.

They would travel along this now-running creek for 140 miles, secure in the knowledge that there had scarcely been a man along it since it was discovered by explorer Sturt twenty-five years earlier. On they went, camping at night by lonely waterholes, watching the cattle in case of a break, a stampede that three men could scarcely hope to turn. Then they came to Artracoona Native Well near Hill Hill, an isolated station, the first sign of man they had seen since leaving their hidden stockyards.

There were, of course, no diaries kept, no notes sent back or forth from owners to stockmen so we can only surmise that they had come this distance in a well-ordered manner, for it was now June, only three months after they departed from twenty-five miles north-west of Isisford, 800 miles away. We do know that Redford's supplies were running low, because the need to restock was one of the reasons for his downfall.

Harry Redford introduced himself to the station storekeeper as Henry Collins, saying that he was droving his brother's cattle to the sale yards in Port Augusta from the family property in western Queensland. He was willing to exchange a few head of stock for money to buy supplies for the rest of the journey. Among the three animals he sold here was a pure white bull that he had gathered in at Bowen Downs 'to keep the cows contented'.

After he had got supplies the herd was moved on further south, away from Strzelecki Creek and down to Mount Hopeless, over the many channels of Petermorra Creek to Blanchewater, 160 miles from Innamincka.

Blanchewater was owned by the Hon. John Baker MP and here Redford sold the entire mob for £5,000, and left for Adelaide. From there he went to western New South Wales—alone, for Dowdney and Rooke had gone to Melbourne, never to be heard of again.

The loss of the cattle was not noticed on Bowen Downs, or rather Mud Hut, until general mustering began in May, and by that time Redford was two months on the way across the southern lands. William Butler, the head stockman of Bowen Downs, had first noted that the big white bull was missing; then the rustlers' stockyard was found, and the tracks of the big herd heading south. So Butler set off after his charges.

He did well. Travelling with two stockmen off Bowen Downs he tracked the cattle down to Hill Hill near Artracoona Well and there saw the white bull and heard of 'Henry Collins'. He recognised Redford by the description given, about six feet tall, of fine physique, and tracked him down to Blanchewater where Redford had sold the cattle. But the cattle had again been sold, in scattered lots to different buyers. Butler had only the white bull as evidence and this stalwart beast began his long odyssey that ended outside the courthouse in Roma two years later.

Butler, as tenacious as Redford, returned to Bowen Downs and the hunt was on for all other rustlers. McKenzie, who had refused to go down through no-man's-land with Redford, was brought to court on 2 February 1871, charged over 100 clean skin calves and 82 cows stolen from Bowen Downs and found on his property. McKenzie had not laid claim to these animals, the evidence against him was circumstantial, and he was acquitted—for the time being.

The next time McKenzie was up before the court at Roma was in November 1871. With him was Redford's old employer, Forrester, and McPherson, whose courage, along with McKenzie's, had failed when faced with the 1,000-mile drove southward over virtually unknown country. This time McKenzie turned Queen's evidence and told how he and the others in court had stolen cattle and brought them down to Forrester's yards where they were re-branded. Faced with this damning evidence the barrister representing the accused wound himself up into a state worthy of one about to save men from the gallows instead of a few petty thieves from the stone-breaking yard of gaol. He addressed the jury for two hours and they, by now exhausted, returned a verdict of not guilty. McKenzie was rewarded for turning Queen's evidence and was also acquitted.

In the meantime, in January of that year, 1872, Redford had been captured and returned to the Thompson River area where he was greeted as a hero. The outback settlers were wild with adulation for the incredible feat he had performed three years before. By now details of the route he took were known and he was looked on with the same awe as one of the early explorers had been.

When the case opened on 11 February 1873 at Roma, the court house was packed, and those who couldn't get inside hung around outside eagerly awaiting any word that came to them through the open door. The calling of the jury began.

Redford rejected any man whose dress showed him to be of the squatter class and after forty-eight men had paraded before him only seven had been chosen. The other five had to be balloted for. Finally, all twelve 'good men and true' were chosen, all local men of Roma.

The white bull was second only to Redford as an attraction in the town. It had been first driven by Redford from Bowen Downs to Blanchewater, 1,000 miles southwards, then Butler had it taken to Adelaide and from there shipped to Brisbane; from Brisbane it was railed to Toowoomba and from there driven to Roma and tied up outside the court.

It was the key witness, or at least it shared the interest with James McPerson, the second man who had reneged and refused to continue driving the cattle after they left the Barcoo River. He now told the whole story—about the duffing of the cattle, the improvised stockyards on the Thompson River, the manner in which mobs were taken down to Forrester's holding ground and his own refusal to trek down Coopers Creek.

It was damning. For the past two years Roma Court House had seen a

Above: Redford came from a part of Australia where duffing—whether of cattle, sheep or horses—was standard practice among stockmen.

Top: Using yards they built themselves on the boundary of the vast station, the cattle duffers rounded up the herd they were to drove 1,000 miles south.

torrent of cattle duffers brought to trial but evidence was hard to find. Now, evidence of such richness was led forth as to make prosecuting counsel rejoice. G. W. Paul, Redford's counsel stood to cross-examine—and he demolished McPherson. The court room 'was trembling with the excitement'. Poor McPherson had stolen cattle more than once, and once at least had pleaded guilty to it, and wasn't he on suspended sentence now after 'surprisingly' pleading guilty to a charge of stealing cattle? And again, had he not been committed to a Lunatic Reception House, and subsequently escaped and wasn't he apprehended yet again and returned and wasn't he promised that he would be set free if he gave evidence for the Crown.

The defence counsel faced the jury and addressed them for one hour, in the blinding heat of an outback mid-summer's day. The jury retired and returned within the hour and handed down its verdict. Not guilty.

Judge Charles William Blakeney, who had risked floods and discomfort to get to Roma in the hottest, most humid time of the year and now had been closeted in the packed and airless courtroom from 9 am until 9 pm, sat stunned. Then he leant forward and said, with anger, 'I thank God that verdict is yours, gentlemen, and not mine'.

Far right: Starlight's theft of a white bull, not the great herd of cattle, was to lead to his arrest. (Starlight, p. 102)

Below centre: Jack Makim (seated) and Reg (R.M.) Williams (standing) at breakfast as sun comes up on the second day of the Glory Ride. (The Glory Ride, p. 122)

Below far right: Out across the western plains, the Glory Riders group up. (The Glory Ride, p. 122)

Below: The route south pioneered by Redford was well watered. The herd travelled along Strzelecki Creek for 140 miles.

Harry Redford was free. He never talked of the great cattle drive, never boasted, and when the book *Robbery Under Arms* was mentioned he made no comment. But to the public he became the pattern for the man Rolf Boldrewood called Starlight in his masterpiece, and Starlight he remained to outback Australians.

He later added to the reputation he had made as the trail blazer down Coopers Creek and the Strzelecki Creek by drives he did in the 1880s. In that decade he remained within the law and took cattle through the Gulf country, drove mobs from Atherton Tablelands of North Queensland, to Dubbo, NSW, and drove the first mob of cattle across to Brunette Downs in the Northern Territory.

He believed that grazing lands would be found in Central Australia and set off from Brunette Downs in March 1901 for Tennant Creek, where he hoped to gain support for an expedition south. On 12 March his body was recovered from Corella Hole where he had drowned in the torrent sent down by the Wet. There, in a lonely grave by the lonely Corella Creek, Starlight was buried.

SINGING THE CATTLE

If heroism is mostly about endurance then Aborigines would be hard to beat. For nine winters I watched them—well past the era when they stalked as tribesmen, but still in the 1950s and 1960s working on cattle stations. I had a reluctant lung in those years and must spend my winters in the dry inland north. Most of the time I camped in the bush, and most of the time there were blacks. Those latitudes drug your energy, and the balmy, dewless night air is made for story-telling round a camp-fire. So mostly I just sat and waited for something to turn up. Even my lung worked in my favour— chest ailments are a thing Aborigines know a lot about. And my obvious lack of capital was also an advantage: you can't hold in awe someone sitting on her up-turned tucker box, someone so hard up for a hat that she is given a stockman's hat, an old 'ten gallon', to keep the sun off her head. And so, I knew them a little.

The times when you sense them in the land but don't see them, when they are like the rock, fastened deep, and living within the soil, attuned to all things as though the sky and the man and grass and animals were not separate, but each a part of the other; these are the times they make poetry on the land.

There was a day when all day long the heat dragged a mirage along the road ahead of the car. This was the road to Wyndham, hot, red, pot-holed, and deep with bull-dust. Isolated small road gangs waved and called out, 'How y' going?'. In the land beyond the Never-Never country, up the Kimberleys area of Western Australia, every man lifts his hand in greeting as you go by, and every second man pulls up for a yarn.

It's the land of the baobab (some call them bottle trees), elephant-hided, bulbous, grotesque; of great grasslands that wave twelve feet high in 'the Wet', where brumbies scatter off into the scrub when they hear a car, and wild cattle threaten to charge as you drive over their fenceless runs. For mile on mile the ranges melt from pale lavender to violet, from pink to the scarlet of congealed blood, rufous, harsh, barbaric and beautiful. When night comes it turns lustrous deep purple, exotic.

My camp was in a circle of baobab trees, fat and leafless. Dust hid the setting sun and the colours of sunset passing through it lay in bars of gold, pink, and lavender. There was nothing to indicate the cause of this low-lying blanket, a red fog from horizon to sky. But the air told me I was not alone on the broad bronze plain.

All other sound was blotted out by the talking of flocks of thousands of rose-breasted galahs overhead, flying on their way to the water at the bore nearby. Numberless finches, budgerigars, and cockatoos settled on the trees around the bore, decorating the bare limbs like clusters of green and yellow and pink and white flowers.

The big birds sat for a time on the edge of the cattle troughs drinking with stilted scoops of their hooked beaks. The little birds darted down and drank

Left: Harry Redford lived in an era when bushrangers were active in all states. But Starlight (as most Australians think of Redford) did not stoop to highway robbery. He went for much greater gain— that of stealing a whole herd of cattle. (Starlight, p. 102)

Concertina, riding boots and ten-gallon hats are regular gear in the Kimberley muster camps. Most of the Aboriginal riders have been on horses since they were boys.

'on the run', taking sips as they flew low over the cool, ground-tasting water, being careful not to be pressed down by the multitude above them and drowned by weight of numbers. The dry river beds, half a mile wide, held nothing for them in this land which is among the hottest in the world.

The birds chattered and squabbled and pushed each other off their perches on the droll baobab branches until dusk. I could hear nothing from that distant blanket of dust, but an excitement was there. It filled the air around me.

Suddenly a little donkey ran by, right beside my camp fire. A bell round his neck went clok-clok-clok as he went. He brayed in ludicrous delight and scampered on to the bore. Then, there in the dusk and the dust and the last of the setting sun was a string of horses with a stockman taking them to water. The donkey was among friends.

I ran to a big rock near the baobabs and climbed it. Sticking out of the top of the dust layer were ten-gallon stockmen's hats and horses' heads and the horns of cattle tossing and dodging as stockmen rode the herd to settle it down for the night. Suddenly it was dark—it's always sudden here—and with the darkness the birds stopped screeching, abruptly, and only then could I hear the complaining of a thousand head of cattle as they were brought into a tight circle and encouraged to lie down.

In the Kimberleys you sleep out under the stars if you're travelling. The night air is gentle, and your fire is always within arm's reach. I travelled 'soft' by outback standards: I had an air mattress. Now, with the fire smouldering low, a soft bed, and a balmy deep purple sky I was comfortable, happy, but for once I couldn't sleep. That excitement was still there. I felt as I do in a theatre when the lights go down and the curtain has yet to come up. There were noises everywhere. Clok-clok went a bell—surely scores of bells? There was a jingling, too, like the tinkling of Chinese wind bells. I didn't think of hobbles. Out there the dark was full of moving animals. I was never too sure whether an animal would tread on a prostrate sleeper in the dark and still can't believe they never do.

The tinkling disappeared and came again. Then the tread of high heeled boots on the dirt track to the bore, past my head. One said, to the other, 'This bin good country. I bin walkem fifty mile. Plenty tucker. Bin catch wallaby, emu, goanna, turkey. Plenty beef. You no starve here.' The scrunch of their footfalls faded away. The cattle were lowing, gently.

And then it began. Gently, softly at first, the stockmen began to 'sing' the cattle, make them content and aware of the presence of men. If one beast becomes uncertain and panics the whole herd will stampede within seconds and no man can stop it. So, they sing the cattle.

I strained to hear the words. They eluded me, the melody too. But inside my head the rhythm was pounding through from the ground beneath me. And the darkness was part of the words and the ugly freak trees and the men who had walked by my camp and the area itself. You knew then that these were Aboriginal stockmen singing their tribal lullabies and 'playabout' songs.

As they rode around the closely packed herd their voices faded in the distance and then grew louder as they neared me. First they were high and clear, then the same rhythm was repeated in the middle register, then came a deep throbbing in the chest. It went on all night, broken sometimes by an elusive whistling and the occasional lowing from a beast. At midnight the watch changed and an older songster took over, but the wild, primitive, disturbing rhythms were the same.

The moon came up, the bloated bottle trees were things of fantasy, great rocks crouched all around, and when the singers passed between me and the moon their tall hats were silhouetted black across the golden ball. And on and on went the song. Sometimes I dozed, hating every minute of sleep that blotted out this thing that might never happen to me again.

Then they were gone. It was daylight. Where a thousand cattle, men, donkeys and horses had been was flat, red plain, scorching already as the sun sprang up, but empty. Even the birds had vanished.

Later in the day I caught up with the herd. First there were the pack donkeys, each with a bell around his neck, clok-cloking as he wandered on, with a pack across his back of bedding, camp gear, cooking gear, pots, pans, buckets, and a spade to dig a cooking trench. Beside them scampered the dog-sized baby donkeys. Droving them were two of last night's singers, astride mules. They were full-blooded Aborigines—there are fewer part-coloured than anywhere else in this area where four out of five are black. One was very handsome, very shy, very pleased that, unknown to him, his singing the cattle had had an audience. Farther along the road the horses were strung out, each with his hobbles around his neck, tinkling as he jogged. Out on the unfenced plain the red cattle moved over the red land. They were weary. They had been six weeks on the track. They were jittery too, for they could smell the meatworks awaiting them at Wyndham.

The drovers smelt the meatworks too. All Aborigines, they said, 'We bin leave cattle quick all alonga meatwork'.

They delivered them to their destination the next day and went away at once. The cattle had shared the long, dusty, dry journey over the lonely weeks with them. The stockmen said, 'Them meatwork plenty rubbish'. For cowed cattle cooped in the slaughter yards are a travesty of the untamed creatures that toss their horns, bellow, and break away in a rush and thunder of hooves, until they learn to settle when stockmen sing them.

I never again camped apart if there was a cattle camp near by and always it seemed as magic as that first night.

Only once was there 'entertainment' and that only because I showed too much interest. I later learnt that wasn't polite. Because of the long hours worked on camp muster or droving, the few hours of darkness are needed for sleep.

This night I was with a camp muster, forty Aborigines and one white man rounding up cattle on the unfenced plains and branding, dehorning, and earmarking them. Two women cooks were with the camp; one, May, was mission bred, the other, Whip, was a 'station black' and they were both the best company I'd had for months. I divided my days evenly between falling off what they called the quietest horse in the camp and watching the girls

The tinkling of the pack donkeys' bells sounds through the twilight as the horse tailers prepare to set up camp for the night.

Above: The cook and the horse tailers get ready to move on to the next cattle yards after the stockmen have ridden off.

Top: May, the cook, shovels hot ash on to the pans in which bread is baking in an earth oven.

cook on the big log fires in the open and in holes in the ground. They cooked the bread in a trench dug in the ground, six feet long by twelve inches deep. Layers of hot coals were shovelled into the trench to heat it, and when the three big camp ovens were ready, the coals were shovelled out, the bread in the ovens put in, and the coals shovelled back on top. The cooked loaves were two feet across and six inches deep, crusty and even-textured.

In another camp oven, on the tree-trunk-sized log fire, beef steak and dumplings bubbled most nights, sometimes a dish of rib bones, the traditional camp-muster tucker. The ribs of a freshly killed beast are broken into eight-inch lengths, dipped in flour, and cooked in hot fat. Another camp speciality was pufftaloons with golden syrup, the same sort of yeast-ball mixture we'd often had as children in the bush. And always there were plenty of vegetables; the homestead truck drove out to the camp at least twice a week with supplies which always included crates of vegetables from the garden.

One night we were just about to attack one of the big meals the girls put on when one of the stockmen pointed to the horizon. 'Here come the boys from Gogo.' Like figures in a scene from a wild west film, men rode in from the sunset. Strung out behind their white English jackaroo, they slumped wearily in their saddles, tall hats silhouetted against the gold and purple bars of the pre-twilight sky, hobbles tinkling around the horses' necks, camp gear jingling on the pack donkeys' backs, while the clok-clok of the bells on their necks fell like notes from a bell-bird in the dust.

They were from Gogo, a neighbouring station, and had come to cut out their cattle the following day—cattle being held in the mob by the camp musterers. There was a lot of yaka-ing when the two parties of stockmen met. As there often is, there were two groups in our camp: the 'bush blacks', an unsophisticated group, apt to prefer fingers to forks, with little English—some with none; and the usually mission-educated people, as sophisticated as the white stockmen in the camp. Tonight, those who ate with forks were having a quiet smoke with the newcomers before turning in, yarning contentedly, swapping time-worn old jokes about the others' station. A hundred yards away, under a tree, the bush boys were kicking up a great rumpus, whoomph-whoomphing away on the didgeridoo, clicking sticks on tobacco tins, and singing their age-old songs, strange when heard on the tape recorder in a lounge down south but here thrilling, utterly attuned to the deep velvet of the purple night in the dark, waiting land.

With great toleration, neither group begrudged the other their differing needs. But I made it clear which group I wanted to hear this night.

The white jackaroo, the man from Gogo, an Englishman, said, 'You're not one of "those" are you?' Before I could ask, 'One of "what"?', the white head stockman of the camp muster told me, 'I've never let them do it before but if you really want it I'll ask them'. I said that it sounded good. 'Oh it's good all right,' the ringer said with real pride. 'All I've got against letting them go is that the day's long enough without having a corroboree all night.'

When our ringer called out to the men under the tree the Englishman from Gogo said he'd turn in. The entertainers took a bit of persuading to get them to perform for an audience, and while we waited the white ringer said of the Englishman, 'They come out here, wet behind the ears, and make a big noise. Still get lost after six months on the run and the poor old Abo's got to go out and round them up with the cattle.'

The artists didn't announce themselves so much as infiltrate our consciousness. The sound of the deep cello-like notes of the didgeridoo were an accompaniment to our talk before the dancers made us aware of their movements on the outer edge of the firelight. The dust rose around their legs, hiding their ankles and feet, and as they moved farther in to the light

from the logs the dust came with them, wrapping our feet in its soft black-gold swirl as they moved around the musician. The stockmen danced barefooted, bare-chested, leaping into the firelight, grunting, twisting, stamping.

When they had done, the dancers faded into the blackness surrounding us; when they returned, they came on stage the same way. They appeared from all directions, as though they had rehearsed, as indeed they had, for all the long centuries before we came to their country. They converged on the didgeridoo player, sitting on the ground with his long wooden pipe propped up with a spread-eagled big toe. Beside him, the rhythm-man clik-clikked with his sticks.

We were so caught up with the dancers that we didn't notice Whip, until May caught my arm. 'Look at Whip,' she whispered in awe. Behind the fire, where once long lines of women shuffled as their men went through the more athletic dances in the foreground, Whip stood alone, arms swinging, feet rapidly shuffling and wearing a hole in the waterless ground three inches deep. 'I've never seen that before,' mission-bred May whispered, unable to take her eyes off her friend.

We asked Whip if she knew any dance peculiar to her own country. 'Bogey Dance,' announced Whip. 'Like bath.' It was unmistakeable. With her body undulating all the time, she went through the motions of bath night, the hair, the arms, the legs, face, all within the prescribed movements of a dance.

And then the men went on again with hardly a pause, singing, dancing, and playing singly and in groups; later they asked me, 'You bin sing or dance, Missus?' So I sang the only song of which I knew all the words, *The Wild Colonial Boy*. They listened politely. I sang the final verse:

After a hard day's riding from daylight to sunset, the stockmen can sing and, if given the chance, dance until the early morning, accompanied by their didgeridoo.

> All shattered through the jaw he lay,
> Firing at Fitzroy,
> And that's the way they captured him,
> The wild colonial boy.

When I finished, there wasn't a sound. Then an elderly man came and squatted in front of me, staring me in the eye, intently. 'They got him?' he asked. 'Yes,' I answered. 'They got him.' He turned and nodded sombrely at the others.

They were still going at midnight. 'See what I mean?' said the ringer. 'The boss'd kill me if he knew.' He called out, 'The last one, eh?' A few grunts seemed to indicate it might be. But half an hour later and three 'The last one, eh?', they were still going stronger than ever; their energy was incredible. I could have watched forever, but already I'd seen the midnight relief horsemen ride out for the change over. In the odd lull their deep sonorous songs drifted over as they sang the cattle. It would be daybreak at four.

'How about you turning in,' the ringer said diffidently to me.

'They'd think I was rude,' I said.

'I know. But it would stop them.' So, I rolled my sleeping bag out on the other side of the big fire and crawled in, and they ghosted out into the darkness and there was no sound from that moment but the lullabies and 'rubbish' songs being whispered into the ears of cattle, and they in their turn moaned back at the tintinnabulation of donkey bells and hobbles a-jingle.

Where the pelican builds

Mary Hannay Foott

The horses were ready, the rails were down,
  But the riders lingered still—
    One had a parting word to say
  And one had his pipe to fill.
Then they mounted, one with a granted prayer,
  And one with a grief unguessed.
    'We are going', they said, as they rode away—
  'Where the pelican builds her nest!'

They had told us of pastures wide and green,
  To be sought past the sunset's glow;
    Of rifts in the ranges by opal lit;
  And gold 'neath the river's flow.
And thirst and hunger were banished words
  When they spoke of that unknown West;
    No drought they dreaded, no flood they feared,
  Where the pelican builds her nest!

The creek at the ford was but fetlock deep
  When we watched them crossing there;
    The rains have replenished it thrice since then,
  And thrice has the rock lain bare.
But the waters of Hope have flowed and fled,
  And never from blue hill's breast
    Come back—by the sun and the sands devoured,
  Where the pelican builds her nest.

KIMBERLEY MUSTER

Every camp muster is the same, every one is different. The best I ever knew, with the best head-man and the best stockmen, was on Jubilee Station.

From where I camped on the banks of the Fitzroy River I could hear the ringer singing in the bar at the Fitzroy Crossing pub. He was singing the rebel Irish song, 'Kevin Barry'. 'That's him.' I knew.

Far out on the track from Wyndham, in the far north-west of Western Australia, I had earlier come on a group whose car had broken down. No, they didn't need help—they had sent to Perth for a spare part and it would be a couple of days, but they did need someone to talk to. They had set fire to a dead tree and prodded this into action to boil the billy whenever they felt like it, like now.

They told me about Gerry Ash. 'You ought to look him up,' they said. 'He's the ringer, head man on Jubilee Station. We reckon he's the greatest ringer in all the Kimberley. Long, lean and hard. Straight as a gun barrel, rides like a whirlwind—a mighty man. He's mustering near Fitzroy River at the moment, and we met him at the pub. He'd come in to wash down the dust of a day's hard riding.'

As an afterthought they said, 'He sings too, Irish songs, when the night grows long.'

The pub at Fitzroy River Crossing is one of the best in the outback. Built on high piers to beat the heat and the white ants, and open on three sides to let in any rare breath of air in that hot, dry land, it is clean, well-run and as outback as a Henry Lawson short story.

The ringer stood six feet three inches in his high-heeled boots. You couldn't mistake him.

He didn't take off his ten-gallon hat while he drank. Neither did the huge, handsome black stockman with him. You got the feeling (and found out later that you were right) that under those hats was hair stirred into a gritty bird's nest by the red dust of the plains where they mustered Kimberley cattle.

It's easy to strike up a yarn with the ringer. He'll talk to anyone provided you don't contradict him when he says this country is the best on earth. Quiet, reticent, and slow-moving, his legs in their tight trousers and concertina leggings seem to creak as he walks with the tender tread of a man who spends most of his waking hours in the saddle.

Next day I drove out to Jubilee bore where Gerry was holding a mob near the stockyards. It was midday when I bumped over the trackless ground past the windmill where the stockmen were lunching. The day-horses were tethered, their saddles up-ended on the ground. Pack donkeys with bells round their necks stumped solemnly by as bronco mules kicked out as they passed. The smell of boiled beef and fresh bread spread out from beneath the trees where the camp cooks had their table.

A group of bush blacks sat beneath a tree further off, and without benefit

A bore on Jubilee Station, Western Australia. Water is scarce in the outback, and wells and bores are zealously looked after.

Gerry Ash, the ringer, head man on Jubilee Station.

of cutlery or other encumbrances, gnawed beef bones with their wonderful white teeth. I joined the 'civilized' group, the white ringer and mission-bred blacks, and juggled with cutlery and plates.

The food at a muster camp is so distinct, so redolent of what cartoonists stress as a bush menu, that it seems an exaggeration. For lunch we had salt beef cooked in kerosene tins on logs kept burning on the ground all day and night; hot bread fresh from the camp oven; pufftaloons dipped in golden syrup; mugs of scalding sloe-black tea; ants, flies, heat and dust.

Two Aboriginal women cooks travelled with this muster, too.

Gerry Ash was the only white man on the muster. All the rest were Aborigines, apart from Mervyn Norton, fourteen-year-old son of an old Kimberley identity.

'Where is your Dad?' I asked him.

Shyly, speaking barely above a whisper, the lad replied, 'He's out on the track with a mob'.

In this great unfenced land of cattle stations limited by law to 'no greater area than one million acres', cattle range far afield and camp musters must be held twice a year and take five to six weeks each time. Unbranded beasts are cut out of the mob of rounded-up herds, and yarded to be branded, castrated, de-horned and ear-marked.

Stockyards are scattered over the property, usually near a bore head. Here at Jubilee bore, Gerry had gathered a mob from the surrounding scrub ready for the cut-out.

After lunch the boys mounted and rode off in different directions. All knew what to do. Each had his stockwhip coiled loosely over one arm and a de-horning knife in the scabbard on the saddle. Alex, looking as though he had stepped straight from a Russell Drysdale canvas, vaulted on to a gleaming black gelding broken only six weeks before and sent it over the land. It was Alex's special job to see to the branding irons.

Anthills as high as a man dotted the plain and at every one the gelding reared and plunged and tried to dislodge the man on his back. But long Alex never shifted in his seat.

'It'll take more than a newchum gelding to unseat that boy,' Gerry said laconically when I gasped as the horse tried to roll.

From men and beasts scattered over the plain, a tight-packed herd of cattle later appeared. The herd was circled by men riding around the mob, pushing them ever tighter. The animals roared and bellowed and tossed their horns. Stretched out from the perimeter of this centre of activity, other men lolled on their mounts like outfielders at a cricket match waiting for the infielders to miss—in this case, for an animal to break away.

High above the tight crush of cattle, horses' heads and the tall hats of stockmen moved—Gerry and another stockman, cutting out. Quietly, unhurriedly they moved the shoulders of their horses, imperceptibly jostling a way through the packed beasts, their stockwhips licking the air above an unbranded animal, leading it out to the perimeter for the other stockmen to take over and drive it to the group of cleanskins waiting to be yarded.

As the horses of men cutting out wheeled and turned and controlled the unbranded animals, I remembered Gerry talking in the pub last night about the stock horses he'd trained, and the cattle-drafting horses like these that he could ride without a bridle if he wanted to.

'Horses you could work like a dog,' he said.

The horse he rode this day would have thrown a lesser rider, turning unguided as it did by instinct and knowledge, rather than by command.

The dust lay like a red miasma above the milling, moving mob. And then it was over. The stockmen holding the cleanskins drove them to the stockyards. Men dismounted, tethered their horses in the shade, drew their instruments from the gear on their saddles and sauntered down to the yards in their mincing high-heeled gait for the main business of the day.

Already Alex was kindling a fire for the branding irons, pulling splinters of wood from the fence to start it. Because the white ants eat wood so voraciously, the stockyards are roughly built and already much of this one was crumbling like borer-ridden furniture in a second-hand mart.

All afternoon the men worked in the searing sun, taking turns with the various tasks, riding among the stock, lassoing a beast and fastening the rope to the harness of Jerry the mule, who would pull the beast to the bronco rail for attention. Stolidly dragging the fighting weight over the dusty ground, Jerry the mule is the pride of the musterers.

'Best mule in Australia,' they claim. 'Can bronco, tail, cut out, anything you want.'

Aboriginal stockmen in the Kimberleys spend much of their year out on camp musters in which the cattle, scattered over thousands of square miles, are systematically rounded up twice a year.

As soon as the mule has dragged the beast to the rail, the action is quick. It is thrown and held usually by the leg or knee on its neck. One man clips the mark on its ear. Another deftly castrates it. Another saws off the horns while Alex casually, languidly, lopes over from the fire and sears the branding iron into the haunch. Then the beast is up and away, bucking, rearing, kicking up its heels, as often as not with one of the stockmen clinging to its back.

Young Mervyn Norton was pretty good at this. His grey workman's shirt stained black down his spine where the sweat rolled off him, he was eager and willing, the black stockmen admiring him openly for it, as though they were all responsible for his good showing.

Alex kicked his fire together with high-heeled boots, keeping his instruments hot and ready, and throwing dust on to the roped ends of the irons to keep them cool.

The essence of the great outback is distilled here, and it hovered on the air. There's the jingle of spurs, shouts, calls, the bellowing of cattle, dust, sweat, the smell of men, cattle and burning hides, and over all a hard blue sky slit with a red ball of sun.

I sat up on the stock rails and watched. Twice the stockmen came over with a billy of water for me to share and it tasted like ambrosia.

When it was done, the rails were let down and the animals charged out to the unfenced plains. The men gathered up their instruments, Alex his branding irons. Alex brought me a mug of water from the can on the back of the old muster-camp truck, and everyone sauntered off to their horses and returned to the camp for the night.

Back through the dust at the empty stockyards, where before no bird had been seen, was a swarm of hundreds of kite-hawks, swooping down to the dust of the arena and scavenging, on the wing, the testicles the castrators had clipped so deftly.

That night Hugh McLarty, Ned McNamara and Jack Huddlestone brought the truck from the homestead with supplies—fresh vegetables, great cabbages, carrots, potatoes, spinach and lettuces. All had been grown at the homestead. These three men—Huddlestone, former manager of the property, McNamara, the present manager, and McLarty, a director of the company which owns this and two other stations—know Kimberley and its problems well. Each has spent the best years of his life here.

Jubilee Station, like many others in Kimberley, has been formed into a company, and with the other two stations combined, totals more than 700,000 acres. This has been necessary for economic reasons, but such things as finance, marketing problems, and business seemed out of place here.

Mostly the men talked of the outback. Jack Huddlestone talked about the time he got 2,000 donkeys in one drive:

They're a terrible menace up here. They were indispensable in the old days. Couldn't have managed without them. Many's the load of stores I've brought behind a team of donkeys. That bread box now, (he pointed at a well-worn, massive wooden crate I was sitting on) that was the driver's seat on the donkey waggon. If you think that's oil that makes it smooth and shiny you're darn right. It's the grease from the moleskin trousers that have rubbed over it for half a century. When motor-cars came, we kept the donkeys, thinking they might come in again. They went wild and now they're a menace. We've got to get rid of them. Some stations claim to have got 4,000 in one drive.

Gerry was directing the dry feeding of the horses—the mules and donkeys must forage. With four horses per man, ridden at the rate of two a day, cartage of food is a large item. But the cunning mules don't miss out on much. As soon as the stockman had turned his back the mules trotted over and nibbled holes in the bottom of the feed bags around the horses' necks.

Above: Gerry Ash on Gerry the Mule hauls an unwilling yearling up to the rails.

Top: The cattle—in their first encounter with men—are hauled in by the long line to the hitching rail. White ants can eat the yards away in the time it takes the camp muster to return.

Above: Thrown with ropes, this steer lies prone, kept down by the Aboriginal earmarker's foot on his neck, while two other stockmen brand and castrate him.

Above left: Fourteen-year-old Mervyn Norton leans nonchalantly on the hitching rail holding the roped steer, while Aboriginal stockmen brand, earmark, dehorn and castrate it.

'Cunning?' said Jack Huddlestone. 'Too cunning. If you bored a hole in a mule's head and let out half his brains he would be twice as good as other animals.'

A mule he hunted off came back again and again, snapping at feed bags to get the horses' food.

'As Wally Dowling used to say,' Jack quoted one of the most famous of Kimberley figures, 'a mule is the most obstinate animal God ever shovelled guts into.'

Gerry Ash the ringer has been in Kimberley twenty years, but still sunburns. He is blond and fair-skinned and will never become immune to the heat.

'He's like chestnut horses,' Huddlestone commented. 'The sun affects them. That's why I breed dark horses.'

As casually as a city housewife might take some stores from her deep freeze when guests arrive, Gerry sent two of his stockmen to cut out a beast. When they had brought it near a clump of trees at the camp, he took a gun, mounted his horse, and rode out to kill fresh meat.

Later there was a great celebration around the carcass. In the light of a lantern you could see the bush Aborigines leaping and yakaing as they put the skinned meat on clean boughs from the bushes.

After tea the bosses drove back the long miles to the station, and two stockmen caught their night horses and rode over to the herd to hold them for the night.

That night, in my bedding roll under the stars, the songs of the men singing the cattle lulled me to sleep. All about the noise of donkey bells and hobbles sounded a lullaby, softened by the low moans of the cattle.

At 4.20 am Gerry bawled out, 'Daylight! Daylight!'. The new day had begun.

All over the plain, men stirred and stretched. Sleeping 'all standing', the men had only to buckle their belts, pick up their ten gallon hats with one hand, their saddles they had been using as a pillow with the other, and they were ready for the day. Each man set off to bring in his hobbled day-horses.

There were buckets of scalding tea, and damper and steaks tossed on coals, for breakfast. Then the men rode off to the cattle and behind us, where the remains of the 'overlanded' beast lay, the kite-hawks were swarming to clean up the carcass.

THE GLORY RIDE

The end of the endurance race doesn't have the excitement of a country horse race since the rules lay down that the horse must remain fit.

There was a time when riding a horse a hundred miles in the Australian outback would have caused no comment at all. The vast inland area could scarcely have been opened up if horses and riders could not endure long hours on the track. Then came the motor car and the skills of long distance riding were forgotten, or at least, the young riders did not gain this experience. Cobb & Co. coaches no longer rattled out of the cities reminding the urban dwellers that out there was the great lonely land. Because there was no longer a reminder we began to believe that it was no longer there, that tough men and women, brave powerful horses and some of the world's greatest spaces were not part of the Australian scene.

And then, the riders themselves decided to do something about it—they set about drawing the attention of all Australians to the grand legends, myths and traditions of their own country. Out of this was born the Endurance Race.

Already there are several annual events in Australia but probably the Warwick to Gold Coast 120 miles and the Tom Quilty, named after a well-known northern rider and stockman, were the best known until recently.

In 1980 another race, the Golden Horse-Shoe Endurance Race of 150 miles from Winton to Longreach in western Queensland was run, and is set to be the classic for the increasing number of riders and horses learning to cover ground in the way it was done when this nation was in the making.

The Australian Endurance Riders Association controls and sets the standards for the rides. The rules for this type of race are simple but stringent: horse and rider must be fit to be accepted and permitted to continue.

The Winton-Longreach race started from the main street of Winton, at 2 am on September 10 with vapour rising from the breath of animals, riders and townspeople in the near zero temperature. The first checkpoint was Natural Bore, 24 miles and a demanding ride away in the blackness of the night. On this stretch the rider must demonstrate bushcraft of the type our forbears had. The Australian bush is relentless, it never lets up. On this first leg, nine riders lost their way and were rounded up the next day.

Here, at the natural bore, one of the many that supply the area with permanently hot water, the strappers for each rider waited with rug and halter and the veterinary surgeons checked the animal's pulse, respiration and temperature. Thirty minutes later the check was completed and a decision made as to whether the horse would be permitted to continue.

The pulse of the horse at this first check must be sixty or below—normal resting pulse of a horse is thirty-two to forty. At the four following checkpoints the heartbeat must be sixty-five or below. As the day wore on there were constant checks for dehydration. A pinch of the skin of a horse's neck will quickly show if he is losing too much moisture.

During the compulsory one-hour rest at each check the riders weighed in. Minimum weight allowed was 164 pounds, maximum 205 pounds, including saddle, tack and rider.

By the time the day's work was done in the cities and commuters were home in front of the telly at night, the leading riders were dismounting at the end of the first leg—a ride of 100 miles. At Maneroo Station they rolled out their swags and rested for the night after attending to the horses. Starting time Saturday was 8 am.

Among those riding into the country that has claimed men and horses since it was first settled was Reg (R. M.) Williams, 71. Now known for his western gear empire, R. M. Williams was once a camel boy and later a noted horseman.

Some riders in the endurance ride were on local station horses (seven horses a man is the ratio on some large properties in the heat and terrain). One such man was Sonny Condren from Mt Isa, riding Cheyenne, a brumby he cut out from a bush mob and trained. Competing with him were six or seven of Australia's leading endurance riders.

Carmen Batterham, one of the sixteen women riders who competed, has been a star since she entered endurance stakes in 1977. A calm, confident rider, this twenty-two-year old has great faith in her gelding, Country. Carmen rode standing in the stirrups, leaning forward, her knees, thighs and feet taking as much weight as possible from the horse—for 150 miles.

She and Country have won seven endurance races, been placed in six, 'got lost in one'. In her first race, the 130-mile Warwick to the Gold Coast in 1977, she came second to R. M. Williams, the doyen of bushriders. She can

Back-country people have been watching races since the time they first took horses out there.

Above: Jack Makim, legendary Queensland stockman.

Centre: Carmen Batterham, with Phil Blackley of NSW, rides in at sunset for the compulsory night's rest for rider and horse.

Top: One hundred and fifty miles later, the groups of riders come in to the finish at Longreach.

ride for 100 miles at ten miles an hour plus and has three Tom Quilty buckles, awarded to those who complete the annual gruelling 100-mile race through the Blue Mountains of New South Wales.

Carmen knows her horse well. 'Whatever speed or style he chooses I go with him,' she says. She rode the Longreach to Winton race in sandshoes, but borrowed her sister's riding trousers. 'I wore the bum out of my jeans,' she said.

The strappers followed the race, over the gidyea stones, red rocks as big as a fist, the sand and bull-dust and spinifex. They passed Alice Tank, Moondarra, Mistake Creek, Bladensburg Homestead, Shanty Creek, Maneroo Shed, Baratria Boundary, Bullock Hole, Scanlan's Dam and Starlight Yards, names redolent of the beginnings of early Australian settlement.

Flocks of emus and herds of kangaroos veered in front of them as they pushed through the bush. Plains turkey stalked by and the dancing bird of Australia, the brolga, went through its paces—as thirty of them did at the end of Winton's main street at the start of the long ride.

They passed the sites where the shearers camped during the strikes of the 1890s that heralded the formation of the Australian Labor Party and the election of the world's first Labor Parliament.

The rest of the night was cold, minus one degree. Neil Batterham, Carmen's husband, had water heated in a bucket over a log fire to warm-wash Country as he came in. At the checkpoint his pulse was seventy, at the half-hour check he was down to fifty-five. He was alert, his ears pricked up, curious about everything, and he ate and ate and ate. And Carmen, his rider? Was she weary after 120 miles in the saddle? No, not her. She kept the strappers awake half the night talking and laughing and bouncing out to look after Country. Country is a most pampered—in a tough way—horse. 'I'll molly-coddle him when we get home,' Carmen told us floor-sleepers in the horse transport in the middle of the night. 'He'll roll in the grass, enjoying himself.' 'Go to sleep,' called her husband from the swag rolled out over the cab of the truck.

Country, of course, was fine although he had run the 100-mile Quilty only one month before. 'You've got to think like a horse,' Carmen believes. Neil says, 'Getting a horse ready for an endurance race is like tuning a racing car. Even his shoes, they must balance perfectly.' Then, they were up and off again.

When Banjo Paterson wrote 'Waltzing Matilda' at Dagworth Station near Winton eighty-five years ago, he would have known many who had done such an arduous ride as this one. What would surprise him today is that many of us Australians, because we are no longer looking at the bush, believe it has disappeared, and with it the tough riders, fine brave horses and the spirit of adventure.

When the city dwellers were heading off to Rugby and Aussie Rules football that Saturday afternoon, the lead riders were coming into Longreach. Backs breaking, backsides sore, thighs paining, faces stinging from the sun and wind, each hoping to win the award for bringing in the fittest horse as well as the Golden Horseshoe prize for endurance. They rode in, congratulating young Carmen as they rode, knowing she had the race won by 1 hour 31 minutes, a total of 15.08 hours in the saddle over the 150 miles. And no one was surprised when Country was awarded Fittest Horse in the race. Of the thirty-five starters, fourteen finished the race, nine lost their way in the darkness, some riders wearied and some horses were 'vetted' out by the five veterinarians who checked each horse at each checkpoint.

It isn't the prize that counts in this race, it is, as veteran stockman Jack Makim says, 'the glory of having ridden as they did in the legendary days'.

DON McLEOD'S MOB

Most of those who fulfil the requirements to be adjudged a hero by their fellowmen can be sure the vote will not be 100 per cent their way. In the case of Don McLeod, perhaps not even history will decide, but for many people he is a great man; to some, a brave man.

You would be unlikely to stumble on Don McLeod and his 'mob', harried and hunted and hounded as they have been from one camping place to another.

I asked for him at a station on my way down from Broome, asked a man in that scorched void. 'I'm looking for Don McLeod.'

'The bloke that lives on the blacks?' he said.

'The man who said that doesn't bloody well know Don McLeod,' the Police Sergeant at Port Hedland told me when I called there to inquire for him.

I knew Don had been in gaol here. 'Yes, I've gaoled McLeod. Often. The law's the law. It's my job. But I've got nothing against McLeod personally. In fact, I admire him.'

He sent me further south to the Roeburne police station. 'Out in the police paddock,' they said there. So I headed off the road, trundled across a carpet miles square of crimson Sturt Pea and arrived at the settlement in the Police Paddock—no paddock by southern standards, it being 1,700 acres. There, several miles from water were 'the shades' of the 200 people of Don's Mob.

In a windowless tin shanty, Don McLeod sat emaciated, gaunt, wiry, his beard white and white-haired chest stark against his leathered walnut skin. Here was the man who was the force behind the first recorded strike of Aboriginal labour. Since then, he's stayed with the strikers who left their station jobs as a result of the strike, and organized their colony into various ventures. Mining had been a big part of their activities and when I met up with them they had formed a company, Nomad Pty Ltd.

His people gave me a place to camp, some damper; Jack came over to make up my fire. He was a big, fully tribalised man with broad cicatrices across his chest and down his arms.

'We decided in our camp council to share tucker with visitors,' he said when I told him I appreciated the hospitality. 'All men today give a little bit for you. We been live hard now. Five months ago we decide to go on damper and tea until we get steam up again. You come in that time and we been have meat and all!' His speech was precise like a schoolteacher.

I pushed more of the lumpy blue damper through my teeth and took great swigs of the thick stewed tea to swamp it down. Next day I saw the meal in preparation, the tea stewed for hours in a kerosene tin to get the most out of the leaves, the damper made from flour and water, the flour bought cheap after damp and mildew had spoilt it and bound it into lumps. Even the toddlers had only this food. They sat on the earth and dipped the chunks of damper into the black tea and sucked it.

Don McLeod.

Right: People of all ages joined the 1946 strike of Aboriginal stockmen in north-western Australia. Old Blind Sally, here ready to bed down for the night, has been with the strikers since the first walk-out. (Don McLeod's Mob, p. 125)

Below right: In the red lands of the Pilbara, before the big mining consortiums moved in, Don McLeod's mob managed to keep themselves with surface mining. This miner is drying the tantalite that he's washed in the tub in the foreground. (Don McLeod's Mob, p. 125)

Far right below: Many children have been born 'in the strike', as their families call it. (Don McLeod's Mob, p. 125)

Jack came to talk. 'Bush tucker him no more gibbit belly-ache, head-ache all a time.' When he spoke of things that affected him internally he lost his pedantic speech. 'In olden time we bin eat seed, goanna, possum, lily bulb. Bin good tucker. No more belly-ache alonga that tucker. After the Wet tucker bin come good alonga here.'

The sun was setting in the sudden disappearing trick it has in that area. Silhouetted in the pink and purple glow of the skyline a long trail of people came filing over the hill. Jack said they were the beryl miners, men, tall, lean, graceful, dusty from work, the women too weary to talk much, babies straddling their hips or shoulders, toddlers trailing them, imitating their energy-conserving walk.

Watching them from outside his tin hut Don McLeod's mood switched from bitterness to passion. 'Things pretty tough?' I asked. 'Our hides are cracking,' he said. 'We need money.' Ideals had been enough to get started with but now, 'We need money. We lived on kangaroo and water for fourteen months once. Now it's bad again.'

He was sixty-two when I met him and after twenty-five extraordinary years what did he have? A gaunt frame, a comfortless lodging with stacks of books, journals, and folders of letters and communiques and documents piled on the earth floor in his little tin hut, unfurnished except for a stretcher. 'I'll stick by these people to the bitter end. They're magnificent. I'll fight to the end for them.'

Over at the camp fire they had finished their damper and tea—the main meal of a day that began at sunrise and ended at sunset. They had a council meeting and the women's voices were as forceful and authoritative as the men's. Since the strike the women have worked on a par with the men and have had their say in affairs that affect the camp. When the meeting was over they began to sing, sweet, sad songs in a minor key, tender, with incredible rapid descents and plunges across several octaves. Don looked across the now dark arena towards their fires. 'I've nothing but contempt for the whites of Australia.'

In 1945, when he first became involved in the Aboriginal cause, Western Australian-born Don McLeod had spent his life knocking around Australia, following the example of his father, old 'Tiger' McLeod (he was a 'tiger' for work, hence the name), a prospector. Don worked sometimes as a casual labourer, and picked up a self-taught education in subjects such as law and geology.

He had no more interest in the Aborigines than the average bushman had until, in the Kimberleys, he met an Aboriginal fossicker named Dooley. Yarning round the camp fire at nights, Dooley told McLeod of the grievances of his people, and particularly about their resentment at their conditions and pay as stock workers on outback stations.

McLeod was biologically a rebel, and Dooley presented him with a ready-made cause.

He took Dooley away into the bush for ten days and taught him how to organise a strike. Dooley did his work well and in 1946 an estimated 600 native stockmen throughout the north refused to work until they had been guaranteed a minimum wage of 30s a week. Some had previously been receiving food and clothing, but no pay; others had been paid up to about 12s a week.

In the history of strike action this perhaps ranks as unique as well as perhaps the most brilliantly engineered, considering the problems involved. Dooley had to encourage a people who, only a generation before, had been living 'in the Stone Age', to take up the weapon perfected only in the twentieth century. The work force he would contact was scattered over an area the size of Ireland. There were no means of communication—not as

known to the twentieth century anyway. And whereas most union organisers come up against a fair amount of apathy, Dooley would have to talk to people who knew that to follow him would put them outside the law: they would be leaving their place of employment without permission, breaking one of the laws made for them alone in this country. They knew the whites could and would arrest them; they would be brought back chained together on the back of the station truck and put to work again, and they would have to leave again and go on until there was some change.

That upwards of 800 people left work that first day and 600 refused to return unless their requests were met is sufficient comment both on the conditions under which they lived as well as the power of Dooley, his friend Clancy, and Don McLeod.

Sitting round fires at night listening to stories of that time, I pictured Dooley relentlessly plodding on across those stoney desert plains, in his pockets the little calenders made of the labels of baking powder tins and cigarette boxes, each square representing a day, until they reached the square with a circle around it: the day the Aborigines, of their own accord, would rise up. As they talked I saw them sitting outside their bag humpies that morning waiting for the boss to send a man down to raise hell; then the boss himself coming and reading the riot act; then the old men, unskilled of tongue in these proceedings, knowing only their belief, 'No pay, no work'.

When the food scraps that used to be thrown to them — the 'salt junk' and flour for damper — were cut off, they organised to hunt greater quantities of game to feed the camps. Then, when the order to get off the property came, the gathering of the children, the wrapping of cooked kangaroo and birds in bark and cloth, ready for the trek on foot. And the farewell look at the place that had been home for their people for so long that not even the scientists know if it was 10,000 or 30,000 years. Those who wouldn't join damned the strikers as they left, accusing them of causing trouble. But still they went.

Dooley, back at Marble Bar when the strike began, was traced as its organiser. He was arrested, chained by the hands and neck as the custom is up there, and held for five days. He was then taken to Port Hedland with the chains from his necklet padlocked to the back of a truck.

In court, Dooley found McLeod waiting to follow him into the dock. He had been arrested on charges of attempting to persuade an Aboriginal to leave his employment. He was found guilty and fined £100 or five months in gaol.

In the years immediately following the strike McLeod was arrested seven times, sometimes for 'counselling natives,' sometimes for being 'within five chains of two or more natives.' On his third offence of 'being within five chains of natives' he was liable to a fine of £200 or two years' gaol, or both. A clergyman who made a special trip to investigate McLeod also found himself arrested for being within five chains of natives and was fined as a first offender, despite his indignant protests to the court.

Dooley made no indignant protests. When fifty-two of his strikers were gaoled he asked, 'How many more can your gaol hold?' 'A hundred', he was told. 'Right! I'll have them for you by Tuesday.'

Dooley kept organising, he went on being gaoled. 'I was in and out like a fiddler's elbow.' He was indefatigable. There is a legend that he once heard McLeod was again on his way to gaol, so Dooley grouped all the strikers he could find about him and marched on the gaol. The police officer who told me the story said, 'If we'd put McLeod in that time they would have taken the gaol to pieces stone by stone even though its walls are two feet thick'.

The gaols up along the north-west never before had such droves of prisoners crowded in them. They were old gaols, with ring bolts in the walls for chains. Some had fireplaces from the early days so the Afghans could

Left: From the Olgas to Ayers Rock and beyond. A Territory tall tale declares that these odd outcrops are the result of a stone throwing contest of long ago!

The women can separate the ore into five minerals by twisting and turning their yandies.

cook their own meals as demanded by their beliefs. Dooley had carved his name in one wall. In the next cell, McLeod had carved his. When Dooley was imprisoned at one time he was herded into the cell, still in his iron necklet and anklets and chains. The policeman said, 'I'll see if I can get you out of those'. 'You can please yourself, mate,' said Dooley. 'I can think just as well in them as out of them.' A prisoner in the next cell heard him. 'That you, Dooley?' 'Yes, who's that?' he called through the grille in the stone wall. 'Me, McLeod.'

All the strikers who were gaoled, and McLeod, were tried time and again by local JPs, men whom McLeod claims were either station owners whose striking stockmen were now brought before them on the bench, or men involved financially or by relationship with the forces opposing the payment of wages to Aborigines.

Don McLeod cannot be said to be free of emotion when discussing the question. It would be unbelievable if he were not passionate to the point of emotion when it comes to talking of people with whom he had thrown in his lot for so long. While accepting that the pamphlets he drew up may appear emotional in content and choice of words, it is a fact that the content has not been denied or proven false.

In eastern states, even to a degree in Perth, thinking people had been in sympathy with his cause, but isolated as his operations were, beyond the ramparts of the distances travelled by most Australians, and outside the limits of news reporting, there was little information to be had. Yet, as far back as 1950 people were saying, 'McLeod is the man who saved Australia from the problems of the USA and South Africa.' Even then they were saying that the revolt he started would never be quenched. They wrote a ballad about the strike—'Clancy, Dooley and Don McLeod'—but they didn't petition the Federal Government to intervene nor did they send money.

Gradually the Aborigines who had given up their station jobs after the strike trekked in to the Pilbara area where McLeod was prospecting. They came to meet their white champion. The colony grew and the white champion realised that he had to make himself responsible for their welfare. He was interested in mining the Pilbara. He'd fossicked a score of minerals out of the ground there, including some most valuable. But mining on any scale would need financial backing and he knew the government would never give that to these people or to him. (The great mining boom had yet to hit Western Australia.) As most of the strikers had been pastoral workers, Don formed them into the North-West Co-operative and started them mining, with the long-range plan of buying their own property.

By 1951 they had paid deposits on four large station properties and had bought a sizeable quantity of station equipment. The work prospered and the community shared the profit. Then, almost overnight, for reasons that have never been made quite clear, the whole venture appeared to collapse. The Co-operative went into voluntary liquidation in 1954 with debts of $30,000. Some of the Aborigines drifted back to work on the stations they had left in the days of the strike.

The antagonism between Don McLeod and the Native Welfare authorities of Western Australia has such complex causes that to quote an article in the *Current Affairs Bulletin* published by Sydney University, 'it would be difficult, perhaps impossible, to describe it objectively or in a way that would be satisfactory to the disputants'.

Don wasn't using a figure of speech when he said they started up again with their bare hands. Apart from a pneumatic drill, and the power unit to run it, all work was done by pick, shovel, and wheelbarrow, as well as a unique piece of equipment in mining lore: a yandy, another name for coolamon, a hollow sheet of curved wood or bark. It is as old as the

boomerang, the woomera, or didgeridoo, and is used for carrying a baby, or as a cradle. You see these curved sheets in many areas of Australia, sometimes tucked under an arm while the family are on the move; sometimes, in towns, held up by a suitcase strap. Often the brown baby is naked, lying on the bark or wood, a healthy hygienic arrangement in the bush.

It wasn't as a baby carrier that the yandy impressed Don. He was watching the women winnowing seeds for food, twisting the yandy around and throwing the seeds in the air to clean dust from them, when he saw its possibilities in mining. By experimenting, he found that by rolling, twisting, and shaking the yandy rhythmically the women could separate the minerals, using one or other of the three movements to bring various ores to the end of the yandy. They can even, for fun, execute patterns of colour with the various ores. To clear the red dust from the minerals they throw the whole content of the yandy into the air. Up it goes, twists like a spiralling tornado, then slowly unwinds and the minerals slip back to the yandy.

Early in the morning they trooped off to the mining fields, old women, mothers, the young children, and babies. Even at sun-up it was hot. The sun doesn't rise here, it leaps up and hits you.

One group went to the tantalite and columbite area where they'd sit all day in the fierce heat, riffling their yandies. The others went to the beryl mine. This is harder work than the yandy-ing. Beryl is a crystal set in hard rock. After the men break the ore the women chip the beryl clear with axe heads, old hammers, or stones. All day they chip away in the white-hot sun, sheltered only by the slight shade cast from the spinifex they cut and spread over scant bushes. The children help if they're big enough; the toddlers and babies are cared for and coddled and fed in the way only the much-loved Aboriginal children are.

There was no morning or afternoon break, only lunch break when they drank from the kerosene tin of cold black tea they'd brought from the camp and ate a very small amount of damper—and then back to work.

Back at camp the raw material was washed in an old tub to remove dirt and spread on sacks for drying, stones are picked out by hand, a dressmaker's magnet picks out the magnetite, a tobacco tin holds the winnings.

'I think they're going to give you a goodbye sing,' Don warned me the night before I was to leave. So I sat, the only white among the two hundred

Above: Jacob Oberdoo, the spokesman of the strikers, and Nancy. Most in the camp have been there since the strike began in 1946. Nancy says 'I been brought up in the strike, married in strike, I won't leave, ever.'

Above left: The much-loved children are part of the day's work. Mothers stop chipping at the beryl to play with any child.

Above: Beryl chippers sit in the blinding sun sheltered only by odd clumps of spinifex.

Middle: Yandying, using an age-old Aboriginal carrying dish to separate the various ores from the red dust.

Top: Washing tantalite at the Nomad camp. Children play at it, imitating their elders.

blacks, flanked on either side and behind me by men who had all been gaoled at one time or another, some many times, and by Nancy who had told me, 'I been brought up in the strike, married in strike, I won't leave, ever.'

Jacob Oberdoo sat beside me. He had been gaoled during the strike. They had told me about his appearing in court charged with knocking a policeman's teeth out. Jacob politely reached out and handed over the teeth. He had gathered them up and brought them to court wrapped up in a handkerchief. I could imagine the scene, Jacob is handsome, has the most magnificent teeth, smiles as though life has been a great joy to him. His physique is impressive and his charm is just the warmth of the man coming out. But those teeth in a handkerchief are what his humour is made of.

Jack Garden, with his tribal markings showing through his open necked shirt, was the other side of me. He has been with McLeod since a year after the strike began. 'We seen many up and downs,' he yarned away. 'But the old man [McLeod] always been stick by us.' 'You're just hanging on at the moment?' 'Been enough to keep the billy boiling.'

Jack had spent the first part of his life on a cattle station:

Ride horse, go after cattle, twelve bob a week. All men like me, some white men too, he not get much wage. We go on strike to get fair money. Everybody, all men, say we no-good blackfella to go on strike, some black-fella say that too. No more [meaning that's not right]. Now blackfella on station get a decent wage all along that strike. White man too. But squatter. He never forget. He hate us still.

We talked about citizenship rights, 'the dog licence', as they called it here. 'What?' Jack was heated about this. 'They been make us citizens of Australia!' They refused to apply for citizenship rights, 'the dog licence'. The very thought of it sent some of them into gusts of laughter. The great tribal dancer, Punch, enjoyed the joke. 'Plenty crazy that one! We bin payem tax but we no belong to country.' Punch said to me, 'You bin sign dog licence?' We all laughed, but mine was pretty hollow.

It was Punch who led the dancing. A big man, tall, with a well-covered frame. I'd heard about him, I never expected to see him dance. He'd pounded the earth, trading dances across hundreds of miles of territory and his name was known to many tribes in the days before he threw in his lot with the strike.

I sat back. With my backside on the earth I could feel the ground tremble when he pounded in, leapt, and stamped, a tour de force that was performed in silence apart from the clacking of sticks. I never knew anyone could dance like that. He hadn't led up to it, he didn't let up on it, he didn't ease out of it. He just started at top tempo and pounded at the same rhythm until your mind was numbed by his power. Then he disappeared out of the firelight.

The following morning Jacob Oberdoo came to wish me goodbye. 'You're a sight for sore eyes, Jacob,' I told him. 'Yes, I am,' he agreed. For the occasion he had donned the outfit the mob had bought for him to wear at the annual Aboriginal Affairs Conference in Sydney. Jacob had addressed the conference and, as well, appeared twice on TV. His khaki shorts, shirt and tie, and knee-length socks were laundry fresh and the creases sharp pressed. He'd kept the outfit in a suitcase, he said.

Jack Garden with the cicatrices shook hands limply in the way these powerful men do. 'We like to see visitor. Things been good then. No one come, things bad.' (Meaning 'outside' gossip about them).

And then I was off, the women calling their goodbyes softly to me as I drove slowly across the camp, Nancy walking at my open window, past the cook-house with the jam tin of flowers on the rough trestle table. 'Thank you,' I said in farewell, 'for everything'. She replied 'That been all right. We agree to look after visitor, share tucker and thing.'

THE DALY RIVER O!

Charlie Dargie and 'Squizzy' Taylor—'Gorgeous Biancous Squizonous Taylor' as Bill Harney christened him, 'his Latinised Maluk Maluk name'—were part of a rumbustious legend-making, end-of-an-era mob. When they disappear we'll righteously say that such things as they did will never happen again and we'll be right. Only men like these have the calibre and stamina to live the way they have lived and we will never see their likes again because we've outlived the conditions that bred such men.

We'll probably forget them, or emasculate them in retrospect by recording them as being 'wild lads'. Already coffee shop folksingers are being gay and wild-colonial-boyish with 'Daly River O!', the song that tells of Dargie and his mates, one of the lustiest songs of an era now gone, and a woman writer has used a castrated version in a book—coyly intimating that other words are used when ladies are not present.

> Now I saw a nigger sitting up an old gum tree,
> The crows had picked his eyes out so he couldn't see.
> Never, oh never a word said he,
> For he was dead as dead could be.
> He was just about ripe, you could smell him for miles
> And his bum was sticking out like a horse with the piles.
> When Dargie threw a gibber and hit him in the guts,
> And the nigger went Whoof! and we all went bush
> Down on the Daly River O!

Squizzy sang and Dargie came in with asides. 'It's true too, the whole bloody lot,' he said as we sat in his dirt-floored tin home on the banks of the Daly River. And the climate of the ribald ditty is as true as the words.

Charlie Dargie and Squizzy Taylor went out to the Daly in the late 1920s. They settled fifty miles from the coast and the area now spoken of generally as 'the Daly' is that area roughly fifteen miles along the banks of the river where the handful of settlers live. They're not overcrowded on the Daly. Dargie lives ten miles from Squizzy and five miles from the Lavaters who live on the grounds of the Maluk Maluk tribe. The first settlement in the area took place in the 1880s when a copper mine opened up, and later the Jesuits built a mission, both of which went into recess for different reasons—the Brinkens, the Aboriginal tribe next to the Maluk Maluk, one night turned up at the copper mine and murdered the five white miners, and in return the scattered white settlers came and wiped out the Brinkens at what is now known as Blackfellows Creek.

The Jesuits were flooded out three times and, as all good Jesuits do, they retired from a fruitless area to gather their strength elsewhere.

When Dargie and the later settlers came, the going was tough. That such pioneering was done in the 1920s and 1930s is scarcely credited if our history books and popular features are to be believed. (The Daly was seventy-five

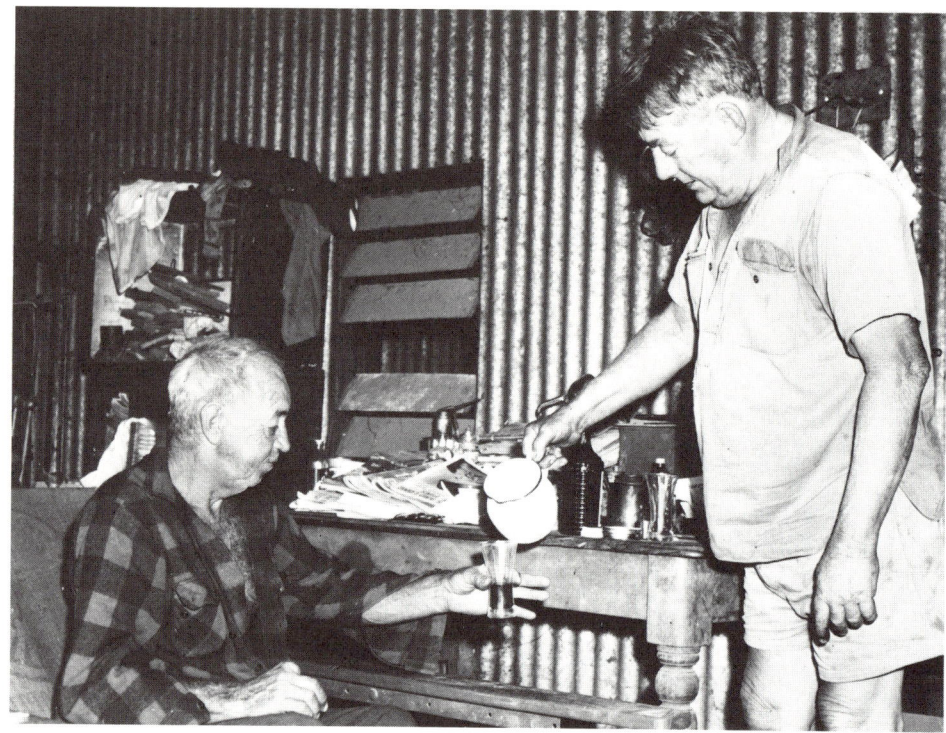

Squizzy declared he'd been educated at Eton and at times played the part. Like all outback men who've endured many hard years, when the whips are cracking the bottle's forgotten and they work in a way that city people could never understand.

miles away from a telephone, crocodiles still bark at the door of the few houses stretched along the river bank, and every snake in the area is poisonous, including the deadly taipan and death adder.) It is no more than a dirt road 170 miles from Darwin, and in the floods of 1960 the settlers were all washed out and rescued by startlingly crude methods, some spending a night in a tree, Dargie himself caring for a woman whose husband was 'somewhere in the river'. This flood inundated 100,000 square miles of land.

Naturally enough, feelings between the few Aborigines left and the white settlers have been strained. The Aborigines of the area were strong and fierce, the white men battlers. It's all very well today to speak of matters in phrases anthropological but the schools of a generation ago gave anthropology no great mention, and even those of us who studied it thought mainly in terms of distant peoples, rarely of our own continent's Aboriginal people. Men with the guts necessary to settle an area such as the Daly had neither the training nor the time to appreciate the ethnic idiosyncracies of the natives when they were battling for their very lives as well as livelihood. Hence the words of the 'Daly River O!' song are offensive today to the city-bound freedom rider and the writer of pamphlets on justice for the Aborigine, but its place in the historic panorama of our history should be demanded. This wasn't milk-and-water living, this was the real blood and guts we admire in other races but deny to our own because it is dangerously unfashionable to walk the tight-rope of a middle line on the colour question.

I believe it is dangerous to the coloured people to do otherwise—and I've had a lifetime of watching ignorant, well-meaning charitable people set out to help to 'emancipate' the Aborigines, only to retreat, revolted and sickened and made bitterly antagonistic both by what they learn of the black and by his reception of them. How many members of committees working for the advancement of the Aborigines would damn Charlie Dargie for his past and have banned the song that so racially sings 'Three whites, two chows, four bucks and a gin,' yet how many could have opened up land as did Charlie. He was not one of the landed gentry who drove their herds across the continent and about whom books are written and about whom it is said they never travelled without a book in their pack, be it to read or to write in. Charlie couldn't and wouldn't want to go down in history as one who read or wrote. I once heard a bloke say to Charlie, 'You oughta written all this into a book', and Charlie said, 'Aw, Jesus, they'da gaoled me'. But it is a sad commentary on our national outlook that while we extol in historical and literary journals our pioneering gentry who could afford to take up the best land and who in these northern latitudes worked whole tribes of Aborigines for no more than scant food and not even that during 'the Wet', we rarely mention the gallant, unlearned, unlettered battler who set out to 'give it a go' without money, property of family to back his sortie into the wilderness. And—this is the important finding—they lived with and formed some sort of alliance with the blacks. Of course it isn't the alliance the city committee member understands, but it is a tolerance based on what they know they and the Aborigines can work on as a basis of co-existence demanded by the place and time.

'This climate breeds good kids,' Charlie said to me as a bare, coffee-coloured kid toddled in. 'My grand-kid.' So, Charlie had children. 'Yairs, I adopted two.' He pointed to a half-caste girl down by the river and a dark boy by a tractor. 'They're mine of course.' A pair of stick black legs passed beneath the foot-from-the-ground tin partitioning wall of the verandah cum living room where we sat and the kitchen. 'Me cook.'

In this way Charlie Dargie has legally guarded his children's and therefore their mother's future in a way most of us would wish the hundreds of other white men who passed along north of Capricorn had done. To me, Charlie Dargie is all man, the type of man you'd expect a real song to be written about.

Charlie Dargie. It's been a hard life to tame some parts of the outback, and only the toughest survive.

> Now come all ye sports that want a bit of fun,
> Roll up your swag and pack up your gun,
> Throw in some sugar, some flour and tea
> And don't forget a gallon of Vic O.P.
> Crank up your lizzie and come along with me,
> And I'll show you such sights as you never did see,
> Down on the Daly River O!
>
> *Chorus:*
> There was Wallaby George and Charlie Dargie,
> Old Skinny Davis and Jimmy Panquee,
> Big-mouthed Charlie and old Paree,
> The Tipperary Pong and Jim Wilkie,
> And whenever you may roam you will find yourself at home,
> For they're noted for their hospitality.
> You'll wake in the morning, and your heart's filled with glee
> By a little nude maid with a pannikin of tea.
> She'll give you such a welcome you won't want to go
> Away from the Daly River O!
>
> *second verse:*
> Now I saw a buffalo bull and a fat Chinee
> Run a dead heat to the foot of a tree.
> The Chinaman flew, he didn't feel the ruts,
> But the buffalo stopped with a bullet in the guts.
> As the bush birds rose at the sound of the gun
> The water dropped a foot in the silver billabong.
> With quacks, duck and feathers you couldn't see the sun
> Down on the Daly River O!
>
> *third verse:*
> While the buffalo kicked we poured in the lead;
> We killed him ten times to make sure he was dead.
> We drew out our knives and we all hopped in:
> Three whites, two Chows, four bucks and a gin.
> We tore off his hide and ripped him up the guts,

*'Gorgeous Biancous Squizonous Taylor',
Charlie's mate.*

Took his little tit-bits and fancy funny cuts,
Then we cranked up the lizzie and shouted 'Right ho!
All aboard for the Daly River O!'

fourth verse:
Now I saw a nigger sitting up an old gum tree,
The crows had picked his eyes out so he couldn't see.
Never, oh never a word said he,
For he was as dead as dead could be.
He was just about ripe, you could smell him for miles.
And his bum was sticking out like a horse with the piles.
When Dargie threw a gibber and hit him in the guts,
And the nigger went Whoof! and we all went bush
Down on the Daly River O!

(Then out with the chorus again, pre-breakfast rum swishing away in the tin pannikin as it is swung in time to the music.)

There was Wallaby George and Charlie Dargie,
Old Skinny Davis and Jimmy Panquee,
Big-mouthed Charlie and Old Paree,
The Tipperary Pong and Jim Wilkie,
And wherever you may roam you will find yourself at home,
For they're noted for their hospitality.
You'll wake in the morning, and your heart's filled
  with glee
By a little nude maid with a pannikin of tea.
She'll give you such a welcome you won't want to go
Away from the Daly River O!

'That Chinese weighed twenty-two stone,' Charlie Dargie told me, 'He had two sticks to help him along. Big-mouthed Charlie and Jimmy Panquee, they were the Chinese who started off at Fletcher Gully gold mine, found nothing worthwhile but kidded everyone they had. You shoulda seen the mining engineers and what-nots that came pouring in to look for gold and Big-mouthed Charlie and Jimmy Panquee smilin' like the chinks they were and nodding and saying "Plenty gold!"'

Jimmy Burgoyne, a mate of Dargie and Squizzy Taylor, wrote the song. 'Old Jimmy Burgoyne and me were chasing the beef, and every detail in the song is correct,' Dargie told me. 'It was my f----- bullet that stopped the buffalo—if you'll pardon the expression. We were hungry. I was hard up in those times, the arse out of me trousers and two left boots.'

Dargie came up to the Daly when he was eleven years old, almost fifty years ago. Squizzy Taylor came a little later. 'And it's about forty years since Jimmy Burgoyne wrote that song. He camped over under that mango tree. He had a squeeze-box, Squizzy had a mouth organ.'

'Oh, they were the days,' Squizzy said and reached for the rum bottle and launched into a poem, '"Oh I've taken my fun where I've found it"—that's Kipling's "Ladies" you know—"She knifed me one night when I wished she was white."' He'd asked me earlier if I wanted a drink. I didn't know how I'd go on rum before breakfast so I said, 'No'—near to midday I was dehydrating fast, so I asked what else was there perhaps except rum.

This threw Squizzy, who claims his father was at Eton, into a flurry. So courteous was he that each time I stood he leapt to his feet too. After the second time when Charlie, having followed suit, said 'What're we jumping up and down for?' Squizzy said, 'Because the lady's standing up,' and Charlie said, 'Well you better sit down or we'll end up bloody well killing ourselves', so I didn't stand again but lolled back as did they in the hessian covered deck-chair-type seats—Charlie reclining like a Roman at a feast with one foot cocked up on the other knee and Squizzy jigging round with his chest display that took all my eyes: it was like the back of a crocodile, as dark in colour and horny, and down below where his navel whorled there were occasional noises that threatened to geyser out in a boiling spurt when he told me, 'I drink anything. Spirits of salts, anything!' 'Surely not spirits of salts?' 'Yes, certainly spirits of salts. A few drops in a glass of water. Tastes dreadful but settles the nerves.' A visiting seed buyer told me, 'I came out here once and Squizzy had been on the Worcestershire Sauce. He was a mess that day!' 'Oh, I'll drink anything,' Squizzy agreed, 'but I'd prefer rum', a hint to the seed buyer that if he had anything in his car the time had come to produce it. 'I've some whisky,' the innocent man announced, 'but I can't leave it here. I only mention it because perhaps your guest may prefer it to rum.' By now I would have settled for 'Spirits of salts, anything!'. The whisky was produced and the seed merchant tried to hold on but couldn't, and then Squizzy went into a flurry. What should I drink from? There didn't appear to be a spare pannikin. 'A glass,' Squizzy cried and stirred around in a trunk and magically came up with a glass, unwashed since something like Condies crystals was last mixed in it. But that was soon fixed: Squizzy has long fingers, particularly the middle finger which reached right to the bottom of the glass where the black nail scraped off the brown sediment before the whisky was poured in neat.

Charlie told me:

There's been plenty seen the possibilities of the Daly. It was the battling they didn't see. We used to have to have a licence to work the blacks. One day a policeman came down the river like a packet of salts, 'Where's your licence to work niggers?' he says to me and I says, 'You can kiss me. I've got a licence', and I did too, but I'd a been a gonner if I hadn't. You know what that track you were on this morning is called? The Pumpkin Road. That's because we carted truck-loads of pumpkins over it once trying to make a go of things. A city scientist fellow came out here once and tried to tell us what to grow, strutting round he was, if you'd a stuck a feather in his bum he'd a looked like a peacock, but every time he told us what to grow we said, we tried that. We tried everything. When the crop was good the market was bad, when the crop was ripening the wallabies came in and ate them to the ground, when we put fences up the floods washed them twenty miles away, even last year when we had a bumper crop and had 7,000 bales of hay and stock down south were starving for want of feed, no one would pay the freight out so our stacks rotted

But the end of the tale is good. Charlie Dargie helped introduce a crop that brought wealth to him and others in the area: Townsville lucerne. This seed was first brought to the Daly by the new Roman Catholic Mission in 1953 to prevent erosion and dust hazard on the Mission airstrip. Charlie got some seed from them in 1959 thinking it would grow good pig food. To quote an Agricultural Department brochure:

As the pigs of Mr. C. Dargie, a well-known resident of the area, did not relish the Townsville lucerne, he later harvested a seed crop for which he was paid £11,000. In the 1964/65 season, settlers on the Daly grew 300 acres of the lucerne, yielding about 60 tons of seed, as well as 287 acres which harvested into 260 tons of hay, and nearby cattle stations seeded 2,000 acres as pasture.

A legume, Townsville lucerne is ideal for north of Capricorn. It establishes readily and survives under the adverse conditions of the flood plains. As Charlie Dargie said, 'Home and hosed'. Who knows, perhaps Charlie will yet live on in official history as the man who introduced 'the wonder seed' to the Daly, and in the way of history he might end up on a stamp in collar and tie and hair neatly parted in the middle. I wish history were the stuff of life and that Charlie could be recorded as 'the man who shot that f—— bull'.

THE ANTI-HERO

When only 300 Europeans lived in Darwin, along with 10,000 Asians brought there as indentured workers, the town was isolated in all ways. How much more so for a lone woman—an unnamed doctor's wife 100 miles south of Darwin in 1905.

The man she writes of would be on his way to Queensland to face trial, probably he will end up in Rockhampton.

Just as we were about to start for home an odd little procession came over the range towards us. A police trooper led the way; he was followed by another at whose side rode a man sitting his horse easily, his travel-stained shirt and trousers telling of hard wear and weary journeyings; two other troopers brought up the rear. As the prisoner passed us he bent his head to his manacled hands hastily slouching his wideawake over his eyes. Swaying slightly back in the saddle he looked up as he passed, and I thought a deprecatory smile trembled on his face.

Seeing the doctor, the leader fell back after they had advanced about fifty yards or so to ask for advice for one of their number.

'You have your prisoner very closely guarded. What is he charged with?'
'Murder, sir, and he has given us many a hard day's work to catch him.'
'Why, it's surely not Dash at last, is it?'
'It's he, sure enough.'

We passed them a little later still riding at a slow walking pace, and once again I caught sight of the prisoner's strange pathetic, quivering smile.

'Poor man, he is "sorry, sorry, sorry",' cried I, terribly overcome at seeing a man under the weight of the law, whose far-reaching arm had penetrated these lonely wilds to secure its wretched captive who was now riding day after day, week after week, for hundreds of miles to answer the call of justice, probably to his death.

We know no more of the lonely prisoner.

The prisoner rides slowly on, across the Northern Territory—1,000 miles to judgement in the nearest court at Rockhampton on the Queensland coast.

THE ENTOMBED MINER

'There is no chance of rescuing the entombed miner alive,' reported the *West Australian* on Wednesday, 20 March 1907. 'Mine Flooded; an Italian missing'. The previous day's report had been from Coolgardie:

Rain came down heavily this afternoon, Tuesday, 19 March, at Bonnievale and a large body of water rushed into the main workings of the Westralia East mine. The water rose rapidly in the shaft. An Italian miner named Varis Scheotti, a widower with five children, was working in the rise from No 10 level in No 2 shaft. The water rose past that level, 100 ft up, up to No 9 level and the Italian was still mining while all the others were safe. There is no chance of rescuing the man alive. The water is still rising in the shaft.

Bonnievale, out from Coolgardie, was an area of many mines, all flooded in the rush of water that ran naturally down stopes, drives, shafts and tunnels, but the Westralia East Extension suffered most of all. 'At about 4 pm the men were working in all parts below when the water with mud and debris came down the shaft with such violence that little time was left for escaping.' Working along a drive out of No 10 level — 1,000 feet below ground — Varischetti (the correct spelling of his name) was now 100 feet beneath the water, the mud and the debris that the flood had tumbled along the drives. None doubted that he was dead.

The other men when rescued and raised in skips were

... utterly unrecognizable when they reached the surface besmeared as they were with the dirty mixture that was rapidly filling the mine. Rescuers assisted all men to escape — all except one, a miner known as Varischetti who had been at work a good distance from the shaft, about 30 feet along a drive.

The following morning mine managers and workmen went down to the 900-foot level to assess the position. With them was Guiseppe Masingoni, Varischetti's 'mate'. While the others clambered about in the mullock and water Masingoni lay on the floor and knocked on a pipe with his fist. Almost immediately came sounds of knocking from below, on the No 10 level. Masingoni beat nine times with his fist to denote No 9 level and he heard ten faint knocks in return. His friend was alive, somewhere about the 1,000-foot mark. Masingoni moved along the wet floor of 9 level, knocking as he went, until the knocking below told him he was immediately above the trapped man. The mine manager, consulting the mine plans plotted the position of the entombed man: he was up a rise — a sloping tunnel with a dead end and most certainly would be in a small pocket of air with water lapping his feet.

The news was rushed to the surface and soon Perth and Australia knew that the miner lived. But trapped as he was, with 100-foot depth of water between him and relative safety, there seemed little hope of his deliverance.

Mines Inspector Crabbe went below with a squad of twelve men after examining the plans of the mine. They cleared debris out of the inclined shaft

The rescued miner, Modesto Varischetti, was an Italian immigrant, the widowed father of five children.

At any time of crisis in the mines, miners used to gather at the post office at Hannan's (Kalgoorlie) to wait for news — as these miners did in 1894.

and arranged for baling to begin at once. In two hours, 'the rescue party had both tanks baling at full speed'. Crabbe then turned his attention to pumping,

but, on going into the matter, I found that it would take ten days to get the water low enough to enable Varischetti to be rescued. Realising that this would be too long a time to keep a man entombed, I began to turn over in my mind the possibility of rescuing him by the aid of divers. I returned to Coolgardie and saw Mr Vincent, who is an old, experienced miner, and, having explained matters to him, I asked him if he thought it possible to get the entombed man out by this means. He replied, that, although bristling with dangers and difficulties, he thought it could be done, and said, 'If you cannot get the divers to undertake the work, get me a diving apparatus and I will take it on'.

The game old man was not required. Two experienced men were sent for, Hughes and Hearne.

'A LOCOMOTIVE RACE FOR LIFE' cried the *West Australian*. 'Encouraging cheers went up from the onlookers at Central Railway Station at 3 pm (Thursday) when a special train with two divers and their impedimenta', steamed off, heading for Coolgardie, 300 miles away. The train—an engine, one carriage and a truck of coal 'to prevent oscillation as the train races over the tracks'—was given an 'open road' to the eastern gold-fields. To save the time of watering and cooling, a fresh engine was hooked on at two places on the long haul and at 4 pm on Friday, the rescue train reached Kalgoorlie (a record that stood for nearly fifty years).

In the meantime, Masingoni had been going regularly to the 900-foot level and knocking out a signal to Varischetti as a comforting knowledge that men were aware of his position. But, 'No idea can be gained of the amount of space the imprisoned man has, or air at his disposal. The terrible position he occupies is being intensified as the hours pass'.

When the divers arrived, Crabbe took them immediately to No 9 level 'and they commenced the work of deliverance'. On examination they found that air was escaping from No 10 level at a point immediately above where

the entombed man was imprisoned. This emphasised the necessity for maintaining a pressure of thirty-five pounds to the square inch to keep the water from rising and smothering Varischetti. As the result of baling operations the pressure was gradually lowered and by 25 March was steady at twenty pounds.

To get to Varischetti it was decided that Diver Hughes must descend to the 900-foot level, climb down a vertical ladder to the 1000-foot level, cross the plat around the shaft, the ladderway being on the opposite side to the level where the man was, and then proceed 200 feet along the rise where Varischetti was imprisoned. For this last 200 feet there was no ladderway and Hughes must climb from set to set along the timber sets, these being several feet apart. This with his 180 pounds of gear and having to drag 900 feet of piping behind him. He was a practical miner and knew the difficulties—and the dangers. He would take an air compressor with him and regulate pressure to thirty-five pounds before he went down. 'I shall want plenty of air.' He knew Varischetti must have very little air space.

On Friday 22 March, after seventy-two interminable hours during which he had been literally in a dark and inaccessible tomb, Varischetti saw a movement in the dark, thick water. There appeared to him, almost as a cruel taunt, a faint aura of light. 'For every second of seventy-two hours the conviction had been hammered home that the last vestige of hope had gone and now . . .' As the man peered through the gloom he saw a great iron orb rise twelve inches out of the water. In the darkness he could make out no more. Hughes had been warned, that in the darkness, for the buried miner, a touch by a hand may well give Varischetti a fearful shock.

Hughes clambered back up the arduous route and reported that the miner was 'entombed in a small air space at the top of the rise.'

On the second descent Hughes took down a zinc tube containing food, paper and pencil, and a typed code of messages to use as signals, that is, 'I want food', 'candles', 'I am well', each signal being a number of knocks. This day the two men shook hands and the Italian 'eyed his welcome and strangely clad visitor with amazement'.

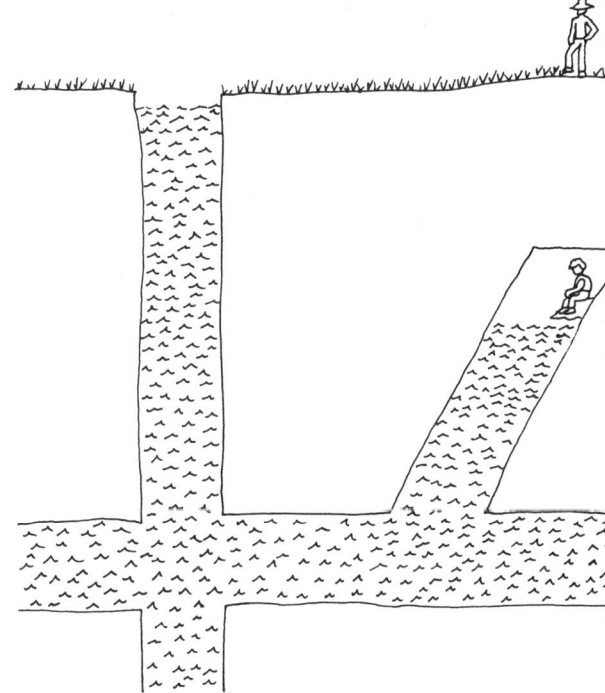

Above: Although the water rose 100 feet above the level where Varischetti was working, he was saved by climbing up a rise and huddling in the small pocket of air held there by water pressure. It kept him alive for nine days.

Above left: When a mine is suddenly flooded, the trapped miner's only hope is that he will be carried into an air pocket created by the pressure of floodwaters rushing up the narrow shafts.

Not knowing how rescue attempts were faring, Varischetti wrote to his friend Giuseppe Masingoni. Hughes brought the letter up in the sealed cylinder and it was opened, translated and read aloud at the mine mouth without waiting for Giuseppe to be located.

Dear Friend Joe, I don't know in what manner I can make you understand how much gratitude my miserable heart has gained by reading your letter that you are so hard at work rescuing me from this tomb. I don't know any more, but wish the most hearty thanks conveyed to all, and have pity on me. Farewell to my brothers, and tell them not to forget me. Farewell to my dear friend, Joe. You will please give the manager and his wife my most hearty thanks, and excuse me for all the trouble I have caused. I wish you peace and good luck, and many greetings to the rescue party. Many thanks to everybody. Have pity on me. As regards the food, I am very well satisfied. I do no more than to open my arms and embrace you all, and thanks again to the manager and his wife. So far nothing remains other than to say farewell to all very heartily. I am your miserable friend, Modesto Varischetti. Adieu!

Those waiting 100 feet above at No 9 level could follow the progress of divers by the length of hose played out.

On 25 March Hughes brought to the surface the tube containing two letters written by Varischetti — in Italian — to his friend Giuseppe which was promptly translated into 'Joe' as the letter was read to watchers on the surface.

Dear Joe, I have given you to understand through signalling that I do not want anything to eat. Because the man that come has told me yesterday was the last day. Therefore, if I have to stay here until tomorrow, bring me some food, because I have nothing more left.

The above message was written while Hughes waited, but the following was already prepared on his arrival:

Dear Masingoni Giuseppe, I cannot tell you, or make you understand how it happened. There is no man that can form an idea at what speed the water was rising from the time I first noticed it. The water was rising so quickly that in a minute the drive was full, and I made up my mind absolutely that God wanted me in the other world; I was preparing to die.

On Wednesday 27 March, Hughes said on returning from the stope:

When I was only about up to my waist in water Varischetti saw me, and came down. He moved about quite nimbly. I could see his face, and he seemed to me to be looking well, and better than you would expect in the circumstances. He has been fed with the right sort of food lately, and that should make a difference. Anyhow, he could move about all right. He took the air-tight tin I brought him, screwed the lid off and seemed to realise everything. He also gave me the letter which I brought up. I shook hands with him, and after staying a few minutes, made my way back. They are talking now of getting him to the surface on Thursday, and I hope it will turn out that way. He has been there a long time. As for myself, the first trip on Friday was the worst. I had the gear on four times that day, and was just about done at the finish. It looks very ugly down at that depth, and you never know what you will meet in the way of mullock, obstacles and holes. It is easier after you have made the trip once.

Although he had now been contacted there was still a considerable risk and danger attached to Varischetti's position, as well as to the work of the divers, Hughes and Hearne, and each day, as the time approached for the divers to descend, a large number of persons congregated about the mouth of the shaft to watch operations and to await news from the miner imprisoned in the rise.

Diver Hughes (second from right) had to don a diving suit of the period, weighted boots, and a glass-fronted helmet to go down into the muddy debris-strewn water of the flooded mine.

The splendid work done by the rescue party to date is the talk of the goldfields. The risk run by the divers in groping their way through the workings has been very great, but the divers are confident. 'Success! Of course we shall succeed!' said Diver Hughes as he put on his 180 pounds of diving dress and groped his way down the ladderway through water to the level below.

Although Varischetti's rescue on Wednesday, or at the latest on Thursday, is now regarded as certain, every possible provision is being made for his comfort in the meantime. On Friday last an assorted lot of delicacies, in the form of beef jelly, liquid, peptonised meat, meal and fruit extracts were conveyed to him, but on Saturday some tasty dishes, composed of minced meat, chocolate sponge, and claret cup, were passed along to him in hermetically-sealed tins by Diver Hughes. On Sunday roast beef, boiled ham, and potatoes were added to the menu, and a liberal supply of cigarettes, candles, and matches was also included in the hamper. To-day the dietary scale was further enriched by condiments, fruit, tea, sugar and milk.

On Tuesday Hughes took down 'an air-tight receptacle' containing the following for Varischetti: 'One and a half fowls, two pounds of ham, one tin macaroni, some bread, two bottles of diluted claret, candles and matches, and tobacco.'

Tuesday 26 March:

It is now believed the rescue can be effected not later than Thursday. The passage down which the divers have descended to the No. 10 level is 350 feet from where Varischetti is situated. Hughes, therefore, has had to plough his way under water through more than a hundred yards of slush and mud, in order to reach Varischetti. There is, however, an opening, now half silted up with mud, some sixty yards nearer the prisoner. It is calculated that a couple of hours' clearing operations would enable a practical passage to be opened at this point, between the No. 10 and No. 9 levels, enabling Varischetti, when the time arrives, to be brought up through it, and thus obviating a heavy tramp for him along the No. 10 level.

On the 27 March Hughes was able to speak with Varischetti:

I had my first conversation with Varischetti in the rise. On the previous visits I could not talk to him. I could only make signs. This afternoon I removed the glass in front of my face and let him hear me speak. I also could hear him. The conversation lasted about six or eight minutes. Yes, I thought he looked fairly well, not exactly well. You wouldn't expect that, but not what you could call ill. He can understand English, and spoke a little. He did not say much, but I asked him questions and he answered. He could not make me out altogether in a diver's dress. He may have been a bit dazed. Think yourself how strange it must have been—a man buried there right below the earth.

This day he brought up another letter, written by Varischetti to his friend Giuseppe Masingoni. It was translated thus at the mine top:

My Dear Friends, I am going to give you my news. First of all, I want you to know God is helping me to keep up my courage, and that He is giving me hope to see again the sunlight and our beautiful country. As to my feeling bad, I do not feel anything, only I think that my strength is diminishing each day. My brothers and dear companions, be quick for me. I also thank you heartily, and I send you my most true and heartfelt greetings. Do me the favour to give me the most sincere compliments and thanks to the whole of the managements and those to whom merit is due; also greetings to all those who ask after me. Dear Joe, I see that they have sent me the shirt and under-clothes, cap, and pair of stockings, but so far I cannot use them, because they are all wet again. I thank you all. I send greetings. Farewell all for the present. I am your friend, Varischetti Modesto. Always with the thought to see you again; the sooner the better. Adieu!

For the rescue, a back-up team fed out a 900-foot line to the divers Hughes and Hearne (in the background).

Crowds waiting silently at the pit head as the entombed miner was brought to the surface.

The water level had been lowered to such a degree that diving suits were not necessary for the rescue. At 3.30 pm the 500 women and men waiting at the mine mouth saw the divers go down, without suits this trip as Hughes would be able to walk to Varischetti. His fellow divers, Hearne, Curtis and Stewart, their assistant, went with him and took bundles of candles and spiders with them (a spider is a spike for sticking into the wall for holding candles). Hughes waded through water up to his chin and reached Varischetti. It was the first time the trapped man had seen his rescuer's face. Slowly he was carried over the floating debris of mine timbers and rocks and helped up the 100-foot ladder to where others waited on the 900-foot level to pull him up.

John Lynch, Mining Surveyor, wrote of the divers:

Theirs is true courage, because they fully realised their dangers. It is those who are acquainted with the nature of underground workings that can best appreciate the risks they are taking in those narrow drives and passes, weighted, as the divers are, with the awkwardly fitting diving dress, and hampered by broken timber and debris, and hauling 900 feet of pipe along behind them.

The forty-four-year-old Hughes immediately became a public hero. He was universally liked and much written about while the slow rescue went on.

On emerging to the surface he was presented with his telegrams of congratulations, one from the Boulder Mines Philharmonic Society, and one from the Melbourne Starch, Soap, and Candle Workers' Union. Hughes is a member of the former society, in which he sings second bass. He seemed particularly pleased that his musical friends had remembered him.

As for Varischetti, the calm and dignity of the man was heroic. In a world of darkness for seventy-two hours and of silence for nine days he remained a stoic.

THE BUSH-LOST BABIES

> Oh, tell her a tale of the fairies bright—
>   That only the Bushmen know—
> Who guide the feet of the lost aright,
> Or carry them up through the starry night,
>   Where the Bush-lost babies go.
>
> *Henry Lawson*

The wilderness was a constant source of fear for the parents of little children. Even in our own time there are vast uncleared and wild areas, some surprisingly near to cities and towns as well as in the sparsely settled country districts. Children, from the beginning of settlement, have 'gone missing', sometimes within a few hundred yards of their own homes, and such instances have been a characteristic feature of Australian life and have a distinctive place in our literature.

Marcus Clarke wrote of '. . . that awesome scrub, silent and impenetrable which swallowed up its victims noiselessly . . . that search in vain, until perhaps some wandering horseman, all by chance, had lighted on a rusty rag or two, a white skull. . .'. He speaks of the 'fathomless gullies, fissured mountain sides, dense thickets and many a weary stretch of sandy slope; solemn wood and deserted scrub, tumbled creeper-entwined rock in swamp-guarded land that lay all unseen'. The awesome variety of that 'strange, dangerous, fascinating, horrible, wonderful place', the great lonely Australian land that engulfed grown men; how much more easily could it swallow up tiny children?

Henry Lawson encapsulated the grief of the parents in his story, 'The Babies in the Bush', with the mother, still distraught, years after her children had been spirited away.

The Babies in the Bush

Henry Lawson
(an excerpt)

She lifted her hands to her head in a startled way, and it was some time before she went on again. There was no need to tell me about the lost children. I could see it all. She and the half-caste rushing towards where the children were seen last, with Old Peter after them. The hurried search in the nearer scrub. The mother calling all the time for Maggie and Wally, and growing wilder as the minutes flew past. Old Peter's ride to the musterers' camp. Horsemen seeming to turn up in no time and from nowhere, as they do in a case like this, and no matter how lonely the district. Bushmen galloping through the scrub in all directions. The hurried search the first day, and the mother mad with anxiety as night came on. Her long, hopeless, wild-eyed watch through the night; starting up at every sound of a horse's hoof, and reading the worst in one glance at the rider's face. The systematic work of the search-parties next day and the days following. How those days do fly past. The women from the next run or selection, and some from the town, driving from ten or twenty miles, perhaps, to stay with and try to comfort the mother. ('Put the horse to the cart, Jim: I must go to that poor woman!') Comforting her with improbable stories of children who had been lost for days, and were none the worse for it when they were found. The mounted policemen out with the black trackers. Search-parties cooeeing to each other about the bush, and lighting signal-fires. The reckless breakneck rides for news of more help. And the boss himself, wild-eyed and haggard, riding about the bush with Andy and one or two others perhaps, and searching hopelessly, days after the rest had given up all hope of finding the children alive. All this passed before me as Mrs Head talked, her voice sounding the while as if she were in another room; and when I roused myself to listen, she was on to the fairies again.

'It was very foolish of me, Mr Ellis. Weeks after—months after, I think—I'd insist on going out on the veranda at dusk and calling for the children. I'd stand there and call "Maggie!" and "Wally!" until Walter took me inside; sometimes he had to force me inside. Poor Walter! But of course I didn't know about the fairies then, Mr Ellis. I was really out of my mind for a time.'

'No wonder you were, Mrs Head,' I said. 'It was a terrible trouble.'

'Yes, and I made it worse. I was so selfish in my trouble. But it's all right now, Walter,' she said, rumpling the boss's hair. 'I'll never be so foolish again.'

'Of course you won't, Maggie.'

'We're very happy now, aren't we, Walter?'

'Of course we are, Maggie.'

'And the children are coming back next year.'

'Next year, Maggie.'

He leaned over the fire and stirred it up.

'And were the bodies never found?'

'Yes.' Then, after a long pause, 'I found them.'

'You did!'

'Yes; in the scrub, and not so very far from home either—and in a fairly clear space. It's a wonder the search-parties missed it; but it often happens that way. Perhaps the little ones wandered a long way and came round in a circle. I found them about two months after they were lost. They had to be found, if only for the boss's sake. You see, in a case like this, and when the bodies aren't found, the parents never quite lose the idea that the little ones are wandering about the bush to-night (it might be years after) and perishing from hunger, thirst, or cold. That mad idea haunts 'em all their lives. It's the same, I believe, with friends drowned at sea. Friends ashore are haunted for a long while with the idea of the white sodden corpse tossed about and drifting round in the water.'

'And you never told Mrs Head about the children being found?'

'Not for a long time. It wouldn't have done any good. She was raging mad for months. He took her to Sydney and then to Melbourne—to the best doctors he could find in Australia. They could do no good, so he sold the station—sacrificed everything, and took her to England.'

It was no good. She was worse in England, and raved to go back to Australia and find the children. The doctors advised him to take her back, and he did.

'And you never tried telling her that the children were found?'

'Yes; the boss did. The little ones were buried. He bought the ground, and room for himself and Maggie when they go. It's all the ground he owns in wide Australia, and once he had thousands of acres. He took her to the grave one day. The doctors were against it but he couldn't rest till he tried it. He took her out, and explained it all to her. She scarcely seemed interested. She read the names on the stone, and said it was a nice stone, and asked questions about how the children were found and brought here. She seemed quite sensible, and very cool about it but when he got her home she was back on the fairy idea again. He tried another day, but it was no use; so then he let it be. I think it's better as it is.'

In Gippsland, Victoria, the great forest held the sad claim to engulfing more children than any other place in Australia.

Lawson's story may well be more fact than fiction. Many babies have been lost in the bush, some never found, and their mother searching for them for the rest of her life. One such mother was Mary Downing.

Sarah

Perhaps the saddest, and yet heroic in a most tragic way, is this story of the Downing children who wandered from their home near Callandoon Station on the McIntyre River (Queensland) in July 1860. William, aged six, was found two days later but Sarah, three and a half, was never traced—for certain that is.

Mary Downing, the mother, searched for the girl for fourteen years, sure that she was alive. The mother, with the little boy safe and well, began to search for the tiny girl in Aboriginal camps in southern Queensland and northern New South Wales, but without success—until 1874. In that year she heard of a 'white' girl who was said to have come from the Callandoon area and had been living with Aborigines near Narrabri (NSW). Mary sent her eldest son, John, to Narrabri and he found the girl working as a servant on a property at Millie. Some of the people who knew her believed her to be a half-caste, others thought she was the child of white parents. Her colouring was such that John Downing believed her to be his long-lost sister; her age, and two scars on her lip identified her for him as Sarah who had been lost fourteen years before.

John reported to his mother and it was decided to bring 'Sarah' home. To do this she must be removed from the tribal people on a charge of 'consorting with Aborigines'. By April 1874, she was placed in the care and custody of the Downing family in Queensland.

The young girl had no memory of her childhood, was domesticated and spoke fluent English, but for all that Mrs Mary Downing finally became convinced that she was not her daughter. She believed the girl to be a half-caste. The poor child was bewildered; she left the Downing's, and the last record is of her dying in hospital of epilepsy.

In 1875 Mrs Mary Downing had at last reconciled herself to the idea that her daughter had indeed died in the bush in 1860, and she wrote a pamphlet titled *The Disappointment* telling of her grief.

More remarkable than the children who have disappeared and been lost for all time in the bush are those who have been rescued—or who have saved themselves. By far the greater number of children who have appeared to have been swallowed from sight by the bush have been found alive. And of these, the vast majority have behaved in a calm, courageous manner.

Jane

Her name stood for courage for a whole generation of bush children and School Readers told the story to further generations. Jane Duff was aged seven when she was sent by her mother on 12 August 1864, to gather wild heath to make brooms. With her went her brothers Frank, aged four and a half, and Isaac, nine.

The Duff family lived in a hut near the home station of Mr Dugald Smith, of Springhill Station in the Wimmera (Victoria). At nine o'clock on the morning of Friday 12 August 1864, the three children left home, and when they did not return the parents knew they must be lost in the bush. The father began to search on horseback and then rallied help from other station hands and they searched for the rest of the day and all that night. On Saturday men from surrounding stations were alerted and the bush was searched by

The Duff children, photographed after their ordeal in August 1864, when they were lost without food for over a week, and had to sleep out in bitter weather.

horseback and on foot. They covered many miles but found no trace of the children. On Sunday thirty men were out all day, and still no sign.

On Monday Mr Smith had a line formed and the country was carefully and systematically searched but nothing was found. On Tuesday, a faint track was seen and followed for twelve miles—this trek took until Thursday night, and the rain washed away the tracks. The search party were 'knocked up', they believed all efforts had been in vain, and further search useless.

Mr Duff, the father, believed the children were alive. He set off to find Aborigines to help but 'they were not located in the immediate neighbourhood' so he travelled a distance. By Friday night he had three Aborigines ready for a first light start and on Saturday morning Duff, Kenna (step-brother to the lost children), a Mr Wilson and the three blacks set off. Mr Wilson had walked while Duff rode off to find the Aborigines and had found the tracks 150 yards from where the track had been washed away on the Thursday night. The blacks immediately recognised the track as being of three children.

They indicated where the three had slept the previous night, pointing out a clump of saplings with a few pieces of broom spread about and a little pillow made from broom. The spot was sheltered and would have protected the children well from the rain and severe cold of the previous night. Further on the blacks pointed to where they said one of the children had stooped to lift the younger one, and further on they found where the child had been set down again 'after being carried a considerable distance; again they pointed out a place where one of the elder children had stooped to carry the little one but this time, they said, the elder child had been unable to rise with the burden, and the three tracks were followed as before.' The day was wearing on and Wilson suggested Duff ride ahead of the tracks as there was only one hour to sundown.

Duff rode to a rise in the ground and saw something white a little distance away—it was Jane in her petticoat, asleep beside her two sleeping brothers, all covered in her dress she had taken off to shield them from the cold and rain. 'It is probable the little ones would never have travelled from this last resting place, unless discovered on this night. The two eldest were almost unable to speak, the eldest woke and said, "Father", the youngest sat up and cried, "Father, why didn't you come before?" Jane seemed utterly powerless and could not speak.'

Later, the children told of their odyssey and a remarkable story it was. The tiny boy's trousers had been taken off because they were badly torn but Jane 'had tied them up in her handkerchief' so they would not be lost. They had taken off their boots and socks when they slept the first night but the wild cats carried their socks away so they slept with their boots on after that. One day, they thought it was the fourth day after leaving home, they came to a hill and thought it was near their own home so they again gathered broom to take home with them. But when darkness came and they knew they were deceived they threw it away again.

There is not the slightest grounds to suppose that the children tasted any food during the time that they were lost, nor that they tasted water more than once. The blacks pointed to a place where the children had travelled in the dark, pointing to where they had stumbled and fallen over logs and brushwood in their way. The little girl had regularly taken off her frock to cover the younger one when he complained of the bitter cold which must have been severely felt because of their famished condition.

The blacks were rewarded for their valuable help without which the poor children would have perished, one squatter gave them £5 and the father gave them £10.

Seldom has brotherly and sisterly love been so beautifully illustrated, seldom has a tale been told that relates so much patient suffering as those little children underwent.

Jane was regarded as a national hero, and in 1865 S. T. Gill painted the scene of their rescue and the work struck an immediate response.

A group of politicians and leading citizens on the train to Geelong donated £19 as a memorial 'to the heroic conduct of little Jane Duff, for her self-denying and self-sacrificing love'. Eventually £150 was subscribed.

So many children were lost in the overwhelming sameness of the Australian bush that it became a constant theme in the literature and art of the country. Nicholas Chevalier, the noted painter, here depicts the lost Duff children, with Jane spreading her dress over her sleeping brothers.

A sequel to the story of the children was told in the *Leader*, 8 April 1905, when Jane, now Mrs J. Turnbull, and aged forty-eight, was 'in straitened circumstances'. The story of her bravery of 1864 was told and a subscription initiated to assist her. 'A children's penny subscription in her favour was taken up and £350 was contributed.' This would be paid to Jane as an annuity of 10s per week. 'An illuminated address was also prepared and was presented to her at the Education Department in the presence of a large gathering of ladies and gentlemen.'

It was not only Jane's stoicism that was being remembered: it was the knowledge that the dark, mysterious Australian bush was always there, seemingly waiting to engulf little ones who wander away from home.

Above: In later life, Jane Duff fell on hard times, and in 1905 a group of Melbourne citizens gathered to make a presentation to help her out of her difficulties.

Top: S. T. Gill, like Chevalier, found inspiration in the story of the lost Duff children.

> Oh! I'll tell you a tale of the babes in the wood
> Of the poor little babes, who were lost in the wood.
> Oh, the night it was dark, and the stars gave no light,
> And they laid down and cried, and they laid down and died.
> And the robins so red, when they found they were dead
> Brought lots of fern leaves and over them spread
> And all the night long they sang them this song:
>   'Poor babes, poor babes, poor babes in the wood.'

Harold Moran, aged ten, lived because he was an observant child of the back blocks. His home was on Mount Nor-west Station in the Tarina district (South Australia) and he was lost on 21 January 1927. He was chased by wild

Right: There's a tantalising sameness about the bush when one is lost in it. Adults have described this—those who escaped—but for a child it has always seemed more of an adventure. Most, after going through the most terrifying experiences, without food and water for days, sleeping on the wet ground at night, have later shown no effects from their ordeal. (The Bush-Lost Babies, p. 146)

Overleaf: Far from the aid of a doctor and the support of their loved ones, the stalwart early settlers buried their dead in the depths of the lonely bush.

camels and escaped and generally showed courage and common sense. He kept to the fences, collected brackish water and carried it to drink as he followed the wire, and kept himself alive by eating saltbush. Three days later he found his way to a neighbour's property where the settler, saddling up to join in the search, saw the boy running towards him.

Another small child, four-year-old Willie Shields, wandered off from his home at Mossgiel in western New South Wales on 31 August 1931. In this rough country there was immediate and real fear for the little boy and at least 100 men from western properties set off searching the rugged area nearby. Five days went by and weary men on horseback were beginning to despair when Willie was sighted: he had wandered forty-five miles from his home. His clothes were torn and tattered and he was weak from exposure and lack of food—there had only been grass for him to eat—but he had reached a waterhole and there he had intended to stay 'until someone came for him'.

Another small boy had earlier survived a similar adventure shortly after the founding of Western Australia. On 11 December 1834, a child aged five, known only as 'the son of the Halls', disappeared into the virgin bush. Two Aborigines, Migo and Mollydobbin, offered their assistance and became the first black trackers used in that colony. They tracked the boy over rocky country for over twenty miles and found him, 'bruised and scratched'. The men had tracked him down in ten hours and their skill, and their delight at finding the boy, 'impressed the settlers' and they were commended in the police report.

Children, as young as two and a half years, have been found by men willing to ride and climb and walk the outlands. Timothy Farmer was only that age when he was found twenty-one hours after he went missing on 5 May 1954 in 'rugged scrubby land' out from Linden (NSW). He had spent the cold night curled up in a cave in the mountains.

Yet another two-and-a-half-year-old, Annette Withers, was lost from Mallara Station (south-west NSW) and never seen again. She disappeared on 11 March 1950, and fifty searchers led by police found no trace of her, nor did Father Higgins, the parish priest, who searched 150 miles of the surrounding country by air on 13 March. Police believed the child had been drowned in the Darling River.

In Western Australia, little Alan West was lost in rough country near Wilga in November 1952. Nearly 3,000 people turned up to search for the six-year-old. Men on horseback, an aeroplane and two Aboriginal trackers combed a wide area until on the fourth day (8 November) the body of the lad was found beside a creek; he had apparently died only a few hours earlier from exhaustion. Near Winton in Queensland in 1953, two aeroplanes and ground parties searched for ten-year-old William Fing. They saw nothing but 'kangaroos, dingoes and wild camels', until five days later when they came on Willie's body in the spinifex: he had died of thirst.

There are many such stories. There were the Kelly boys, Stanley (seven) and Maurice (five) of Brodribb (Victoria) who were lost for three days and nights; 500 men were out searching for them, lighting great beacon fires in the Gippsland bush in an attempt to attract the children. When they were found on 22 July 1933, the bushmen praised their fortitude and level-headedness. 'They had been without food for three days and nights, their feet were severely cut, yet they appeared unconcerned. At night they had made beds of bracken in hollow logs.' The rescue of these boys was known as 'the Three Signals Rescue' because of the three shots fired as an indication that the boys had been found alive.

Jack O'Riley, a black tracker, found the remains of two-year-old Desmond Clark, fifteen miles from Coonabarabran (NSW) seven months after he went missing on Christmas morning, 1940. The almost

impenetrable scrub had been searched thoroughly but O'Riley had always believed the child would make for the mountains south-east of Bugaldie. He doggedly searched until he found the body of the small child—near the top of the mountain.

Many of the children have walked great distances when lost. Joyce Fielding, only twenty-two months old, wandered from Goondabluie Station, near Mungindi (NSW) on 3 February 1936. There was rough sand-ridge country here, riddled with deep rabbit warrens; added to this was the fear that wild pigs would attack the child. An Aboriginal found the baby three days later sleeping beneath a log. She had walked at least fifteen miles. A five-year-old girl from Andamooka Station, sixty miles from Pimba (South Australia) wandered fifteen miles in bare feet when she was lost for thirty-six hours in the bush in April 1939. 'She was not affected by the ordeal,' and like little Joyce Fielding recovered quickly. But not all were so lucky.

Willie (seven) and Thomas Graham (four) and their friend Alfred Burman from Connells Gully (Victoria) were lost on 30 June 1867, in cold, rainy weather. Hundreds of volunteers searched but found no trace of the boys. On 13 September, three months later, the dog of a timber-splitter returned to its owners with a child's boot in its mouth, and the following day the bodies of the little lads were found lying in the hollow of a tree.

The story of the bush-lost babies in the Australian countryside is a tale of courage by the children, and a history of dogged and persistent endurance by the bushmen searching for them.

Above: Black trackers brought in to search for the Duff children on the ninth day, found marks that indicated that one child was carrying the smallest.

Left: Many a bride went with her husband in the old bullock dray, far from the towns and the loved-ones she had known.

Women of the West

George Essex Evans

This page and above right: The pioneer women of outback Queensland contended with white ants, mosquitoes, heat and sometimes total isolation from other women.

Bottom right: With a wood-fired copper or a kerosene tin over an open fire, the outback woman would still manage to dress respectably for the family walk through the bush on Sundays.

The 'West' of the poem's title, incidentally, refers to the western plains country of eastern Australia, although it could apply with equal validity to the Far West of the continent.

They left the vine-wreathed cottage and the mansion on the hill,
The houses in the busy streets, where life is never still,
The pleasures of the city, and the friends they cherished best:
For love they faced the wilderness—the Women of the West.

The roar, and rush, and fever of the city died away,
And the old-time joys and faces—they were gone for many a day;
In their place the lurching coach-wheel, or the creaking bullock chains,
O'er the everlasting sameness of the never-ending plains.

In the slab-built, zinc-roofed homestead of some lately-taken run,
In the tent beside the bankment of a railway just begun,
In the huts on new selections, in the camps of man's unrest,
On the frontiers of the Nation, live the Women of the West.

The red sun robs their beauty, and, in weariness and pain,
The slow years steal the nameless grace that never comes again;
And there are hours men cannot soothe, and words men cannot say—
The nearest woman's face may be a hundred miles away.

The wide Bush holds the secrets of their longings and desires,
When the white stars in reverence light their holy altar-fires,
And silence, like the touch of God, sinks deep into the breast—
Perchance He hears and understands the Women of the West.

For them no trumpet sounds the call, no poet plies his arts—
They only hear the beating of their gallant, loving hearts.
But they have sung with silent lives the song all songs above—
The holiness of sacrifice, the dignity of love.

Well have we held our fathers' creed. No call has passed us by.
We faced and fought the wilderness, we sent our sons to die.
And we have hearts to do and dare, and yet, o'er all the rest,
The hearts that made the Nation were the Women of the West.

Past Carin'
Henry Lawson

Now up and down the sidling brown
   The great black crows are flying',
And down below the spur, I know,
   Another milker's dyin';
The crops have withered from the ground,
   The tank's clay bed is glarin',
But from my heart no tear nor sound,
   For I have got past carin'—
     Past worryin' or carin'—
     Past feelin' aught or carin';
     But from my heart no tear no sound,
     For I have got past carin'.

Through Death and Trouble, turn about,
   Through hopeless desolation,
Through flood and fever, fire and drought,
   And slavery and starvation;
Through childbirth, sickness, hurt, and blight,
   And nervousness an' scarin',
Through bein' left alone at night,
   I've come to be past carin'.
     Past botherin' or carin'.
     Past feeling' and past carin';
     Through city cheats and neighbours' spite,
     I've come to be past carin'.

Our first child took, in days like these,
   A cruel week in dyin',
All day upon her father's knees,
   Or on my poor breast lyin';
The tears we shed—the prayers we said
   Were awful, wild-despairin'!
I've pulled three through and buried two
   Since then—and I'm past carin'.
     I've grown to be past carin',
     Past lookin' up or carin';
     I've pulled three through and buried two
     Since then, and I'm past carin'.

Above: The strangeness of the new order for both black and white produced reactions that ranged from hostility to kindness and trust.

Above left: On the lonely edge of a vast property, the shepherd and his wife and baby camped in a dirt-floored hut. Supplies would be taken to them once a month.

Below left: The kitchen may have been primitive, but in it the bush woman cooked the hearty meals needed to feed both the menfolk and the children who were growing up in the wilderness.

Taking their children and travelling in tip carts, drays and wagonettes, the great women of last century shared with their husbands the dangers and hardships of settlement beyond the ramparts of civilisation as they knew it. They not so much endured the difficulties as triumphed over them.

TOM BARTON AND THE BURDEKIN

The watershed of the Burdekin River covers an area of 50,730 square miles. The largest river in Queensland — 400 miles from source to mouth — it is fed by a score of rivers and their tributaries from north, south, and east, waterways that in the monsoon season become powerful torrents half a mile wide which roll one into the other, joining up until they come together on the way to the mouth of the Burdekin near the coast of north-east Queensland.

The river level here in flood time has been known to rise ten feet in two hours, six feet nine inches in one hour. It is here on the old Inkerman Bridge that some of the greatest sagas in Australia's railway history have been played out.

Tom Casey, at that time Fireman on the Queensland Government Railways tells the story:

Tom Barton should have been given the VC that time we were caught on the Burdekin. It was February 1930. We were working the mail train Townsville to Bowen with 280 passengers on board. We knew the Burdekin was rising. At the general manager's office in Townsville a train's clerk gets rainfall readings and river levels from as far away as Einasleigh up nor'-west to Alpha down south and over to Cardwell and with this information plots on a graph the expected time of arrival of flood waters at the Inkerman Bridge.

We arrived at the Burdekin at 11.45 pm and the ganger met us. He thought the water looked too high to cross although he had just walked over and the river was still clear of the line, but the flood was coming down fast. Once it arrived there would be no train for a fortnight. If our train didn't cross, our 280 sleeping passengers would have to be woken up, got out of their bunks and ferried across the river in the two rowboats kept there for that purpose.

'Did you get your boots wet?' my driver, Tom Barton, asked the ganger.

'No,' said the ganger.

'We'll give it a go.'

The ganger said he'd ride the footplate with us.

We rolled gently down on to the bridge. It was quite clear (and there's few old drivers who haven't gone over the Inkerman with their whole engine hidden in a smother of foam, going through a foot of water in flood time as many a photo album will show). But we had passengers on and were taking no risks. There was no water on the bridge. We were keeping a look-out on both sides and were crossing steadily. Then we stopped. The brakes were on. We were fastened to the bridge. Something had fouled the Neilds Patent [the braking device that automatically halts the whole train; in carriages of that period a chain exposed in each compartment, if pulled, had the same effect: the brakes were applied to the whole train].

Tom Barton and I climbed back over the top of the train — we couldn't go along the side of the train on the track because the carriages overlapped the bridge — we had the mail van next to the engine. We found the trouble: a springy stick had stuck up through the bridge and struck the Neilds Patent.

Right: The twin terrors of the Australian countryside—flood and fire—have constantly thrown up from among the battlers men and women of courage and endurance. (Operation Flood, p. 170)

Below right: When the great watersheds of the outback do run a banker, homesteads are cut off for weeks at a time. Nowadays army ducks come to the rescue of many a stranded family.

The water was not over the transomes when we went on to the bridge. In fifteen minutes' time it was over the rails, in forty-five minutes it had risen five feet six inches. It was decided I should go to Carstairs a mile away for assistance so I set off with the Slush lamp from the engine to walk the bridge. I phoned Control. The nearest engine was forty-two miles away. Too far. The water was rising faster than he could travel to us. There was a train at Gulhabunga. We must have the engine cut off from this. It could run light, at speed, to the river.

While I was away Tom Barton climbed down over the side of the bridge and re-set the Neilds patent—this freed the brakes on the engine and mail van. We now had power. But each of the carriages was still fast. While Tom worked, the water rose higher and the passengers hung out the windows watching him hanging on for life while he worked. When he was finished the water was so high he couldn't get up and one of the passengers pulled a sheet off his bed and threw one end out to Tom and a group of passengers hauled him in through the window.

We moved the train forward a short distance then, dragging the locked carriages an inch at a time. Tom went back and applied more Neilds Patents. All the while the water was rising, debris was smacking the side of the train and foam flying over us. We couldn't get the train out like this but we could make a start. We'd take the mail van and the two leading coaches into Carstairs. We got as many passengers as possible into these carriages. One man said he wanted his luggage. I said it was back in the luggage van and I showed him how to climb along the top of the train but he said he'd be out of his mind if he tried that caper!

We came back and cut off another two coaches and hauled them up to Carstairs with the remainder of the passengers. We could now set to to save our train. There were no lives in danger any more.

We had our boots off and every time we climbed back on the tender bits of coal must have speared our soles. We found them next day but didn't notice it them.

We hooked on to the train and tried to haul it with the brakes still on but could only move it a short distance so we took them two by two. Each time on our return to the bridge the water had risen higher. When we hooked on the last two coaches and the van the engine couldn't pull them up the steep one in thirty-three grade. So Tom held them clear of the water while I ran to Home Hill and piloted the light engine on to the bridge. In the meantime the Inkerman sugar mill had got steam up in one of their engines and it came to assist with the last pull, and we were out.

It was now 5 am and we had gone on the bridge at 11.45 pm.

The water rose ten feet above the bridge and traffic was held up for over a week.

The old bridge had been built in 1913 only ten feet above normal river level, in the belief that the debris brought down by the flood waters would float over the top of the bridge leaving it undamaged. In the second flood of 1946 the water was so high that this principle was proven and the bridge was unscathed, but in the floods of February 1925 when the water was twenty-six feet over the bridge eight spans were wrecked leaving a 240-foot gap in the bridge. In 1940 spans were washed away. It was the only weak link in the 1,043-mile line from Brisbane to Cairns, but what a tyrannous one!

The only years the Burdekin did not flood was during droughts. For the rest, trains were diverted annually out through the western lines, adding up to 600 miles on to a journey.

And there was the loss of life.

On 8 March 1945 at 4 am the goods from Ayr to Home Hill was crossing the bridge. As in the trip Tom Casey described the water was not yet over the bridge and as in that other case the train was stopped on the bridge: debris had stuck up through the sleepers and fouled the Westinghouse braking system between the engine and the tender, causing the train to stop immediately.

Because of the awkward position of the train the driver was not able to effect repairs on the spot, and the water had risen fifteen inches over the top of the line in the fifteen minutes it took to locate the trouble.

The whole tragic story can be told in a few words from this time on to the

end. The fireman clambered over the tender and uncoupled the engine, and the driver moved the locomotive forward. As told in the preamble to the later inquiry, events then moved swiftly, fearfully. 'During the absence of the engine a wall of water ten feet high came down the river. The train was thrown off the bridge into the river. Two of the six passengers lost their lives. The guard and the remaining four passengers saved their lives by grabbing the tails of passing bullocks which they had released from the cattle wagons.'

The witnesses gave evidence concisely, and with no attempt to dramatize the night, but the events piling fast one on the other are drama enough.

The driver, W. C. E. 'Bill' Thompson, told of reaching the bridge at 4 am. Two trains had crossed the bridge just prior to his leaving Ayr and neither crew spoke of the Burdekin. He had had the report gauged in Townsville as to expected time of arrival of flood water at the bridge. This report estimated that the waters would sweep over the bridge at 8 am. He had four hours to spare.

Left: Flood, fire and drought: the fearsome trilogy of Australia.

There was wreckage on the bridge on the upstream side although the track was clear but I hadn't expected this debris. Half way across, the engine was struck a blow, right beneath my feet, and the train came to a stop. There was a rush of air beneath my feet: the Westinghouse. I lit the Slush lamp and said to my mate, 'The trouble is down here'. I tried to climb down but the debris prevented this. I then knelt on the apron plate and leaned well down. I could see nothing for foam. At this time the fireman was standing behind me. Suddenly he called, 'Look ahead'. I looked and saw the water rushing over the rails carrying debris with it. It appeared very savage. He said, 'We're becoming trapped. Get the train out!' I would have to get the engine away to where I could get under it to repair the Westinghouse. The fireman climbed over the tender and hung down and uncoupled the engine while I bled the air from the engine and tender. As we began to move we collected debris and a log with a girth as big as a man's body was caught on the cow-catcher. We got out. At the top of the bank I climbed down. There was foam up along the side of the engine. I proceeded to reconnect the Westinghouse.

The gauge then showed the water to be two feet three inches over the bridge and the time was 4.30—half an hour since we had rolled down to the dry bridge.

Joined by the ganger of the section, the driver and fireman were well aware of the position. They couldn't now take their engine back on the bridge. Their mate, Guard 'Darcy' Ford, and six passengers were trapped. The driver tried to get a rake of empty trucks to roll down the bridge over which the trapped guard and passengers could clamber to safety. But there weren't trucks available. They phoned to the station on the opposite side of the bridge but they had no trucks to roll down either. They ran to awaken the police to get a boat but there was no boat there. The driver's evidence continued:

We then took the engine back to the river. It was getting towards 5 am. The gauge showed five feet of water over the rails. It was dark and a fog had settled. But we could see the guard's light on top of the train. A white light. The fireman then said he thought he saw the light fall and go out.

Jim 'Darcy' Ford, the guard, next gave evidence.

Before I left Ayr I made enquiries from the Station Master, Ayr, and was informed that the river was three feet six inches under the bridge and stationary. I was also informed by Guard Grose, who was spare on 501P, that the water was under the headstocks and that I would get across to Home Hill but had no chance of getting back as the river was rising. Therefore there was a big margin of safety seeing that the level of the water below the headstocks corresponded with the gauge reading. 501P was the last down train across the bridge before we departed and this train came in not very long before we departed. We arrived on the bridge at 4.05 am.

The infamous Inkerman railway bridge across the Burdekin.

We stopped on the bridge, the van being about the middle of the bridge, when I noticed that all pressure had gone from my gauge, and I assumed we had blown a hose bag. There was no water on the bridge when we stopped, but within a few minutes the water rose and I was cut off from going round the back of my van. I was going to protect the train against 998G, as I was on ticket ['a ticket' being the safe working method of forward movement; a following train would give half-hour safety margin to such a ticket before proceeding]. I was unable to do so as there was more than a foot of water over the bridge at that time. I then climbed along the 3 VTS and VR, with the intention of finding the broken hose, but to my amazement I discovered that there was a defect in the engine as I saw the fireman climbing over the back of the tender. I noticed him because I could see his Slush lamp. I watched and saw him return to the engine and the engine proceeded out of the river and up to the south bank. I then returned to my van, got my six passengers out, three or four of them stripped, locked their clothes in the van, and we assisted one another to climb over the top of the train to the lead thinking that the train was on the up grade out of the river, and we could escape from the river from that end, but we were surprised to find the buffers were under water when we got there at the lead of the train and our escape was cut off. I noticed the engine coming back from the top of the bank towards the train and I exhibited a red light to stop him as there was no chance of him getting down into the river. I kept my passengers together as we went along and they were with me at the lead of the train. I called out to the people on the bank that we had no chance of escape unless a boat was sent to help us. At approximately 5.05 am, I noticed the time, the empty N wagon in the lead was then heeling over so we uncoupled it and let it go. The water was then over the top of the N wagon. While we were on top of the leading K two of the passengers, I think they were Linton and Christeson, were down on the wagon of bricks in water. These were two of the passengers who had stripped. One of them uncoupled the H wagon and let it drop into the river, under my instructions. After this was done we then decided to release the stock in the K wagons. In releasing we took the trailing K and released the doors where we could, in some we could not release the bottom doors. The water by this time was over the bottom door, with only the backs of the bullocks showing above the water. We released three trucks and they started to cant over into the river. We were working on the fourth with one door open when we were thrown into the river with the truck. Just previous to this three passengers had jumped into the river with the stock, two of them being those men who were lost and the other a lad named Pemble who was rescued. The two that were lost went into the river with their clothes on. I am not sure about the lad Pemble, but the remainder had stripped. I did not have time to strip, when the wagon toppled over being pulled by the two leading Ks and the others as they fell into the river. Christeson and I were thrown on the upstream side. I fell on my shoulder, hitting the wagon as it heeled over. We went under the bridge, and as I came up on the downstream side I got hold of the tail of a beast and he pulled me out of the churn of the debris and water. I hung on to the beast until about a mile downstream, when it got mixed up with a number of cattle which were milling and ringing around in the water. I left the beast and got on a log. I heard Christeson calling out that if there was anybody with the bullocks to come over to him as he was on a tree. I could not see him but I called out to him and noticed him about twenty yards away downstream floating down on a tree. I swam over and he assisted me to get on to the tree. We continued to float downstream and shortly after picked up another passenger (either Felstead or Linton) and shortly after picked up a fourth man. We continued on downstream until we struck a ti-tree scrub in the centre of the stream, which held our tree broadside on and allowed us to take refuge holding on to the ti-trees. By this time it was daylight, and the river was continually rising, and ultimately had risen to such an extent that the original tree was floated over the top of the ti-tree and threw us into the river again. Each man then swam for a different tree, and held on to the tops of these for about an hour until we were rescued by a boat which took us to the Home Hill side, about five miles downstream from the bridge.

The Swenson brothers were never seen again. The last man to sight them said one of the brothers passed him going downstream clinging to the tail of a bullock. The young boy Pemble who could not swim clung to a bullock's tail and the beast swam to a sandbank that stayed clear of the water and the boy stood there until he was rescued.

For months there were volumes of correspondence with the stock owners about the 124 cows that had been on the train. For months they were being mustered over many miles and when ninety were recovered it was found they all had the same brands although they were owned by different people (they were being delivered from a saleyard at the time of the disaster). The sellers volunteered the information that forty of the beasts had been bang-tailed and would be thus recognizable. They forgot that with the passage of time such identification might have faded.

(In 1957 the tyranny of the old bridge ended. A new, high-level bridge was opened over the Burdekin.)

This Victorian train steamed safely across a railway bridge almost submerged by floodwaters. Tom Barton's train was not so lucky—debris brought the engine to a stop in the midst of the floodwaters.

OPERATION FLOOD

Above: Neighbours and even strangers turned up to bolster the levees. Some stood for days filling sandbags.

Top: Like bushfires and droughts, floods are a recurring disaster in outback life. A helicopter and a motor boat round up cattle at Brunette Downs Station during the Queensland floods of 1974.

Sometimes the city, the big towns and the back o'beyond are all suffering together, but there is an old custom, an unwritten law, that 'upcountry' must be helped. And it has always been easy to learn when the bush is in trouble.

The people of Sydney knew when they opened their *Sydney Morning Herald* on Thursday, 24 February 1955. 'Warning on Trunk Calls' the heading read. It was the Director of Posts and Telegraphs, Mr C. C. Smith, appealing to the public not to attempt booking calls to towns north of Maitland, and west and north-west of Orange.

'The serious floods in these areas have disrupted communications and contact is extremely difficult.' The rain that had delayed the cricket in Sydney between England and Australia had been widespread: 60,000 square miles of New South Wales was covered with water, about sixteen per cent of the whole state. (Had such flooding been in the northern hemisphere it would have covered all England and Wales. It covered an area equivalent to forty per cent of California or a quarter of Texas.)

It became a flood the likes of which the state had not seen before. The water had poured down the rocks and creeks of the Divide and split to go one way to flood the lovely Hunter Valley while the rest spilt over the Namoi and rolled over the flat miles of north-west New South Wales carrying stock, homes and men and women with it. This flood was so gigantic that one-quarter of the police force of the state, 1,000 men, were rushed to the rescue and the Army, Air Force and Navy called in.

On 25 February the whole of the front page of the paper was alerted: 'Thirty-two towns suffer as flood waters rise. The Hunter River is expected to burst its banks today.' Army ducks had left Sydney for Dubbo, Muswellbrook and Maitland. Three people had been washed away and not seen again, only one wheel from the truck they were travelling in had been found.

The people of Maitland were being ordered to evacuate their homes, immediately. It was the seventeenth flood to roll over Maitland since 1949. Army ducks racing to rescue people marooned on rooftops and in barns were having trouble. One 'duck' was stranded on top of a fence post, and another was marooned between two swiftly flowing currents. The Glen Innes Express had been derailed. 'The engine and tender tore free and plunged into a mud hole. The side of the engine was only a foot out of water and men could only reach it by swimming. "It was a queer trip", one passenger said.'

The people of the central west were preparing for record floods. 'Mr O. Male and operators in the Mendooran telephone exchange worked in two feet of water yesterday afternoon but abandoned the post office when the rising water short-circuited the exchange equipment.' Near Trangie nine valuable Bundemar stud rams were drowned in the swiftly rising waters; the manager of the stud, Mr Sutton, had taken the remainder of the champion

It would have taken more than a stop sign to halt the vast waters that swept over the land at twenty miles an hour.

flock into the homestead for safety. The rail line between Warren and Nevertire had been washed away. A widow living alone in a cottage was isolated by the sudden flooding of the Bogan River—until police made a dramatic dash by tractor to rescue her. 'The Bogan, normally a mere trickle or entirely dry, now is a raging torrent flowing swiftly over Tabratong Bridge.' Farmers at Gunnedah were moving stock to higher ground. Gangs of volunteers were out building levees, filling sandbags and bolstering old levees.

By Saturday morning, 26 February, the monstrousness of the rolling yellow waters filled the newspapers.

Sixteen believed drowned in flood. 23,000 homeless. Two men died when they fell onto high tension wires from the rope ladder of a helicopter which was rescuing them from a railway signal box. The helicopter, the only one in the area, crashed—and four men are then believed to have been drowned when the signal box was washed away. At Dubbo 300 people have not been accounted for, 3,000 are homeless and most of the 11,000 people are expected to be without food by tonight.

Police in rescue boats found men marooned on the top of fences, and on the roofs of houses, 'with water up to the eaves'. And the worst of the flood was yet to come.

Monday, 28 February 1958:

DEATH TOLL, LOSSES MOUNT
The peril has now moved to Warren in the west.

But the picture was as muddied as the rolling water. With communication gone it was hard to get the most sketchy picture.

Top: Helicopters were used in the 1955 NSW floods in an attempt to rescue men stranded by the fast-moving floodwaters. Here two men grasp the helicopter grappling line thrown to them and the crew wait to haul them aboard.

Above: The men lost their grip and fell, hitting high tension power lines. One was electrocuted; the other drowned.

There was one story of a woman, due to give birth to her baby, being swept five miles on the flood water. She had been on the roof of her house. 'But then the roof "seemed to disintegrate".' The crew of a duck picked her up. Flood waters were sweeping past cottages and farmhouses to whose slippery roofs clung terrified women and children. There was only a localised and often fragmentary picture of the extent of the flood, the plight of the people and the heroic work of the rescue-aid organisation—and scarcely any reports of the constant individual acts of heroism.

Apart from the 1,000 police in the disaster areas there were 2,000 soldiers with thirty rescue ducks and hundreds of trucks (a conservative estimate put rescues by duck crews at 6,000 people). The RAAF used nearly fifty aircraft—Dakotas, Lincolns, Ansons, Fireflies and Vampires—with 1,000 men to man them. One army helicopter flew across from the Woomera Rocket Range in South Australia. The RAN provided six helicopters (including the one lost attempting the rescue of men from the railway signal box). PMG and Forestry Commission radio operators, over 100 amateurs ('hams'), hundreds of telegraphists, switch girls and technicians worked and stayed awake at their posts trying to maintain any communication with the endangered area. Thousands of women and children joined men—many from dry areas who went in to the danger zone to help—and worked against the rising waters at the levees ... and that is only a part of the people involved. This flood was so gigantic and so dangerous that an operation of almost war-emergency was mounted: Operation Flood.

The Police Rescue Intelligence Centre for NSW is in Sydney and here, eight hours before the great flood rolled over to the west, the Chief, Superintendent J. D. McAuley, assessed the danger and pressed the requisite buttons to alert authorities and call for help. His HQ became the nerve centre, the central directive in the emergency.

Flood medical supplies, blankets and sand bags had to be got to the danger points. As they worked, all were conscious of the figures of the past: since 1949, over 170 people had lost their lives in NSW floods, thousands more had been injured, thousands had lost their homes, stock, crops and the soil itself, which swept down the Darling at a rate of 3,500,000 cubic yards in five years. Floods had beset the state from its beginnings, and in 1806 had forced the colony to the edge of starvation. In June 1852 the Murrumbidgee River swept eighty-nine people to their deaths; year after year the floods rolled out. Only the previous year, 1954, there had been 26 lives lost and damage of £4,000,000.

Now disaster was upon them again. Planes were dropping rubber dinghies to people on the last scraps of land above water in isolated areas. Mae Wests and food dropped down: 300 tons of food, clothes, blankets, shovels, tents and supplies such as 200 'storepedoes' packed with medicine were parachuted down; 115,000 sand bags dropped to men on the levees—and that included 11,000 dropped at midnight to Warren with car headlights aiding the drop, and other night drops to Brewarrina and Nyngan. From planes and helicopters above muddy rips, where one mistake meant death, came the nonchalant radio messages that told of epic achievements:

> Ten rescues, two maternity cases.
> Picked up badly shocked case from scrub.
> Lifted bloke from top of tree. Was he happy!
> Spotted five on roof. Directed duck.

There were hundreds of these—little lonely dramas of death or survival. One helicopter made air history when it became the first to be 'talked down' to the runway by radar using GCA (ground controlled approach) in darkness. It was this machine which crashed the next day at Singleton, when trying to rescue the two men from the railway signal box who fell and died on high tension wires. The duck that rescued the helicopter's two pilots (after following their yellow Mae Wests downstream for five miles) also hit a high tension wire the following day—the second tragedy in twenty-four hours. Two soldiers, Sergeant William McGrath, Signaller Eric Chard, and policeman, Constable Brian Orrock, were killed.

These were pioneering days for helicopters, and heroes were there in plenty:

It is known that they directly saved the lives of at least 110 people at Dubbo, Narrabri and Maitland, twenty-four of those people at Narrabri alone in twenty-four hours. One helicopter hovered twelve inches above the water flowing over the Dubbo Showground and in a series of trips rescued fifteen people. Others went on reconnaissance and located marooned and endangered people and directed ducks and boats to them. They acted as carriers, flying penicillin into Narrabri when the power went off, and they lifted a kerosene refrigerator in (swinging it at the end of a rope) and lowered it to the hospital to enable penicillin to be kept.

Twenty-two lives were lost in this one week, but the number would have been multiplied had it not been for the army ducks that snatched victims off roofs, fence posts and lonely hillocks in the water—victims who on occasion gave their lives trying to save others. Mrs M. Eckert of Maitland was saved by a neighbour: 'I'm alive today because a woman who was drowned told the men who rescued me to take me first because I was a sick woman. That woman was Mrs Frank Dickson. She got into a tree but was washed off later and drowned. I owe my life to Mrs Dickson. I'll never forget her.'

The courage, the uncounted hours of toil, the selfless bravery make the story of this tragedy one that can be told with pride.

Bottom: An Army 'duck' rescues a farmer and his family from the roof of their flood-stricken home. They had taken refuge in the ceiling of the house and were rescued through a hole in the roof.

Below: RAAF personnel evacuate children from a low-lying area during the 1955 NSW floods.

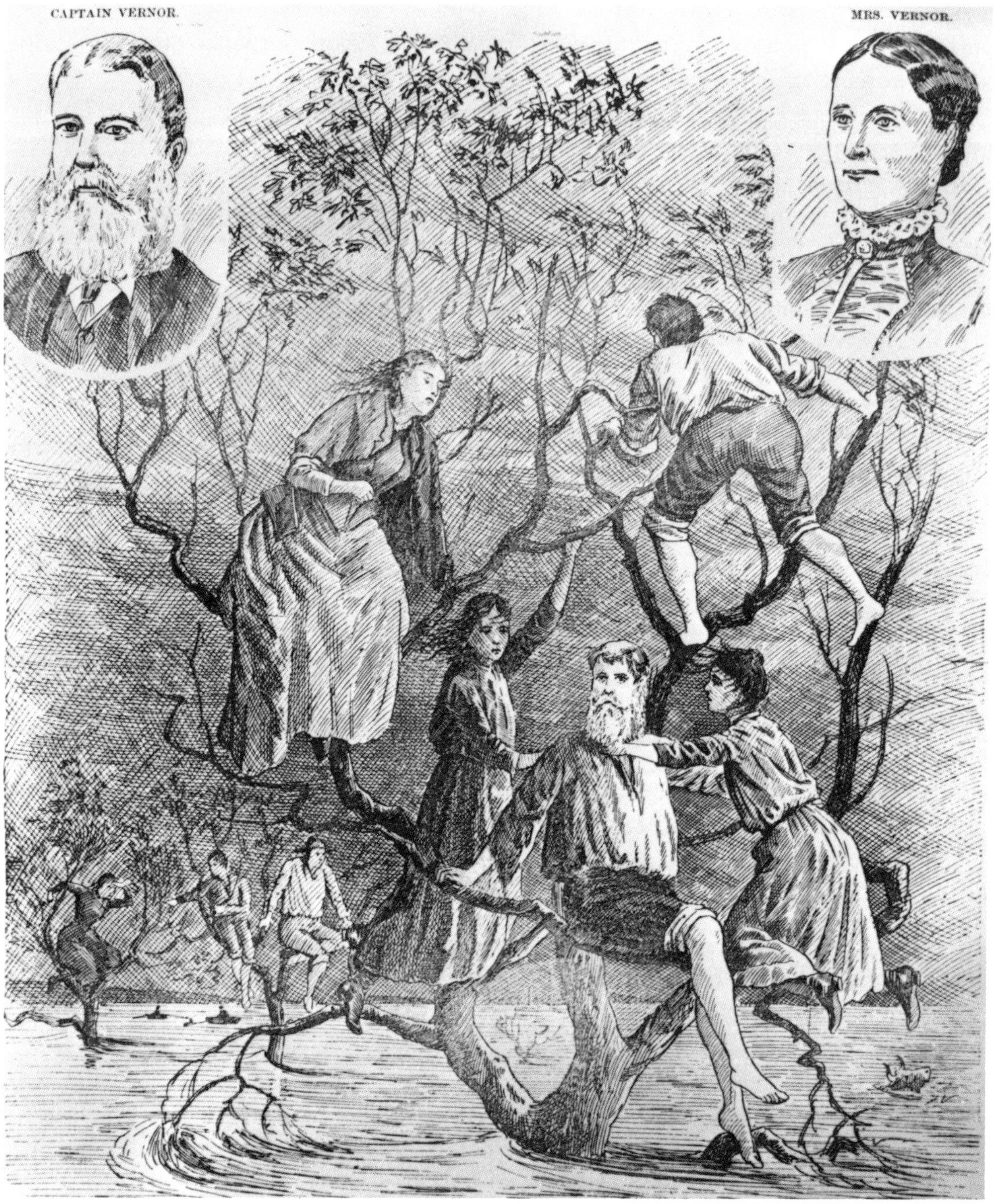
CAPTAIN VERNOR.
MRS. VERNOR.

J.E WARD.

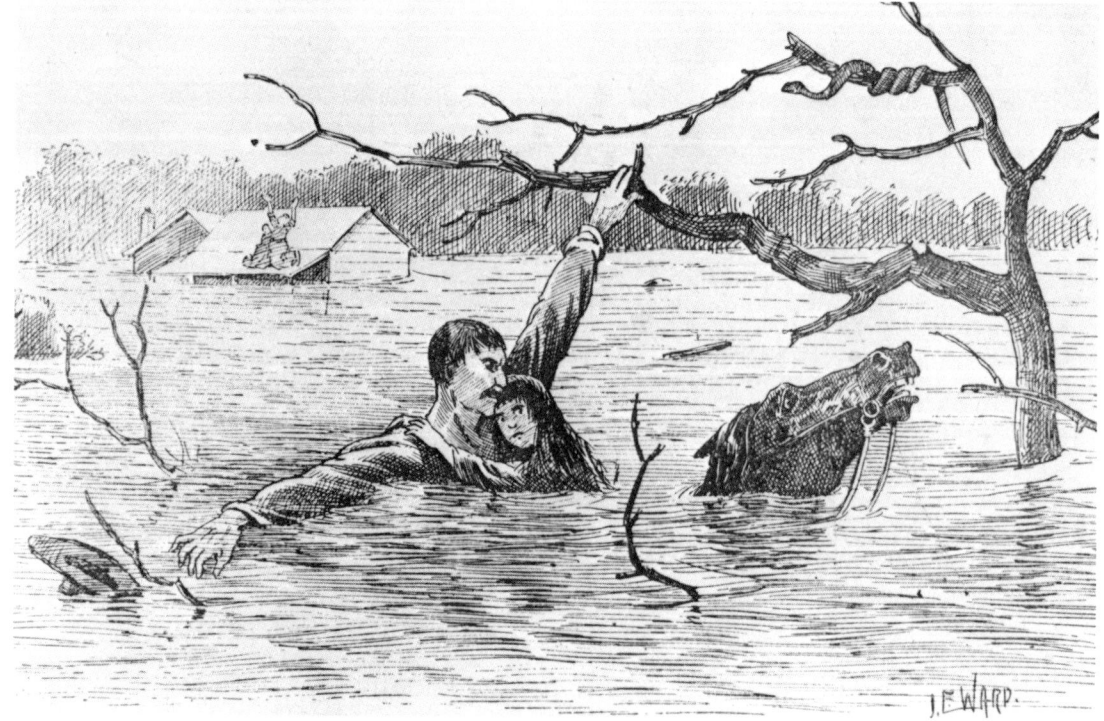

FIRE

Even today, there are pockets in the forested ranges of Gippsland, Victoria, that are most difficult of access, hamlets where, if the phone is cut off in times of disaster, the embattled settlers are as isolated as were the earlier pioneers. Because of the terrain where the settlers 'could not see the sun overhead at midday for the closeness of the trees' bushfires have always been disastrous here. The awe-inspiring sight of a 'crown fire' in an Australian forest cannot be imagined except by those who have experienced it; the sound, the roar, the hissing, the swishing of displaced air as the fire leaps from the top of one tree to the top of another; the atmosphere of complete futility in facing a fire jumping up to half a mile—even one mile—ahead of the main blaze is heart-stopping. The impotence, the knowledge that there is nothing but the hand of God that can save you and yours and the home you have made in the clearing, makes firefighters liken themselves to gnats attacking a rampaging elephant.

For a puny human being to joust with an Australian bush fire takes courage that is valorous beyond understanding. They move in the presence of death and know it.

In 1857 one of the most devastating bushfires ravaged what was then the recently settled Gippsland area. 'Garryowen' (the pen name of E. Finn, author of *The Chronicles of Early Melbourne*) wrote that on 6 February of that year 'there was a Black Thursday in Port Phillip, so called from the country being overwhelmed with fire and smoke, as if an avenging angel had winged its way through the air, scattering fire brands far and wide; its wake lit up with flaming forests, the fire and smoke, as if waging a war with each other, spreading consternation and dismay throughout the length and breadth of the Province.' By noon-time, city dwellers had left the streets where vast gusts of smoke and dust enveloped the town and obscured the light of the sun. 'Every mouth of air was like a flame puffing out of a furnace. Short, hot, blinding spurts of winds were so stunning as to make a wayfarer imagine himself ablaze, as though his hair was burnt and his clothes singed.'

At noon the Fahrenheit reading on the thermometer was 110° in the shade and 129° in the sun. At 4 pm it was 113° in the shade. There was no telegraphic communication and the dirt roads to the hinterland were such that no news escaped, so the townspeople for some days knew nothing, except that disaster was walking over the land.

The stories of pain and desolation came trooping down from the hills. East, west, north and south were ravaged. The fire was thought to have escaped to run widdershins through the land from a camp fire of two bullock drovers at Diamond Creek. The whole countryside was so rapidly 'turned into an ocean of billowy fire' that the few settlers looked on half dead with fear. 'They thought the end of the world had come.' Some sank to their knees believing the crack of doom had sounded. They recorded seeing their first crown fire: 'Not content with rushing along the ground, it ran up the

Left above: Among the disasters that have beset the Australian countryside since time immemorial, that of fire and flood come most swiftly. In southern Queensland at the turn of the century the eight members of the Vernor family embarked in a punt and tried to make fast to a tree until the water subsided. But the force of the water swept them broadside on to the branches of a gumtree, capsizing the punt. The family struggled to safety in three different trees. Captain Vernor constantly cooee-ed and eventually the plight of the family was seen. By 3 pm on the second day they were rescued—cold, hungry and exhausted.

Left below: Floods have ravaged farming lands regularly since the first years of settlement. This picture illustrated the report of a father's heroic rescue of his daughter. 'After a desperate struggle horse and riders reached high ground safely.'

highest trees, and the flames leapt in monkey fashion from tree to tree. A shepherd saved his flock and rushed to the house of his master, Dr Ronald, and helped him save his wife and child by taking refuge on some burnt ground over which the fires had already passed. More than 100 persons were left homeless. Edward Doversdale was with a mate herding cattle when the flames suddenly encircled them. The mate ran to a clearing they had already carved in the timber, Doversdale rolled into a creek where he was later found so maimed that he was taken down to hospital in Melbourne, 'and died after lingering in excruciating agony for a week'.

There was lamentation and misery over the countryside. The dead carcasses of sheep and cattle blocked the creeks and the cart tracks. In Diamond Creek 'a pile' of burnt sheep and bullocks lay, most of them dead, but some bullocks in the last agonies of life. 'When anything approached the poor creatures they emitted a yell enough to freeze the blood in one's veins. About twenty bullocks were blinded and half-roasted, though alive and writhing with torture, and moaning in a heart-rending manner.'

'Another remarkable occurrence was the finding in several places of hundreds of dead opossums and snakes.' Bush creatures had run before the fire and been captured by it. Much of the state had been razed, 'from the almost Terra Ignota of Gippsland, up to the Murray was burnt. In Gippsland they had truly stood and trembled under the expectation of the coming of the Lord: the darkness at noon remained as a scar in the memory of those who survived'.

John, James, Joseph, Mary Anne and William McLelland, aged from one year to eight years, were in their hut in the ranges, with their parents. The mother looked out the door of her cabin and the fiery wind hit her and she came back inside, 'declaring that it was like the Day of Judgement'. She had scarcely spoken when the cabin exploded in flames. The parents tried to save the children, pushing them out through the flames. McLelland grabbed Johnny, the eight-year-old and tried to run to the creek but it was too far for the little burnt boy who 'faintly begged, "Daddy, lay me down" and with the words died from heat and exhaustion.' McLelland, maimed and half dead himself, plunged into the creek and submerged himself up to his neck in water and so stayed alive. The mother and the other four children had forced their way out of the hut but died a few yards away in the bush. The six corpses were placed in a bullock cart, accompanied by the half-dead father, with one arm 'little more than a charred bone'. The roasted corpses were laid out for an inquest, 'unshapen masses of blackened bones and grilled flesh. Stretched on a bed was the invalid husband writhing and groaning piteously.'

There were ten known deaths on this day, but it is believed there may have been others of pioneers, unknown to a living soul, who had tucked themselves away in the bush, clearing a little land of the tall timbers and planting a small crop, milking a cow or two. When the earth cooled the settlers went back to the hills, and Gippslanders can tell stories of being burnt out three times in the great conflagrations that followed Black Thursday.

In the fires of 1926, the whole state was again affected, but the greatest loss in life and forest lands was in Gippsland. In the mountain country Powelltown and Noojee were badly hit. Near Powelltown, Florence Hidges, a fifteen-year-old was severely burnt saving the lives of her three younger sisters. As the fires swept past, Florence crouched over the little girls, taking the brunt of the heat and flames on her own body. Thirty-one deaths were recorded.

But the worst of all their fire disasters was yet to engulf the tiny mountain communities.

Black Friday

Because of disastrous fires in 1926, timber millers in the tall timber country of Gippsland had been required to dig underground dug-outs near each mill. The space was to be commensurate with the number of mill workers and their families. Because of these refuges, many lives were saved in 1939 when the most terrible fire drove along a front of many miles, 200 feet high, and engulfed the small groups of houses that made up the two score of mill towns. Every woman and man who turned to face the holocaust was a hero.

The front page of the Melbourne *Herald* on Friday, 6 January 1939, ran a small item headed 'Rain still eludes the countryside'. The drought was over much of Australia. At Boree, in the Riverina (NSW) water was so short that residents were preparing to travel seventeen miles to Lockhart to where a special train was heading with 6,000 gallons of water. 'There, for the nineteenth day in succession, the temperature has been above 100 degrees with verandah temperatures of 117 degrees. Last night at 11 pm it was 98 degrees with high humidity.' As much space was given to Australia's Prime

No part of Australia has been swept with bushfires so repeatedly as the thickly timbered and lush forests of Gippsland in Victoria.

Above: Since Gippsland was settled late last century, families have tried to shelter in creeks and hollows in the ground from the inferno that has come down regularly upon them. When the rescuers went into the Rubicon Valley in 1939, they stood for a moment, heads bared, around the shelter where three men seeking refuge had died in the fierce heat.

Top: When the immense conflagration of January 1939 ended, the timber-mill workers went into the blackened forests to carry out the dead.

Minister, Joseph Lyons, who had rebuked the visiting H. G. Wells for having called Hitler 'a certifiable lunatic' and Mussolini 'a fanatic renegade'. Both items underestimated the tragedies inexorably moving closer. Melbourne's Saturday *Herald*'s front page had a leader banner 'Northern Heat Due in City'.

'With temperatures nearly up to 100 degrees by 9 am . . . the whole of the state sweltered yesterday.' In small print, 'already two serious fires are burning in the densely timbered mountain ash country near Powelltown and Noojee. All available men, sawmillers and fire fighters have been rushed to danger points.'

Monday's headlines: 'Two Forestry Officers dead in bushfire. One gave life to warn mate of peril. Worst yet to come.' The two firemen, Charles Denby, 55, and John Barling, 31, were working in the Toolangi district of Gippsland. Denby, who was exhausted after a week's fierce fire-fighting, lost his life trying to warn Barling that he was in danger of being burnt to death. He was in charge of a gang of men who were trying to check a swiftly moving fire four miles from Toolangi and three miles from the road. Winds, suddenly rising to gale force, swept the roaring flames to the side of the gang, then towards them. All men dropped their beaters and ran for their lives. When the gang was in safety, Barling went to reconnoitre and make sure in which direction they could move in least danger. Denby saw the wind suddenly change again, carrying the fire at tremendous speed towards Barling. He ran to warn his colleague but had not covered 200 yards before both men were cut off. 'The rest of the gang were unable to do anything and within a minute their two officers were hidden by raging flames.' The following day a search party was able to pick their way through burning timber to find the two charred bodies; they carried them on stretchers out of the forest.

'These men died in self-sacrifice, each trying to save the other and his fellows,' the chairman of the Forests Comission said. 'Each had done splendid work whipping up volunteers and organising gangs to fight the fires which had been burning near Toolangi for several weeks.' Denby had been in charge of the district and Barling had gone there to relieve him because he was absolutely exhausted after days of strenuous fighting. 'Yesterday however, Denby joined the gang again although he was tired, when the fire became serious.' The sad fact was that the fires had been deliberately lit by farmers burning off.

The day's paper did tell of a race for life of women and children from Monnett's Mill, where only four of the seventeen houses in the outpost escaped destruction. The little school 'went up like a match box.' The fire swept along in a face 200 feet high, the flames leaping from the front of the fire from ridge to ridge, at times a jump of a quarter of a mile. As it came racing down on the tiny, isolated settlements, the roar of the flames was punctuated with bursts like explosions as huge trees went crashing down into the gullies. At Monnett's Mill all the women and children were ordered into a sixty-foot dugout. The flames burned right to the edge of the dugout, but the women and children were safe. At Morgan's Mill the men took shelter in holes in the creek, while the flames raced through the tall timber lining the banks above them. 'Izzard's Mill, eight miles from Erica, was practically surrounded by fire late today. No word has been had of six unemployed men camped about six miles north-west of Erica.' Mills, farms and labour camps were surrounded, cut off. 'While fires raged round Mr E. Riley and his housekeeper of Lundi's farm, six miles from Erica, they fought desperately to save the house and buildings, beating out flames as they started from falling embers and carting water from tanks to spray on fires.'

The report on this Monday, 9 January, ended, 'Carrying the few possessions they had saved, families struggled down to Erica where they are being cared for by residents, while some are quartered in the hall.'

And the headlines next day, Tuesday:

Erica showered by blazing embers in fierce northerly gale. Urgent appeals for aid from six milling centres in the Erica district were made soon after midday today. Earlier hopes for rain were abandoned at 3 pm and the tension increased.

All work has been stopped at Powelltown, scene of the 1926 fires in which twenty-nine were burnt to death and every man is out fighting a fire bearing down on the town from the north.

Much of the state was on fire. In the north-east, near Benalla, 800 square miles were blazing and four townships were threatened with destruction. The pending disaster was smelt in the city:

Melbourne awoke today to find the city and suburbs enveloped in a dense, pungent smoke haze, which brought home the appalling extent of the bushfires and gave grim evidence of the terrifying conditions facing settlers in the danger zone. The haze covered the whole of Victoria except for a small corner in the south-west.

In the north-west rain began to fall on Nhill after the worst dust and wind storm in the district since 1897. The heat—over 113 degrees—was the highest recorded there until that time. Clouds of dust and smoke greatly restricted visibility.

Much of Australia was suffering. Ivanhoe (NSW) reported its twenty-seventh day of temperatures over 100 degrees. The settlers of that district had just passed through a day of 122 degrees. Broken Hill passed its record-breaking run of ten centuries with a reading of 113. At 9 am that morning the reading at Bourke was 105 degrees, its twenty-fifth successive day of temperatures exceeding 100 degrees. Both Bourke and White Cliffs had minimum overnight temperatures of 96 degrees. Water was being brought more than 120 miles from Menindee to Ivanhoe to the town water supply.

South Australia sweltered. At 9 am it was 110 degrees, by midday just on 116 degrees.

Grafton (NSW) was reporting a plague of millions of flying foxes, driven from the dry inland. 'They are settling over miles of country near fresh water.' Canberra recorded its highest ever, 106 degrees.

Reports of men, women and children fighting for their lives were coming in from all corners, but the tiny announcement that presaged the real tragedy—and the heroism— read, 'Warragul is enveloped in a heavy bank of smoke from surrounding fires. A fire swept the Tarago Valley and jumped three miles at Neerim. Glen Nayook has been ravaged by fire.' Warragul was at the heart of Gippsland, and here the townsfolk stood staring at the hills, the tall timber country, where the country folk who trooped down to the 'big town' to market on Thursdays were fighting for their lives, running over burning stubble to lie in small ploughed pockets, scattering to the creeks, mothers holding babies to their breasts with only a face above the water as the flames soared overhead, old couples who had pioneered the land—later than most other areas of Australia because of its inaccessibility—stumbling down the tracks they cut so long ago, using the wits a lifetime in timber land had taught them. Isabella Adam-Smith, aged ninety-five, who had gone to the hills when she wed at the age of sixteen, now stood at her gate in Warragul peering through the smoke. 'Jessie's up there,' she told her granddaughters. Her daughter, our Aunt Jessie. 'She's been burnt out twice. Rebuilt twice.' She said no more for a while, just stared and stared. Then, 'They've ploughed a patch for potatoes. Down the back paddock. They might be able to reach that.' And because she stood at her gate in Kent Street, Warragul, staring through the gloom towards the hills, we stood staring too.

And then the Wednesday's paper: 'Eighteen Burned to Death in Last

The rails were left swinging over what had been the highest wooden trestle bridge in Australia.

Night's Inferno'. This was in the Rubicon Valley. 'As the searchers move up the blackened gully, steep-sided as a gorge, they are finding more bodies of trapped men as they advance.'

The weather forecast indicates that the whole of the eastern half of Victoria is still in the gravest peril. Lighting a mile ahead of itself, the barrier of flame set twenty square miles of country alight in half an hour. While mill workers' families dashed for dug-outs, their wooden homes disappeared in flames. Men, with smouldering hats covering their faces, were found where they had fallen, exhausted.

Mill on mill was being wiped out and the lovely gullies of fern and bell bird were seeing a continuing tragedy that had not yet reached its apogee. The Kerslake family—a mill hand, his wife and six-year-old daughter—were found, their bodies charred. They had used their bushcraft, made for a rough bush track that took them to the boulevard-wide Acheron Way—where the tall trees above them burned with such intense heat that they fell exhausted, dehydrated, dead.

Walhalla, the town at the pit of the great canyon of mountains that defied the building of a road until recently, was ringed by flames. 'Hospital patients evacuated. All available men in town fighting to keep the blaze back.' The fire, at 1 pm, was half a mile from the little town, with a following wind. 'Walhalla people, who remained fairly calm through a night of extreme anxiety, are beginning to pack belongings and prepare to leave home at a moment's notice.' Noojee and Powelltown were fighting for survival.

Thursday, 12 January, reported 'Grave news in the bushfire peril came from the weather bureau today when it forecast at least two days of scorching northerly winds. 1,150 Forest Commission officers and 5,000 volunteers are struggling to consolidate temporary gains.' Stories were seeping out of 'the hardihood of bush workers, their wives and families.' One of the most graphic was that of the night of terror spent by eleven workers and their families in the dug-out at Cecil and Brown's mill, in timber country. Mrs Foster Potter, lying in bed in a refuge, her voice reduced to a whisper from the effects of smoke, told of the survival in the dug-out:

When the fire came roaring down on Tuesday afternoon we rushed to the dug-out. Mrs Mason, the last woman to get there, was black with smoke and covered with glowing embers. We could hear the fire roaring over the top of the dug-out and several times the timbers holding up the roof caught fire. As the hours dragged on the dug-out filled with smoke. There were four other women, five children and eleven men. My baby Ronald is only eight weeks old, another baby there was eight months old. We held the children down to the ground so they could get as much air as possible. We kept Ronald's face plastered with plenty of mud from the bottom of the tunnel to keep it from blistering.

A cockatoo and a parrot which we had taken in with us died in twenty minutes. As the smoke became denser we could not see one another, but called out in the darkness to find out how the others were standing it. Gradually the replies became fainter. I could hear Mr Bert Murphy reciting the Lord's Prayer, and then his voice drifted off.

Several of the men who were at the back of the tunnel were out to it when at last the fire began to ease and we could drag them out. None of us could have lasted another half hour. We tried to sleep in the bush that night, and then came on down the train track. My husband was blinded by smoke, but I led him as he carried baby, and it took us four hours to walk seven miles.

With the raging temperatures and fierce winds, Friday the thirteenth was tragic. The afternoon Melbourne *Herald* told the story:

Six hundred take refuge in rivers as wind drives blaze on. Hundreds flee from sweeping bushfire peril. Towns ringed by fire in record heat. Township of Erica reported to be doomed.

Fanned by scorching northerly gales on the hottest day Victoria has ever experienced—two separate fires have converged on Erica, and the fate of the people in the mill area is not known. Grave fears are held for the safety of twenty-five Greek lime-workers near Erica.

At Noojee, practically the entire population has been evacuated by goods train to Warragul. The town of Noojee is surrounded by fire.

Fires covering three-quarters of Victoria, leaping into new life under the drive of searing northerlies, are burning through forest, countryside and townships from the Murray to the sea.

The difficulty of communication makes it impossible to gauge the full toll of Victoria's worst day of bush fires.

The Rubicon fire had razed 1,200 square miles. Down in the capital, Melbourne sweltered while breaking an all-time heat record—114 degrees—two degrees higher than that of Tuesday, and this torrid heat gave them a small taste of what the bush dwellers were suffering: on that day, by 9 am, most country thermometers were already registering 100 degrees. City men answered the frantic appeals for volunteers.

> Saturday:
>
> 42 More Burned to Death in Fires.
> Many Others Missing.
> Victims Now Total 63.

Many others were feared to have perished, dozens being reported missing.

Noojee was wiped out late yesterday, and the victims there were burnt to death in two timber mills. Armed with axes, a party has left Warragul to recover the bodies. Noojee's disastrous fire leapt on the town with devastating suddenness, giving the fighters no chance to save buildings of which, today, only two stand. Past Noojee, the small settlements of Icy Creek and Fumina are destroyed.

Icy Creek and Vesper are cut off, and in both places there are a number of people not yet accounted for. There were grave fears for five men, a woman and a child, at Brown's Mill, seven miles from Noojee, but today they reached Warragul, after a terrifying night, spent by three of them in a dam, and by the other three in a dug-out. Benambra is in a desperate position and Cassilir has been wiped out. Fire swept Omeo last night, wiped out a hotel, the hospital, twenty houses and at least eleven shops. Yarra Glen lost thirty-two houses. St Bernard's Hospice and Hotham Heights Chalet have been wiped out. The proprietor of St Bernard's Hospice, Mr. B. Bush, his wife, daughter and mother-in-law escaped down the deep gorge into the Dargo River where they are still marooned. A rescue party has left Harrietville. Every available man is out fighting at Healesville.

East Gippsland is ablaze and help is wanted everywhere. Omeo and Swifts Creek are still without sufficient man-power to fight.

Whole families were dead: 'Mr and Mrs Fawley, Noojee, and their children, John, Ben and Agnes; Therese, 13, Mary, 12, Vera, 10 and Paul, 8, the Robinson children from Kawarren.' 'An Italian, name unknown, his wife and three children, at Noojee.' In a welcome touch of levity we learn of 'an eighty-year-old man found sitting in the Goulburn River smoking his pipe'.

In the continuous stories of heroism coming out of the desolate black areas time and again were heard the names of post mistresses, women who ran the tiny telegraph offices in isolated hamlets—the switchboard and office often being in their 'front' room.

Mrs Sanderson, post-mistress at Noojee who was in the 1926 catastrophe, rang the post master at Warragul soon after 2 pm and told him that the building was on fire.

She put all valuables in the safe, tied the key to her wrist, and made for the river where she remained for three hours. When she returned only the safe was standing In the river were fifty people, the oldest ninety-two, and the youngest a baby of three months. Mr Devine, who ran the mail service between Noojee and Warragul, put two invalids, Messrs Padsett Senr and Junr in his new £1,000 car, backed it out of his garage, and drove it straight into the river with its passengers.

The plucky young post mistress at Erica, Miss Hazel Binns, was the last to leave when the women were evacuated as the fire roared down on the town. She had worked without cease, standing by her switchboard since the outbreak and left only when she could give the final report, 'All women and children left town. Valuables secured. Closing office.'

Of another postal family it was reported:

Mr Hugh McKinnon, who stayed at the Loch Valley Post Office answering telephone calls while the building was in flames, died in the Warragul hospital yesterday. With his wife who is Post Mistress, he escaped in a car but a falling tree blocked their way. They had to take refuge in a creek for five hours and Mr McKinnon contracted pneumonia. He was employed by the Forestry Department.

Calls were still going out for fire fighters and 1,200 were transported out in eight hours. They marched in to death and desolation. It was all far worse than the 1926 holocaust when, at Noojee and Powelltown thirty-two lives were lost, a million acres of forest burnt, 1,992 people claimed for relief. The aftermath of that fire saved lives in the blaze now covering the same area. Dug-outs had been built, underground shelters, roads and tracks for escape routes and communication had been built and underground pipes for water had replaced the open wood flues used in 1926.

By Monday, 14 January, the end was in sight. 'Rain brings respite.' The grim reckoning was seventy-one dead, 1,500 homeless refugees, and damage of at least £1,605,000. Twenty victims were in a critical condition in hospital suffering severe burns. Sixty-nine mills had been destroyed and millions of acres of fine forest of incalculable value were destroyed. The Red Bull had ravaged the land.

'The Noojee'

Noojee has been destroyed by fire and rebuilt again—three times. Driver Roy McDuff tells of the last great rescue bid to the mountain town:

It was 23 March 1954. I was on Warragul yard. Stan Stewart, a Melbourne driver, rushed up and said he had to relieve us as we had to go to Noojee. We told him someone was pulling his leg as we didn't run Noojee's at 8 pm on Saturday nights. Jim Steer my fireman went off to find out who was the joker but in minutes flat he was back shouting we had to go to Noojee as the biggest trestle bridge was on fire.

We collected six water tanks and engine number N460 and took off for the bridge. After a wild ride we arrived to find the points of the bridge burning, dry leaves and rubbish had been blown into the points and now it was all ablaze. We took the train to the middle of the bridge and the repairers, the gang, worked their way past the engine hanging on by their finger tips with nothing between them and a 100-foot drop. They were magnificent. There was no railing on the bridge, but they crept on the end of their toes past us. We had 10,000 gallons of water. The gang—us too for that matter—believe to this day we could have saved the bridge if we'd been allowed to use that water. Instead, they tried to bring hose pipes over the hill.

Well, as the time went on I wasn't any too happy with us there on the loco in the middle of the burning bridge. I was squinting back along the track in the darkness lit up orange by the fire and as soon as I saw the guard's lamp move sideways I backed

Right: When the Red Bull is loose, fires rage over the land and have been known to jump a half-mile ahead, through the treetops.

Below: The railway line to Noojee, though small, is one of Australia's most famous, owing to its wooden trestle bridges that straddle the deep valleys through the mountains.

Far left top: The sight of an Australian bushfire is one of the most awesome sights in the world, as the towering flames consume the atmosphere and feed their own progress through the forest. (Fire, p. 175)

Far left below: As night falls, the flames can be seen leaping from crown to crown of the eucalypts. The sound of the explosions of the gases can be heard miles away. (Fire, p. 175)

Left: Courageous navvies crept alongside his engine attempting to fight the fire raging beneath them.

off the bridge without waiting for any further invitation. We sat there and watched the bridge crash down into the valley; it was a terrible thing, then we backed up to Nayook.

Australia Phoenix

Higher and higher his red arms grasp,
Tighter is drawn their burning clasp;
From tree to tree the red flame goes,
Searing the grass that beneath them grows;
Yet wider those blazing arms stretch forth
Eastward and Westward, to South and North,
Till all the land, like a funeral pyre,
Is a blazing furnace of liquid fire.
Wide flung are the blood red gates of hell,
And dancing devils the red tide swell.

Like a far-off whisper of coming ill
The hearts of God's creatures with terror fill,
The lyre bird starts in the shadows dim,
And the jackass' laugh has an echo grim,
The parrots fly with frightened shriek,
And the wallaby leaps o'er the reddening creek:
The snake and possum go side by side,
Blind fear, to their flight, the only guide.
The fire-fiend comes, with his red arms spread,
Gathers them living, and leaves them dead.

The whole wide land, that has glowed with life,
Laughed with brightness, and throbbed with strife,
Lies charred and blackened, as formless things
To which no semblance of life now clings;
Nor bird, nor beast, nor thing that crawls,
No sound on the deathly silence falls,
And Autumn's fingers are powerless quite
To soften destruction's awful blight,
And Winter comes with its cold and rain,
But brings no help in its bitter train.

Above: When Roy McDuff took his engine out in 1954, high winds swept the bushfire through this bridge.

In lighter, open country, the firefighters are able to defend homesteads using gum boughs or beaters to thrash out the flames at ground level.

Mary Gilmore, when a child, saw one woman's stand against the elements, and set it down for posterity:

How quickly the mind had to act and meet great issues when settlement was sparse! Perhaps it acts as quickly now, but the occasions are different.

There was a woman whose husband either had a selection on the run where my father was building, or else was working for sheep as payment for his labour. This was often done when barter was easier than to obtain currency.

Where a station-owner did not have a good enough banking account, he paid (or part paid) his boundary-riders and stockmen sometimes in stock, and sometimes in land. Whether the man in the present case was a selector or merely a paid man I have forgotten. But, stores being needed for his family, he harnessed the dray to go to town to sell his skins (such as he had) and buy supplies. Men shopped then, not women; and while he would be away the wife and children would be alone.

He was only gone a day of the four that he must be absent, when, as night came, the wife noticed the glare of a bushfire on the horizon behind the house. No help was near; no one who could be called in or given a message was likely to pass, as the hut was just a tiny nest in the midst of miles and miles of grass and forest. Did she know the danger? She did. Did she fall into panic? She did not. A bushwoman, she looked at the glare (it was a thirty mile wide front of fire as it happened), and estimating distance judged that it would be quite safe to go to bed.

When morning came this woman, who knew distance and direction as men knew them, made no hurry for all that the fire was enormous. She dressed the children and got the breakfast as usual. When this was over she took the dog, and the little ones, and went out and rounded up the small handful of sheep that was to be the foundation of their future flock.

She brought the sheep to the hut after having watered them. There she let them rest for half an hour. Then the dog and the children behind them, and herself on the outside, she drove them round and round, round and round the place. They were so pitifully few, and the grass so strong and thick, that their little hooves trampled but little more than a couple of furrows wide at a time. An hour passed, and she rested them. At noon she let them feed and go to water. Then she began again. All day she kept them resting and going, resting and going, till dark. Six miles a day is sheep travelling at stock rate. Because they were so few, and her one narrow chance depended on them and their endurance, she did not dare to overdrive them. If they began persistently to lie down she would not be able to get them up after a while; and if, at the end their hooves foundered from being too long on them, and later sweated off them, the flock would be ruined and her husband's toil lost.

When dark came she could smell the fire on the isolated puffs of wind. These puffs came from the sudden ballooning of masses of air from the cooler spaces of the forest as opposed to the warmer open areas of grass. Rising to a high altitude as they heated, there they cooled somewhat and fell again, forming air puffs that reached earth miles ahead of the flaming front itself. The sheep were done. The dog had such swollen feet that he whimpered as he licked them, the children were so dead tired they fell and slept where they had stood. Her own boots were worn through and she went barefoot in the last rounds to ease the tension of the muscles on the ground.

She could do no more than the next thing, thought was dead, but automatically her body did what her mind had earlier set it to do; so she looked at the narrow ring of trodden grass, put the sheep and the children inside the hut, and lit her return fire. Whether it would go forward to meet the on-coming monster now roaring on the wind of its own heat, or whether when started it would flare back across the narrow trodden 'break', she did not know. But all that could be done she had done. She nursed the trickle of flame as it began to run, then as it widened forward she went inside, laid the children on the bed, gave the panting dog a drink, and after making a billy of tea, sat by the fire and sewed.

I have forgotten what their name was. But I remember the released wonder, joy and relief in my father's voice, when, though the horses still danced in places from the heat of the earth, the ground was sufficiently cooled for us to get across to see the family, and we found it safe. Through the burning logs and still falling timber we went, my sharp eyes the first to see that the hut was still standing. It stood with a little ring of trodden earth about it in a sea of ashes, some of the tussocks still smoking and glowing as an air moved, or a tussock-puff rose. The dog's feet had to be dressed and wrapped in oiled rags, and two of the sheep were broken and would never do any good again. But that was all. Even the one solitary hen they owned was saved. We camped by the dried-up waterhole and stayed till the husband came home.

'Because,' said my father, 'after what she has been through she might suddenly break up and go mad . . .' The physical strain, alone, had stretched endurance to the limit.

The husband came home nearly frantic. The slow travelling with the dray, after he had heard there was a fire, made every mile seem ten. On the last afternoon he took the horse out of the shafts, packed him with tea, sugar, flour, and a tin of jam, and sometimes riding, sometimes walking, did the last miles home. When he heard the barking of a dog (ours) he said he could hardly breathe for the leap of his heart, and in spite of himself burst into tears.

The fierce heat of an Australian bushfire can be imagined only by those who have experienced it. By the time a fire reaches the stage shown in the photograph, it is all too late: the flames have reached the tops of the mountain giants and will now roar from treetop to treetop—the infamous Gippsland crown fire.

The Bush Fire

Henry Lawson

On the runs to the west of the Dingo Scrub there was drought, and ruin, and death,
And the sandstorm came from the dread north-east with the blast of a furnace-breath;
Till at last one day, at the fierce sunrise, a boundary-rider woke,
And saw in the place of the distant haze a curtain of light-blue smoke.

There is saddling-up by the cocky's hut, and out in the station yard,
And away to the north, north-east, north-west, the bushmen are riding hard.
The pickets are out, and many a scout, and many a mulga wire,
While Bill and Jim, their faces grim, are riding to meet the fire.

It roars for days in the trackless scrub, and across, where the ground seems clear,
With a crackle and rush, like the hissing of snakes, the fire draws near and near;
Till at last, exhausted by sleeplessness, and the terrible toil and heat,
The squatter is crying, "My God! The wool!" and the farmer, "My God! The wheat!"

But there comes a drunkard (who reels as he rides) with news from the roadside pub:–
"Pat Murphy—the cocky—cut off by the fire!—way back in the Dingo Scrub!
Let the wheat and the woolshed go to —" Well, they do as each great heart bids;
They are riding a race for the Dingo Scrub—for Pat and his wife and kids.

And who are leading the race with Death? An ill-matched three, you'll allow;
Flash Jim, the Breaker, and Boozing Bill (who is riding steadily now),
And Constable Dunn, of the Mounted Police, on the grey between the two
(He wants Flash Jim, but that job can wait till they get the Murphys through).

As they strike the track through the blazing scrub, the trooper is heard to shout:
"We'll take them on to the Two-mile Tank, if we cannot bring them out!"
A half-mile more, and the rest rein back, retreating, half-choked, half-blind;
And the three are gone from the sight of men, and the bush fire roars behind.

The Bushmen wiped the smoke-made tears, and like Bushmen laughed and swore
"Poor Bill will be wanting his drink tonight as never he did before."
"And Dunn was the best in the whole damned force!" says a client of Dunn's, with pride;
"I reckon he'll serve his summons on Jim—when they get to the other side."

It is daylight again, and the fire is past, and the black scrub silent and grim
Except for the blaze in an old dead tree, or the crash of a falling limb;
And the Bushmen are riding across the waste, with hearts and with eyes that fill,
To look at the bodies of Constable Dunn, Flash Jim, and Boozing Bill.

They are found in the mud of the Two-Mile Tank, where a fiend might scarce survive,
But the Bushmen gather from words they hear that the bodies are much alive.
There is Swearing Pat, with his grey beard singed, and language of lurid hue,
And his tough old wife, and his half-baked kids, and the three who dragged them through.

Old Pat is deploring his burnt-out home, and his wife the climate warm;
And Jim the loss of his favourite horse and Dunn of his uniform;
And Boozing Bill, with a raging thirst, is cursing the Dingo Scrub,
But all he'll ask is the loan of a flask and a lift to the nearest pub.

Flash Jim the Breaker is lying low—blue-paper is after Jim,
But Dunn, the trooper, is riding his rounds with a blind eye out for him;
And Boozing Bill is fighting D.Ts. in the township of Sudden Jerk—
When they're wanted again in the Dingo Scrub, they'll be there to do the work.

THE VALLEY OF THE SHADOW OF DEATH

Some men make a heroic stand by enduring, and the Chinese community in Australia has a fine but tragic record here, one that ennobles an otherwise shameful period of our history.

When all else failed, many early Chinese migrants 'hung on', displaying that spirit in adversity that Australian pioneers normally so admired. Many died for no other reason than because of their industriousness on the gold fields.

Mary Gilmore wrote about Lambing Flat, New South Wales, where, on 30 June 1861, 2,000 rioting white miners armed with bludgeons and pickhandles drove the Chinese from that field.

Earlier, in 1854, there were only 2,341 Chinese in Victoria; by 1857 there were 30,000 (and the following year, 1858–59, 42,000). At Buckland in north-east Victoria in 1857, the Chinese diggers suffered the most violent, brutal day in goldfields' history. There were over 1,000 'white' men involved, and of these, Police Trooper J. S. Duffy was the only man whose behaviour brought honour to the Europeans. For the rest, it is as well that the Valley of Death mining camps have all gone, and with them the memory of that dishonourable day.

The Buckland diggings were more isolated in 1857 than are the nickel deposits north of Kalgoorlie today. It was as easy—or as hard—to reach the gullies of gold from New South Wales as from Victoria, and once there, escape was difficult. The small police camp consisting of Troopers Duffy and Gilroy was hard pressed to control the turbulent miners; this new field was sixty miles from the nearest police depot at Beechworth.

The Chinese were unpopular because of their long hours of work, their clannishness, and their ability to exist on little food. Resentment was burning in the Europeans because these hard-working men had, in the previous twelve months, shipped £500,000 in gold to China from Melbourne. In 1854 the white miners at Bendigo had driven the Chinese off the fields, and the date of this hostile injustice, 4 July, is an indication of some of the root of the trouble. The Americans who flocked to Australian fields in the 1850s were mainly men who had failed, or been late, for the 1849 rushes in America: they were 'forty-niners', tough men who had spent their lives living tough in frontier lands of at least two continents. They chose their own Independence Day to drive the hard-working Chinese off their legitimate claims. These men already knew of Judge Lynch's law in California, and were ready and willing to deal out the rough justice of goldfields the world over. The Melbourne newspapers were openly critical of the American gold seekers. Thirteen ships had arrived in Port Phillip in 1852 with American diggers and more in 1852. On 5 March 1853, the *Argus* claimed these men were 'unprincipled idlers who live only for scenes of anarchy and excitement'. The following year their behaviour on the

The Aborigines resented the coming of the Chinese as much as they had the coming of the white men, but the Chinese had the added burden of also being resented by the whites.

Above: Hardworking and persistent, the Chinese were successful miners, which drew the enmity of other men who followed the rush.

Top: The artist S. T. Gill named this painting 'Might versus Right'.

Bendigo diggings caused the government to fear that the Chinese might be slaughtered; they rushed police and troops to the area.

In 1855, in an attempt to prevent further trouble, Chinese immigrants were restricted to one per each ten tons of the weight of the ship transporting them, and a poll tax of £10 was imposed on each. Victoria was the only state with such restrictions and it was impossible to police the smuggling across the state borders. In the first six months of 1857, 14,486 Chinese landed at Guichen Bay in South Australia and crossed the border. At the time of the Buckland violence it is thought that 30,000 Chinese were on the various Victorian goldfields. This 'swarming' angered the already anti-Chinese miners and they were constantly troubling the hard-working Asians.

When the rush to the Ovens Valley began, 5,000 men had rushed to Beechworth, Buckland Gorge, Reids Creek and the valley of the tributaries of the Ovens River, and among these were the Chinese looking for a less potentially dangerous field on which to search for gold, seeking to escape the harassment elsewhere. They had all scarcely staked their claims when disaster struck: a malady known as Colonial Fever, which killed many white diggers. Others left Upper Buckland, the 'Valley of the Shadow of Death', as they named it, but the Chinese stayed on, impervious to the disease.

These men struck gold, and by 1857 this drew miners back to the valley, but of the 4,000 diggers, the Chinese outnumbered whites by three to one. They had built solid huts of wattle and daub or logs, had Chinese stores well stocked, and several camps of some hundreds of tents. The whites congregated four miles away near Tanwell's Hotel and the police camp, on the edge of the richer claims already taken up by the Chinese. The white camp seems to have spent more time and energy seething with bitterness, on 'indignation meetings' and plots to rid the valley of the Chinese than it did on hard work — the only way to win gold in those harsh regions. Those who had been at Bendigo knew that resistance to the Chinese must become widespread if it was to succeed. Hoping that other groups in the Ovens goldfields would also riot, they again planned their attacks for 4 July.

Trooper Duffy was apprehensive. He sensed the powder keg was about to go up but he could get no news of the date or the method. On 3 July he sent his only man, Trooper Gilroy, to ride sixty miles to Beechworth, the nearest police station, with an urgent request for help. Thus, when the riot began Duffy was alone. Again it was American Independence Day. Duffy patrolled the whites' tent town and at 11 am he watched about 100 whites in front of Tanwell's Hotel. Instead of being at their claims they were there, armed with shovels, picks, mattocks and some with stout pieces of wood, being whipped to a frenzy by one John Thomas Bell, who was urging the driving of the Chinese from the goldfields of the Ovens Valley.

The men began to move, and then to run. Duffy ordered them to stand, but the tide swept past him, shouting, running up along the bank of the Buckland River, going to Louden's Flat where the Chinese were working. They were not too inflamed when they reached the first camp; they permitted the Chinese to take some personal belongings and escape unharmed. Only then did they burn down the two stores and forty-six tents of the camp; but as the rioters progressed from camp to camp more and more men joined them, the excitement became hysteria, and fear and hatred boiled over into open violence. They poured onto Louden's Flat where the

Above: Thousands of Chinese miners flocked to the gold rushes of the 1850s and 1860s.

Top: Ideal hard-working citizens, with a model family life, the Chinese were nevertheless the butt of ridicule, criticism and physical attack.

191

Above: Arriving in the country with little money and few possessions, the Chinese cheerfully set off to walk long distances to reach the new fields.

Top: Their swags on a wagon, Chinese miners trekked over the countryside, following the rumour of gold finds.

Right: Self-sufficient and sensible, the men from China carried large water bags and little weight to help them across the harsh territory.

Far right above: Among the hundreds of men heading inland from the coast to the goldrushes were files of Chinese, who carried their worldly goods on bamboo poles on their shoulders. (The Valley of the Shadow of Death, p. 189)

Far right bottom: The lusty, crude, hard-working days of the goldrushes bred tough, rumbustious characters. (The Valley of the Shadow of Death, p. 189)

Chinese had built a dam in the gorge; there they saw 600 Chinese miners busily working and decided to blast the dam, flood the big camp and trap the miners. The Chinese ran to their tents hoping to save their gold; the whites followed them using their picks and mattocks as cudgels, battering the Chinese as they ran. The miners fell to the ground and were kicked with the hob-nailed mining boots of the whites; as they died, they saw the fires begin as the looters ran amok in their big camp.

There are many stories told of those short terrible hours. Perhaps all of them are true, perhaps none of them, but we do know that whatever happened was violent and vicious. Some say there was a white woman in the camp married to a Chinese miner, and this woman resisted the white men and was battered insensible. The Chinese made little resistance. They watched their stores burnt down, their camps looted and gold stolen. But they rushed to defend the Joss House, and many claim that several Chinese died in the flames trying to protect their place of worship. The whole of Louden's Flat was razed.

Worse was to come. In groups, the frightened men hid in the bush. July in Buckland is bitter cold, mountain winter weather, and the men were all in light clothing, some only in loin cloths as they were dressed for the manually hard work of digging when they were attacked. They knew their only means of escape was across the river, but the white men patrolled there, with lighted fire-sticks for torches and picks for weapons, barring their way.

Trooper Duffy had now returned from his camp with all the firearms he could muster—his and Trooper Gilroy's. The rioters had split into two, one half barricading the exit up the gorge while the others drove the Chinese down into the cold, icy river. Somehow Duffy got through the rioters, doubtless smashing his way through their kicks and blows, and he made a stand between them and their victims. Perhaps he 'read the Riot Act' or as near to it as he could muster in such a time, perhaps he just shouted the truth of their infamy to the rioters, but when the police from Beechworth arrived Duffy was in control of what was left of the Valley of Death.

This outbreak has been poorly documented. We do know that no official figure has been recorded of the number of Chinese dead, but Robert O'Hara Burke laid charges against nine white men. (Burke, later to lose his life in an attempt to cross Australia, had been sent from Melbourne with fifty mounted troopers when word of the riot reached the town.) But anti-Chinese feeling was so high that the court refused to convict five of the nine men, and four were convicted on minor charges only.

Four years later, over the border to the north, Lambing Flat erupted, and the sorry business was repeated, but no attacks against the industrious Chinese were as cruel as at Buckland and nowhere did one man stand between so many enraged miners and their victims as did Trooper Duffy on American Independence Day, 1857.

THE DISASTER

On Tasmania's west coast there used to be a greater complex of railway lines, both state and private company owned, than on any area of similar size elsewhere in Australia. This complex had grown because the mountainous terrain defied road builders. No road entered the area until 1936.

In 1912 there was no transport to the area except by rail. (The sea coast is one of the most daunting in Australia.) On 12 October of that year there began a tragedy that involved all the workmen of the small mining town of Queenstown. The railwaymen of the west coast, in an attempt to save their mates, the miners, made one of the greatest dashes in the history of railways in Australia, and until the small gauge trains carried the coffins on flat tops to the graveyard they were involved in the drama.

Gus White, a guard for the Mt Lyell Mining and Railway Company, was on duty when the fire began:

A shunter came past on his way to the station. 'Did you hear the mine is on fire?'
I said, 'Don't be silly.'
'It's on fire all right and there's ninety-six blokes trapped down below.'
It seemed then as though everyone in Queenstown suddenly knew. Groups of people came out in the street, all looking over at the mountain. The mine was behind the other side of the one-in-two rail haulage. There was a small stream of smoke rising. Then a woman ran by. She must just have heard.
I thought it wouldn't be serious. A fire wouldn't spread below in the damp timbers, and the chaps could get up in a stope or a drive and sit it out. This was the general feeling, even at the mine. The fire had broken out in the pump house on the 700-foot level. There were 165 men down the mine at the time but 69 escaped soon after, leaving 96 entombed. These would come out, it was said, when the fire died down.

The *Zeehan and Dundas Herald* carried its usual ads that day and Queenstown people read them, not too perturbed about the fire. Bill Burge, a fettler from Crotty on the North Lyell line, was issuing, 'A CHALLENGE to E. M. Bone, Zeehan, to CHOP for a subscribed purse of One hundred pounds (£100), nothing less, any size log', and the MARRIED LADIES' CONCERT which would end with a MIRTH PROVOKING ONE ACT COMEDY was advertised for Monday next, October 14.

But by Monday there was no mistaking the danger. Deadly carbon monoxide fumes were filling the mine. No man had come out of the mine since midday Saturday.

There are dread and sickening fears. It is possible that 100 men may lose their lives through being suffocated. Queenstown is at a standstill. People are gathered in knots in the streets, the greatest crowd being near the railway station, because it is here that any rescued men ... would be finally landed.

The Married Ladies advertised: 'Owing to news of the Disaster' their concert would be cancelled.

Left: S. T. Gill, the painter of many an early bush scene, was never more sympathetic to the spirit of the brave early settlers than he was in this painting of 'A Bush Funeral'. In this way, the painting has the nobility of a great funeral march, with the slow plodding steps of the bullocks pulling the coffin matching those of the mourner beside them.

Overleaf: The speed of a crown fire through an Australian eucalypt forest is unknown in any other country. Since settlement, men, women and children have regularly had to fight to save their homes from 'the red bull'. (Fire, p. 175)

At the mine, 'there are about 100 women at the tunnel mouth, most of whom remained all night'. Large coal fires were kept burning all night. It was alternately snowing and raining. At midnight, across the snowfields from Mt Lyell mine, the lamps of 200 miners flickered as the men coming off the 11 pm shift came for news of their mates.

A suggestion had been made that smoke helmets or a diving suit should be procured and some smart work was performed by means of rail motors.

The suit had come from Burnie and this was the first of the many anxious train journeys down this line in the next few days. But the suit was found to be useless in the conditions below.

Chickens were lowered down the shaft and each lot lowered were hauled up dead. The fumes and smoke defeated every attempt made to get the men. Then the cage jammed in the shaft. All efforts to free it failed. The miners were now cut off from above and the fire still burned below.

At midnight on Sunday a loco drawing one carriage steamed out of Hobart carrying Superintendent Trousselot of the Hobart Fire Brigade who was bringing diving equipment. As the coastal paper wrote of the train:

The most casual observer could not fail to notice that the train was a stranger in these parts, being made up of an engine and one wagon. The rolling stock belongs to the main line and had made the run right through [from Hobart].

Superintendent Trousselot, who, by the way, stands six feet nine and three-quarter inches, had with him his smoke helmet and 1,000 feet of three-quarter inch piping.

At Zeehan where the engine that would take him over the rack rail was coupled up, Trousselot went up town and bought another 120 feet, 'busying himself making the necessary connections as he continued his journey to Strahan'.

Meanwhile, a rail motor had left Launceston for the 250-mile dash to the mining town with oxygen, and across Bass Strait the tiny *Lady Loch* was steaming to Burnie with helmets and oxygen masks. The now famous 'Race across the straits' had begun.

Bad weather in Bass Strait buffeted the *Lady Loch* and her foredeck opened up. She limped on, her speed gone, herself in danger. At 4 pm on the Monday the SS *Loongana* of the Union Steamship Company, the 'greyhound of the fleet', left Melbourne with firemen and rescue gear from the mines of Bendigo and Ballarat and, in a record-breaking run that has not yet been beaten, crossed the Straits to Burnie in thirteen hours forty-five minutes. She arrived at 5.45 in the morning, shortly after the *Lady Loch*, and by 6.04 the equipment she was carrying was on board the Emu Bay Company train and the engine was steaming south with the men from Melbourne and those from Hobart—rescue workers and 'relatives of miners who had been franked through on the motor'.

The journey of eighty-eight miles to Zeehan, the 'Silver City', was cut out in four hours twenty-six minutes, the railway station being reached at 10.30 am. The Mt Lyell engine Abt No. 3, which had never been past Strahan, now came up the Government line to Zeehan to meet the Emu Bay and in eight minutes men and equipment were transferred and the little rack engine was off. Peter Jack was driving, Paddy Hartnett firing, Peter Connelly guard. On the twenty-nine and a half mile run to Strahan the little Dubs engine gave all she had. Fettlers patrolled the line keeping it wide open for the speeding train as it went round horse-shoe bends and over severe grades. In one hour twelve minutes the engine stopped at Strahan. They'd cut thirty-five minutes off the run. Again there was a transfer. The rescue gear was rushed to the company's rail motor; the passengers would be taken on the special train to be dragged over the rack section. Barney Westerman was driving now and he could drive! This day the trip that normally took two hours five minutes took one hour. The whole run was done in five hours ahead of the normal time from Burnie.

By now, Tuesday, the paper had something to report. A cord had been left hanging down the shaft and, at a time when the men making the rescue bid were out of the mine, the cord twanged and tattooed out the message, 'Men to come to surface'. In the darkness below, scarcely able to hold on with smoke exhaustion, a miner's hand had touched the cord and rung out what must have been the most thrilling yet poignant message to come from a mine. At the surface the joy was tempered because there was no way to bring the men up. They rang again, 'Haul up'. The cord was pulled up. There was a note tied to the end. 'Forty men alive at stope 40 the 1000-foot level'.

But by Wednesday the paper would record that at the 600- and 700-foot levels: 'Four rescued; fifteen dead; twenty-seven unaccounted for'. On Thursday, the men from stope 40 were reported to be out. The rescuers, still unable to use the shaft, had broken a way through, a tortuous, dangerous path but possible. Two thousand watchers waited silently at the mine mouth.

At intervals chickens were lowered in cages, but always they were brought up dead from the fumes.

After being entombed for 102 hours, miner L. Lennell is helped out of Mt Lyell mine.

As the hours and days wore on nerves began to snap under the strain of waiting, and 100 men rushed the shaft, thinking they were being kept in the dark by the company. But the poisonous air was seeping right up through the shaft. They realised that nothing more could be done, and dispersed.

Men down below never went near the shaft fewer than three in number, so that if one collapsed the other two could drag him back to safety. Some escaped, only to go back to look for mates and be trapped again.

Others, like Joe McCarthy, died thinking of their loved ones. 'I will say good-bye,' McCarthy wrote on a page from a rent book. 'Good-bye to all. Your loving husband, J. McCarthy.' He pinned the note in the timber with a miner's 'spider' and died.

There was no easy way to bring the men still alive to the surface. Devious, laborious routes had to be taken by the men, who had already spent 100 hours in darkness, mostly without food and water. Trembling near the mouth of the shaft, mothers and sweethearts, sisters and fathers watched for the first flicker of the candle coming up from the darkness.

When the first eleven men were raised, the crowd was told not to cheer, because of the exhaustion and weakness of the rescued. Some of the miners walked out unaided; others were carried. 'Good lad, Jack,' some one murmured quietly as Jack Lees came out. 'There's Jimmy Elliott,' another whispered.

Gus White, a guard, saw some of the men come out:

It was about two o'clock they started to come out. One by one, long periods in between leading some out. Some walked all right, others staggered and had to be held up. Some were carried. We didn't cheer or anything. We kept quiet. They'd had enough. The only sound was the loco running on the line above. When the whisper went around, 'They're on their way out,' the loco stopped for a moment and just when I saw the first candle flicker in the tunnel the loco set off again—the sound the men were used to when they came up to the top. About forty of them, half the trapped men, came out. They'd been down below for 109 hours.

These were the men from stope 40. There were still the others. No word had been heard of them for four days. More rescue equipment was on its way. Trains shuttled down from Burnie. One train on the Wednesday did the

Three of the heroes of the disaster — Fireman J. Caldwell, Penny Peasnell, and Fireman A. Moore. Moore and Peasnell were the first rescuers to reach the men entombed at the 100-foot level.

Burnie to Zeehan run in four hours four minutes, twenty-two minutes less than the famous Tuesday dash. At Zeehan the Mt Lyell motor left at 9.42 am and reached Queenstown at 11.35 — sixty mountain miles in less than two hours.

All the state's railway systems were thrown open for use, cleared when rescue trains were on their way. The whole state watched the trains rush by. Sometimes the transfer of equipment took only four minutes and the relay loco streaked off on the next line. Prime Minister Fisher, himself an old miner, interrupted a speech in parliament to announce, 'The train with the rescue gear has arrived at Queenstown' — and it is said the politicians cheered.

The busiest line was a little one-in-two haulage over the mountain to the mine. It ran almost non-stop, taking rescuers and equipment up, and bringing down stretcher cases. Women collapsed there at the tunnel mouth from fear and exhaustion. By Wednesday some had been waiting for four days and nights.

Thursday's paper recorded the rescue but recorded the worst, the final word for the waiting women. 'Twenty-five bodies discovered, seventeen missing — no hope for their safety.'

On Friday, horse wagons carrying forty-two coffins rumbled through the little mining town of Linda Valley and up to the mines. Made quickly, overnight, the coffins had handles at both ends for easy movement in the confined space of the mine, but they could not yet be used. The fire was not yet out and thirty million gallons of water flooded the mine and then had to be pumped out before the bodies could be recovered. It was 5 December before the first of the dead miners was brought up.

It was 8 June 1913, before the last of them was buried. It was said that the fumes had killed bacteria in the mine and so delayed decomposition. Some of the miners found their dead mates much as they had last seen them.

The coffins were brought out of the mine and lowered down the one-in-two haulage on bolsters. The fettlers spread tarpaulins over them. At the foot

The haulage way used to take men to work, later bore the coffins of those who died in one of the worst mine disasters in Australia.

they carried them over to the two-foot gauge and put them in the railway wagons.

'It wasn't too good. Most of us blokes knew one another in Queenstown.' The first five were buried on Tuesday, 10 December. The papers told of the coffins being slowly lowered down the haulage on wagons, with the miners sitting on open trucks behind.

At the Queenstown railway station from which the cortege proper was to move there was an immense crowd waiting even though night was approaching and heavy rain falling. Slowly, very slowly, the engine and wagons approached with its strange freight and passed by the carriages which were standing at the station. The points were then thrown over and the engine quietly backed in to take its place in front of the mourning carriages.

There were five in number (all the line possessed) and nearly all had their full complement, mostly men. Large numbers of women remained in crowds around the station and when at last the engine slowly moved off for the cemetery more than one handkerchief was raised.

Away to the front of the engine hearse the members of the F.M.E.A. and the Friendly Societies marched in one long column and formed a procession that reached into the far distance. In the wagon with the coffins, and immediately behind the engine, stood the funeral directors.

Driver Harry Westerman helped to prepare the funeral train. 'We tied black and white ribbons on it and scrubbed it clean and laid ferns down on the floor. For the big funeral in March, the Company itself prepared a train. This was the biggest number of bodies yet buried together in Tasmania. That day we buried eighteen men.'

Today the Emu Bay Railway is the only line left of those four little railways that worked so hard to bring relief for the forty-two miners who lie side by side in the graveyard beside the old railway track.

In Queenstown, where no grass or trees grew for many years because of the sulphur fumes from the mines, they still talk of those long, grim days of 'the wait'.

THE IRON MAN

On Tasmania's west coast they call Ernie Coleman 'the Iron Man', a title he has been given even in his hometown Zeehan, a mining area where tough men are taken for granted.

He earned his title as a distance runner over and around the bush tracks of his rugged home district. He might have become an Olympic champion had he left his birthplace and really put his mind to serious training and competitive athletics.

Ernie Coleman began his marathon running when he became an assayer in the Queenstown mines, 26 miles from Zeehan where he had always lived with his mother, to whom he was devoted. To see her at week-ends, he decided to run home every Friday night.

When Ernie started his long runs there was only an ill-defined bush track from Queenstown to Zeehan, so he chose to run up the rough clearing that followed the electricity lines. He made the Queenstown–Zeehan run 360 times, his best time being two hours fifty-seven minutes. He always beat the train that ran between the two towns, but he doesn't claim any particular credit for that as the West Coast trains are noted for their rambling gait.

In between his week-end home jaunts Coleman tried himself out on other marathon runs. His longest was in 1937 between Strahan and Queenstown and back again, a distance of fifty-two miles which he covered in eight hours forty-five minutes.

To assess that performance it was necessary to consider its hazards. Between the two places there isn't a town, not even a house, because the country is too rough, the ravines too deep, and the mountains too steep for anyone to want to live anywhere along the route.

There was an unsealed road, a nightmare of curves and hairpin bends. When Coleman did that run the road had just opened and was so full of holes and dangerous ruts, he had to keep to the barely cleared sides of the road. Included in his time was fifteen minutes he spent 'chasing' a creek for a drink and thirty minutes he took for a meal in Strahan.

Tasmanians predicted great things for Ernie Coleman, but he decided to give up marathon running. While reading through his cuttings on athletics he came across an announcement that the only man in the world, a Swiss, who has had more distance runs than Coleman, died after making his four hundredth run. Coleman had made 370. 'It's time to stop,' he said.

Iron men are the rule rather than the exception on Tasmania's west coast. Isolated from the rest of the state until a road was put through in the mid 1930s (it was only in the mid Sixties that a road was put through from the west coast to the north part of the island) the area was a breeding ground for tough men. In 1960, at Tullah (the town that had no road at all until 1961), two men walked in from Cradle Mountain, fifty miles away. Ted Foster and Murray Wilcox had taken a bushman's holiday. Both bushmen, they used

Ernie Coleman, the Iron Man.

their Christmas holiday to walk across a stretch of country that had not been traversed since 1902. They reached Tullah on New Year's Eve, four and a half days after they had left Cradle Mountain on a walk they had thought would take only two days. The country they crossed is marked on maps as 'inaccessible bush.' It is covered with the dreaded horizontal scrub and thorny bauera. 'The bauera was the worst,' Ted told me. 'We tried every way to get past it. Sometimes we rolled over it, crawled under it, other times in desperation clawed through it. Once we covered only one chain in one hour. The distance as the crow flies is 50 miles but the way we went is 150 miles.'

The conventional way into Tullah was by the two-foot gauge railway line. This was an enchanting journey to survive until this day and age. The little engine, 'Wee Georgie Wood' chuffed and puffed along and pulled up at a creek to enable the engine driver to haul water for the boiler. The small town existed for the silver-lead mine, and because of its strange isolation had remained quaintly in the Steele Rudd period of folklore. 'Shut the door,' a miner called during the showing of a newsreel of the Melbourne Cup in the old Mechanics Institute. The projectionist was having trouble focusing his lens and the movies were flicking off the screen on to the walls. 'Shut the door or the horses will get out!' On the wall were posters of bygone shows including *East Lynne*, whose players had trod the boards here in 1912.

DORFER'S HONEYMOON

The story is still told of an extraordinary and loveable man who went to a wild mountain for his honeymoon, taking with him not only his bride, but also a tent, 800 sheets of blotting paper, a flute and a violin. The new century had just begun, and though the man and his bride are dead, his memory still lingers in one of the wildest, most beautiful, but at that time inaccessible, parts of Australia, and the story of that honeymoon, once told with laughter, is now told gently and with deep affection.

The man was Gustav Weindorfer, born in Austria in 1874, who came to Australia 'after an unfortunate love affair' as they used to say in those days. The mountain that he 'discovered' on his honeymoon, Cradle Mountain, is now one of the chief attractions of the Lake St Clair National Park in Tasmania. It is sixty miles inland from Devonport in the north-west of Tasmania. With today's roads and transport ending at either end of this national park, bushwalkers can gain some idea of how rugged and isolated a place it was in Weindorfer's day. Even now, rangers have been isolated for weeks at a time by bad weather. The park has an area of 525 square miles and measures roughly forty miles by fifteen. For seventy years it has attracted men and women from many parts of the world who find joy walking amongst the mountains — and camping near Waldheim, the 'forest home' of Weindorfer. Waldheim is all things, a shelter, a tradition, an outpost, the stamping ground of a gregarious ghost and a shrine for pilgrims.

Gustav Weindorfer built Waldheim in 1912 of King Billy pine, a timber peculiar to Tasmania. He had, until that year, camped nearby. This chalet still stands, it has never been despoiled by paint, and nestling as it does in a forest of myrtle and native pines with little Loose-Leaf Creek trickling by its front door, it is as natural as a large grey rock on the landscape. Life here today still revolves round the memory of 'Dorfer' as he is affectionately remembered, the man who lifted his eyes up unto the hills.

When I first went to Waldheim in the 1940s there were still old men and women who knew Dorfer walking in the mountains. I asked Major Ronald Smith, 'What was Dorfer like?' and he spread his hands wide to encompass the mountains, the hills and the forests. 'Look around you.' You look and you listen. 'Dorfer came here when he was a young man and he stayed until he died. We buried him here. He never left except to go out and coax visitors to come and see the forests and hills and regenerate their spirit. He had the courage to find strength in beauty.'

Dorfer first saw Cradle Mountain when he was on his honeymoon. From the altar he set off with his bride into the hills to honeymoon in a tent with the blotting paper to press the wild flowers and mosses they would gather.

'They played the violin and flute at night in the hills and when the flat-lands people heard of this they thought he was cracked!'

Dorfer.

Weindorfer sent the hundreds of specimens he collected back to a museum in his native Austria.

Dorfer died in 1932 but his presence is strong in the area. Fables and folk lore have grown up around him but the facts are enough for him to be placed in the pantheon of our heroes of the wild woods.

Born in Austria in 1874 of a well-educated mother and a father who was Bezerkshauptmann (Governor) of the province of Carinthia, he finished his schooling on a grant from the Emperor Franz Josef and after a love affair that ended badly he emigrated to Australia.

When he arrived in Australia he had the impressive title of Chancellor of the Austro-Hungarian Consulate in Melbourne. But he threw that job up overnight and trekked off to the unexplored mountains of the wild west of Tasmania, and stuck it out there through all privations—and there were plenty.

With little money he battled along, 4,000 feet above sea level, imprisoned during the long bitter winters because he couldn't afford to go elsewhere. His beloved wife, Kate, died, and also his faithful dog Flock.

'Since my dog is dead,' he wrote to a friend, 'it is not only awful to be quite alone at times but the tiger cats are getting so bold I am afraid they are going to eat me.'

'He stayed,' say his friends, 'because of the hills.'

Weindorfer learned how to fell trees and split palings so he could build Waldheim. Alone he built the large chalet of eight rooms and it is as solid today as when he built it—the shingles he split still roof it.

It is a mark of the respect his memory is held in that though thousands of tourists have passed through it none of it has been harmed by vandals. Even the bark is still intact on the huge pine logs he upended in the living-room to support the steep snow-shedding ceiling and roof.

There he entertained many tourists, cooking and cleaning for them and acting as guide in the hills and friend in the camp. The story is told of the day he stayed home to bath and care for a baby so its botanist mother could scout out specimens on the hillsides.

The legend sprang up that he was a hermit—'The Hermit of Cradle Mountain', the newspapers called him. But Weindorfer's life had not one ingredient of the hermit. He was never alone by choice and he had many friends all over Australia. After his death these friends banded together and bought Waldheim and Weindorfer's land there to stop timber interests getting it.

On 6 May 1932, a shepherd found him dead in the valley beside his motor bike. There was a rough road to within a mile of his forest home, but for the last stretch (and bush miles are long ones) he had to walk and manhandle his cycle up and over the swampy yet rock-strewn slope. Years before he had written, 'I cannot smoke now. My heart it is beating so.' And now the extra exertion had stopped its beating.

His body was taken by horse and cart to Sheffield forty miles away for the post-mortem. But it was not buried there. Weindorfer's friends hurried from many parts of Tasmania and received permission to carry it back to Cradle Mountain Valley. By horse and dray they went at first. Then, when a sudden storm broke, eight men carried it the rest of the way to Waldheim.

Next day in the rain and mud they dug a grave for him facing Cradle Mountain. 'Such men as he are rare,' a speaker said as they filled in the peaty soil.

Ronald Smith, a stalwart mountaineer who had entered Cradle Mountain Valley with Weindorfer on one of his first trips in 1903, and Lionel Connell, a great Tasmanian bushman, helped to bury him. Fred Smithies, who had walked many of the peaks with him, cut a rough cross from King Billy pine and carved DORFER into it for the tombstone.

And there, had he been an ordinary man, his story would have ended. But he wasn't ordinary and since his death Waldheim and his forests and nearby hills and mountain tarns have drawn more visitors than ever. And many come quite frankly to 'see where Dorfer built his forest home'.

Ronald Smith, when he was on Gallipoli in 1915, received a letter from his wife at Sheffield—near the foothills of Cradle Mountain. 'When Dorfer heard that we were at war with Germany he came down from the mountain to see if they wanted to intern him as an enemy alien.' He had been afraid that in the snow and ice of September in the wilderness, it would be uncharitable to have men risk their lives to attempt to come up after him. In later years Smith told me, 'I thought, when I received that letter, ah, there's a truly heroic man, a man of vast compassion and heroic strength'.

'Waldheim'—the house that Dorfer built—is now the mecca of bushwalkers from all over Australia.

MOTHER BUNTINE

The new land threw up heroines of a different cast from the old world. In the British Isles, a female heroine was lauded if she once rode out to the rocks where a ship was wrecked and helped save the passengers. In Australia she would have had to find many wrecks for her peers to elevate her to the rank of heroine: she must continue to defy the elements, opposition, or the terrain without thought or wish for recognition. And, ideally, she must rear her family, care for her husband, and act circumspectly at the same time if she was to be elected by that strong body, her peers.

Agnes Davidson was such a woman. Born in Glasgow in 1822, she came to Australia in 1840 and worked as a dairymaid for a farmer named King. At the end of 1840 she was earning £12 10s per half year, plus her food, and before she turned nineteen had married Hugh Buntine and begun her remarkable career. With Buntine, who was eighteen years her senior, she set off for Gippsland, an area not easily accessible by land. With the newly-weds were Buntine's five children by his first marriage. (His first wife died of typhus on the voyage in the ship *William Rogers*, which reached Sydney Harbour and flew the yellow flag of quarantine.)

The new Mrs Buntine sailed off around the coast to Port Albert with her husband and five children—to which were rapidly added another six bringing the total to eleven—and took up 'a run', a large area of land on Bruthen Creek between Carrajung and Port Albert. This was only a few months after the first explorer had managed to reach the area—Angus McMillan had come south and penetrated to the coast, being frustrated first by timber so thick that he had to squeeze through the gum trees and then skirt the swamps and deep, fast-running rivers that kept the area isolated from easy access to other areas except by sea for years. So we know one thing for certain about Mother Buntine as she became known: she could not have been one of the swooning crinoline-skirted damsels literature of that period seemed to favour. Gippsland was among the hardest areas to tame with its forests and mountains, sharp valleys and tremendous morasses that made overlanding to Melbourne virtually impossible for the average settler. And these lush mountainous timber lands add Australia's worst bush fires to its dangers.

The Buntines landed on 3 July 1841, and were soon well-known pioneers, partly because they ran the Bush Inn at Bruthen from 1845 to 1848 and partly because Hugh, who some believe had studied medicine in Edinburgh but not graduated, began helping the sick and injured and became known as Dr Buntine. Agnes had her first child (and the first white baby born in Gippsland) in 1841 and seems to have set off on her unique career almost simultaneously. She became a bullock driver.

At the time, she and Buntine were running a general store. Leaving her husband to care for the store she developed the carting business in the inhospitable mountains.

Agnes Buntine, known as the 'White Mother of Gippsland'.

Mother Buntine took her bullock teams through some of the toughest country in the Gippsland mountains.

She worked hard and long. In 1851 she drove a bullock team from South Gippsland on the 'rush' to the diggings at Forest Creek. Her cargo was one ton of cheese and half a ton of butter. Arriving at the diggings she opened a store and went on to Bendigo and opened yet another store at Eaglehawk. Recognizing that as much money—or more—was to be made from carting supplies to the miners as from mining itself, she set up as a carrier between the goldfields and Melbourne. An indication of the size of her business is that at this time she had two bullock teams and nine horses stolen. She and her husband were an enterprising pair. They opened yet another store, this time at McIvor at the beginning of the gold rush there, and obtained the contract to cart police stores as well.

Life was moving fast for the new colony of Victoria and Agnes Buntine maintained the pace. In 1855 she and her husband were back at their property at Bruthen Creek, again working as carriers, this time taking supplies to Donnellys Creek with Mrs Buntine driving the ten packhorses herself. In 1862, when gold was discovered at Walhalla she showed her true hardiness. Walhalla quickly became 'a lusty, booming gold settlement, populated by thousands of diggers, traders and adventurers', but it was so inaccessible to all except those spurred on by the lust for gold that today, the ghost town of the once boom-town is still remote because of the difficulty of access. Lying in the foothills of the wild Baw Baw Ranges, it was discovered by Edward Stringer, the ex-Tasmanian convict, in the decade when men were clambering over any obstacle looking for an Eldorado.

Walhalla's challenge was that, although geographically it was in Gippsland, there was no outlet south, and supplies had to be got in from the upper Goulburn River area from Melbourne by way of Jamieson. The cost of cartage was enormous—£97 a ton in 1863. The retail price of goods was correspondingly high, with flour at £10 a bag. Then, as was happening all over Australia, a local man, Tom McEvoy and his partner 'Portugee Joe', 'hit on a roundabout trail from Glenmaggie Station', and won the £50 reward offered by Sale businessmen to the first man to find a reasonably accessible route through the forested hills to the new strikes. Packers and drovers hurried to the newly blazed trail and in the van was Mother Buntine—or the White Mother of Gippsland as she was sometimes known. She imported goods from Melbourne by sea to Port Albert, hauled them by bullock wagon to the staging point at Bald Hills, which was as far as wheeled vehicles could go, and did the rest of the haul with packhorses.

On her first trip in with supplies the trail had not then been blazed and she could not get her packhorses nearer than five miles. By her third trip she pushed through the whole way and on her fourth took a mob of cattle—and promptly became the first person to slaughter a beast for food in Walhalla. To be the first person to lead a packhorse in to a settlement over ranges that even today make a car driver quail was an extraordinary feat for someone not born to the bush, and over country which had bested the resolute men who had penetrated Gippsland.

There is a legend in that country that once in the 1860s, when packing through the rip-roaring little mining town of Bald Hills, she took her bullock whip to a man. He is said to have 'pawed' a young girl and to have been drunk. The girl had been frightened, and Mother Buntine, large, indomitable, and adept with the whip, lashed into the ruffian and 'thrashed him nearly sober'. She would have been no stranger to violence and hardship. An active, enterprising and strong woman, a real pioneer, she could ride after stock, kill and dress a bullock, use a pick and shovel, split posts and rails, build fences, and, of course, handle horses and bullocks. On 'Black Monday'—2 February 1863—she was almost killed, and escaped with burns, while fighting to save her wagons and freight from the bushfire that engulfed most of Toongabbie—then a major supply depot for the trails into the goldfields in the hills.

For much of their time together Hugh Buntine had been unwell, and in 1867 he died at their home in Rosedale. At about this time, J. J. O'Connor, himself a pioneer, met Agnes Buntine:

> I once had the good fortune to meet Mrs Buntine at a little roadside pub at Toongabbie, and we two being the only guests sat all the evening in the bar parlour. I had been travelling the road all day with cattle, and was wet and cold when I arrived, and as I saw a boiling kettle on the fire, I thought a hot whisky would be fine.
>
> Just then in walked this great, big, rough-looking woman, and the landlord introduced me to Mrs Buntine. As she looked wet and cold, I invited her to join me.

When the teamsters were setting off with supplies to the new settlements, Mother Buntine was either there with them—or had gone on ahead.

We spent all the evening by the fire and she told me of many of her experiences in the old carrying days.

She was a superior type of woman and all her children had brains. She impressed me as being a wonderfully fine and interesting character. She did not make a boast of anything she had done beyond rearing and educating her family.

I ventured to ask her why she took up bullock-driving. She said there was no money to be made at anything else; she had to keep her family, and as men were making good money at the carrying trade, she though she could do the same.

She undoubtedly succeeded, as she was living a quiet, retired life at the time and her family is well provided for.

Her family were very well provided for. All had opportunities for education in an area and era when few working-class children did. The Buntine children became doctors, clerics, teachers and army officers. (One, William Murray Buntine, was, from 1896 to 1933, Principal of Caulfield Grammar School, Melbourne; another descendant, Dr Martin Buntine, was headmaster of Geelong College, 1946–60.)

Mother Buntine lost none of the spirit that sent her up rugged mountain trails with bullock wagon and whip. After rearing eleven children, caring for an ailing husband, winning an income from unbelievably hard, lonely, dangerous work, she re-married. On 14 February 1873, the fifty-one-year-old married Michael Hallett, aged 29, and settled on their farm until she died in 1896. She was buried at Rosedale where her bullock wagons had often laboured from the coast to the 'imprenetrable hills'.

In the densely wooded Gippsland hills Mother Buntine was unexcelled at her trade.

The Bush Girl
Henry Lawson

There were those other, the silent ones, the girls who were left behind when
the men with wanderlust rode out where the world was wide.

So you rode from the range where your brothers 'select',
   Through the ghostly grey bush in the dawn—
You rode slowly at first, lest her heart should suspect
   That you were so glad to be gone;
You had scarcely the courage to glance back at her
   By the homestead receding from view,
And you breathed with relief as you rounded the spur,
   For the world was a wide world to you.

Grey eyes that grow sadder than sunset or rain,
   Fond heart that is ever more true,
Firm faith that grows firmer for watching in vain—
   She'll wait by the sliprails for you.

Ah! the world is a new and a wide one to you,
   But the world to your sweetheart is shut,
For a change never comes to the lonely Bush girl
   From the stockyard, the bush, and the hut;
And the only relief from its dullness she feels
   Is when ridges grow softened and dim,
And away in the dusk to the sliprails she steals
   To dream of past meetings 'with him'.

Do you think, where, in place of bare fences, dry creeks,
   Clear streams and green hedges are seen—
Where the girls have the lily and rose in their cheeks,
   And the grass in midsummer is green—
Do you think now and then, now or then, in the whirl
   Of the city, while London is new,
Of the hut in the Bush, and the freckled-faced girl
   Who is eating her heart out for you?

Grey eyes that are sadder than sunset or rain,
   Bruised heart that is ever more true,
Fond faith that is firmer for trusting in vain—
   She waits by the sliprails for you.

THE LADY MIT THE VEIL OR 3,000 MILES SIDE-SADDLE

The citizens of Perth watching the 'cultured, quiet and somewhat frail-looking lady' walk down their streets could hardly credit that a woman of her physique could have contemplated such a journey. 'One of the most arduous trips that any lady has ever undertaken, she had established what must almost be a record in the endurance of the "weaker" sex.' The year was 1902 and Daisy Bates was the woman.

Later to be known for her work among Aborigines, she was, at the turn of the century, living on a cattle-station. In order to gain a thorough experience of the most challenging part of station life, she had decided to buy cattle herself at Roebuck station and travel them down to her homestead. During the period of six months which the trip occupied, she travelled over 3,000 miles on horseback.

When she undertook the long ride she was thirty-nine years of age. She set off on 23 April 1902, from Roebuck Plains, eighteen miles from Broome, Western Australia, and helped drove 770 head of cattle to Peak Downs on the Murchison River, almost 700 miles as the crow flies to the south. Another of the reasons for travelling personally with her cattle was to test the capacity of the wells on the Kimberley–Murchison stock route for watering a large mob, the mob which she accompanied being the largest ever travelled in one lot down from Kimberley up to that time.

Daisy had done many tough trips and was to do a few more, but this was the toughest. The glamour disappeared as civilisation receded. Writing about the journey for the *Australasian* newspaper in 1924, Daisy said:

To watch a mob of 770 Hereford cows placidly browsing round the fringe of Lake Eda, some forty miles east of Broome, or wandering in small groups to little clumps of herbage or shade was to bring vividly to mind the drover-poets, Gordon, Patterson and others whose stirring verses raised droving to the realms of romance and high adventure, where one journeyed over country of luscious herbage, water, ideal cattle camps, and contented animals that lay down in obedience to the voice of the drover. To ride after that same mob, day after day for six months, was a different proposition.

The Ophthalmia Ranges where her run was situated, and Peak Hill, where cattle were to be delivered, were about 1,000 miles as the route ran from Roebuck, but 3,000 miles as they zigzagged behind the cattle. Before leaving Broome they had obtained stores and equipment, a Maori cook and 'droving hands' whose knowledge of the art of droving equalled that of Daisy herself.

We all armed ourselves, as a matter of course, with the long stock whip of story and poem, and while the station hands and the head drover were mustering and branding, we tried to flourish our whips in true stockman style, practising on horseback. After much climbing into trees to disentangle our whips and strong

Daisy—who moved in society in Dublin, London and Australia—was presented to the Duke and Duchess of York in 1901. Throughout her long life she continued to wear clothes of the era when she arrived in Australia.

One of the overnight camps on Daisy's way south with the cattle.

One of Daisy Bates' mobs of cattle.

objections from our mounts, the whips were quietly rolled up and hidden away in swag or dray, a humble buggy whip or a less ambitious instrument of sapling and twine taking their place.

But she was, as ever, a practical woman.

My equipment was a good English saddle with ordinary stirrups, three pairs of wallaby-skin shoes, laced, with smooth soles; three habits, one of good British cloth, the other two of stout holland; a felt hat; three pairs of riding gloves, and plenty of fly veiling. A compact hold-all and portmanteau carried all necessaries, and was always easily accessible on the dray, which also carried the drovers' swags and the stores. Besides the four fine draught horses there were thirty riding horses for the drovers, myself and my twelve-year-old son. But not one of the drovers owned a cattle dog.

(It is hard to imagine droving such a mob for such a distance without dogs. Few droving trips of any sort have been undertaken without 'the drover's right-hand'.)

On the first day the head drover assigned each one his position and duties. Some guarded the flanks; the leader and his second headed the mob; the Maori cook, Davy, took complete charge of the dray, provisions and spare horses; and the others became 'tailing' hands.

A travelling mob of cattle usually shapes itself into a triangle, the strongest beasts forming the apex, while the stragglers make an ever-widening line at the rear in their efforts to find food, as those in the lead consume every blade of grass as they go along.

All the cattle had been accustomed to surface water and while going over the well-grassed country south of Broome the big mob travelled easily. The leading drover always went ahead after the cattle had been started on the way, to pick out the night camps. My place, and that of my boy, which we retained throughout the trip, were the wide base of the triangle, zigzagging to and fro behind the 'tailers' as the lagging beasts are called. All went well until the Ninety Mile Beach was reached: here surface waters ended and wells began.

Six canvas buckets, each twenty gallons capacity, with pulleys and all gear, were brought for emergencies. Most of the wells were in a bad state, in most cases too far

After her long days of droving sidesaddle, Daisy left for her next trip in a buggy.

apart—and cows in calf were slow walkers. The huge mob of thirsty beasts, used to surface water, made for hefty work at the end of each day's droving. The canvas buckets were rigged up here and there but the long disused timbering and platform more than once gave way, burying buckets and gear and effectively closing the wells, so there was nothing for it but to move the beasts on to the next well.

The thirsty animals 'broke' when they saw the sea, 'With a sort of "Hurrah!" swing of their tails they ran back', but the tide was out and they were recovered. Daisy, always observant, noted at Nambeet well a corrugated iron headstone telling of the murder of a traveller. 'The place was once a favourite camping ground of the natives but since the murder none of them will stay there.'

At this place, some of their cattle were affected by a weed that stupefied them. Not a day went by without some drama.

A species of bloated rat with thick tails, makes shallow burrows on the plain and these pitfalls added to the difficulty of manouevring the thirsty mob.

Along the whole length of the beach firewood had to be carried in the dray, for only one tree, an unburnable 'Sandy thorn-paper' was left standing.

The first stampede occurred in the Barn and Church hills, the mob heading back towards home and water:

Standing on Barn Hill I caught a glimpse of horns and tails and dust in one long line. Out on the flanks were the drovers, making their own dust line as they galloped along after the herd. It was a long time before they got them headed, but presently the long line of dust widened, and then gradually slowed down, and the runaways were soon under control again.

As they rode, the drovers watched the smoke signals from the inland tribes 'always the same, a spiral inclining to the south', as the tribesmen relayed word ahead of the coming of the big mob. As the weeks wore on Daisy records that the long, wearisome day tailing was made easier by frequently 'changing to the off-side' and then, 'I noted that many of the drovers rode "side-saddle" now and then'.

But the quick and arduous work at the wells was an antidote to saddle-weariness. It had been expected that the drove would be over before any calves were dropped so no conveyance was provided, but the difficulty at each well slowed the progress and more and more calves were dropped. Many could not travel, they were killed, and the night was made hideous by the bellowing of their mothers who constantly broke back, searching for their calves. All-night watches with great fires at various points became the rule, yet in spite of this, cunning mothers made their way back. More drovers were needed, so Daisy was sent off to La Grange station to telegraph to homesteads and stations for extra hands.

Because of the stampede she had to leave the horses she usually rode for the drovers and take a 'pig-jumper'. This bucking horse sent her flying over the plain, still pluckily hanging on to the reins, 'though now and then the flying hoofs came closer to my head than was "comfy"'. With a twisted ankle and no mounting block the little Irish lady led the fractious horse to an anthill, 'from the top of which I mounted him, and proceeded on the journey'.

With the additional drovers, they moved on. One day, tailing along in the dust . . .

we were surprised and concerned to see the whole mob suddenly split in two, leaving a clear lane along the centre. Every beast's head seemed to be turned to the opened lane, and along this opened lane slowly walked a Jew pedlar, with his huge pack closely strapped on his back. Drovers, horses and cattle stood like statues while Moses passed through the open ranks, never once hastening his steps, and taking it as a matter of course that these wild cattle were doing the ordinary thing in opening their ranks to let him through. On he went, the beasts so astonished that they kept the lane open after he had passed. The two leading drovers were waiting for him — fortunately out of earshot — and his only remark at the end of the double-barrelled harangue was: 'Who is the lady mit the veil?'.

Daisy had a small six-by-eight-foot tent, quick to put up at sunset and as quick to strike at first light. Excepting for this comfort she and her son shared the tailing work with the other hands all along the route. 'Now and again the water tasted odd, and at one well, when tea was finished and the final bucket drawn up, it brought the remains of several very dead crows with it.'

She declared that side-saddle riding was no more tiring than the cross-saddle riding of the men, but if she were to undertake another such journey she thought she would have a saddle made with adjustable pommels for the off-side, 'for a change of position now and then is desirable'.

The stock horses were a delight. Daisy describes 'Rock':

He used to watch the long stock-whip tip or the stockman's eye, and on whatever beast either alighted, Rock soon had it on the edge of the mob and out of the way. It was beautiful work. His feet might be described as dancing feet; they were so light and agile. He not only knew his work, but he enjoyed doing it.

There are no eight-hours-a-day work in droving camps. All hands are roused at break-o-day. 'Davy had breakfast steaming and ready and no one dallied over the meal for the hobbled horses had already been brought in and the mob was ready to be started again on the route south.' Daisy wrote charmingly about the dray being packed full of calves too weak to travel — 'To watch a cow hide its calf behind a four inch tussock is an education in wild mother-craft.'

Then, for Daisy, it was back and forth, zig-zagging along the ever-widening tails of cows and calves, while the head man rode ahead to find a camp for noon and another for night. Davy the cook followed the tracks in his cart. They spelled for a few days at a beautiful well by Wallal, and did some repairing before they set off again, this stretch being hills and stony ridges.

Range after range of irregular hills branched in all directions. Nat Cook was the pioneer who opened this part of the country, but mine was the first dray that ever passed through the Shaw Gorge there. Flood marks showed some sixty feet above the bed of the river. Our final night in the Gorge was a nightmare.

Just as darkness set in it began to rain. We were all in a cul-de-sac—cattle, men and horses—with gorge and stony hills around and above us. Our only outlet was that along which the floodwaters would run. Everyone had had some experience of the quick rise of these rivers. No one retired. The cattle lay along the sandy bed within the gorge, and a silent group sat in little shelters under the rocks.

All night they watched and waited, and at daybreak got safely away.

Before the journey was over, there was another stampede and this caused some of the hardest work Daisy had done so far. It was at Battle Tree Well, adjoining Ray Hill Station, and the owner, Sam McKay, had offered a paddock in which the herd, now a thousand strong, could be rested. With a fence as security, the drovers relaxed, had a mug of tea and lay down beside the dray. It had been an exhausting day and it was thought the cattle too would lie down and rest, but at midnight, some troublemakers rushed the fence and headed for the pools at Ray Hill. About six hundred beasts headed off, leaving four hundred tailers, cows and calves to be watered by Daisy, her boy and Davy the cook. As the other drovers headed back to many days of trouble rounding up the stampeders Daisy and her boy began work with the double buckets.

We managed to satisfy our charges by steady lifting and emptying. Bucket-lifting from a 170-foot well, the buckets being two heavy drums, emptying the full bucket into the trough while the small boy held the windlass steady, was strenuous work for two amateurs, but it was done, and when night came we divided the watch between us. I took the first and middle watch of the night, round the now contented mob, all lying down chewing the cud or sleeping quietly. The night was still and cloudless, the stars traversed their route into the mystical light of the west. No sound was heard except the quiet breathing of the sleeping herd—the little calves

Overleaf: Daisy Bates droved through waterless country that still takes its toll of cattle.

Daisy Bates is best remembered for her work among Aborigines. She poses here with a group of Ooldea blacks rehearsing for the visit of the Prince of Wales in 1920.

Daisy Bates.

snuggled up beside their mothers in full content. One felt thankful that their hard times were over.

Daisy here ends her account of the long drive, a cheery enough report. The truth of the matter is that when the trek was completed the tiny woman collapsed, worn out by the labour, long hours and strain. At Glen Carrick there was only a bough shelter to offer her, but here she rested until her strength returned. She was at first prostrate, she could neither eat nor sleep; she had lost fourteen pounds in weight from a figure always spare; her hair was greying and she later believed the journey aged her by fifteen years. When it was time to return to Broome she travelled to Port Hedland by stretcher, but the sea air must have revived her because on arrival at Broome she rode off inland for eighty miles looking for some cattle that had been left behind.

In all the years left to her, all the journeys and work she was yet to do, nothing could exceed in tenacity and determination that ride of 3,000 miles, side saddle, in the fog-like dust tailing behind 770 head of cattle down a lonely route.

HAWKERS

> Dust, dust, dust and a dog—
>   Oh, the sheep-dog won't be last,
> Where the long, long shadow of the old bay horse
>   With the shadow of his mate is cast,
> A brick-brown woman, with her brick-brown kids,
>   And a man with his head half-mast,
> The feed-bags hung, and the bedding slung,
>   And the blackened bucket made fast
> Where the tailboard clings to the tucker and things—
>   So the hawker's van goes past.
>
> *Henry Lawson*

There were some men who were not interested in land but followed the first settlers out and faced even greater dangers because they travelled alone. They were the hawkers, often Jewish, more often 'Afghans' as the Pathan Indian travellers were called. One of the most remarkable endeavours of a hawker was recorded by John Lewis and Alfred Giles who were working on the construction of the telegraph line from Port Augusta to Darwin in 1870. This was a perilous area to traverse, it only having been crossed three times before, and men travelled in parties of five or more. But 'Chawner' the hawker went alone.

This hawker had started from Port Augusta with a load of goods to sell to the telegraph construction parties, and intended travelling through to Port Darwin, thinking there was a road all the way. He was joined on the Finke River by a Dane named Anderson, who had with him a little blackboy from the Macumba named Jim Crow, only twelve years old. On their arrival at Mr Harvey's camp (the furthest of the construction parties going north) they were advised not to start through to Daly Waters, as there were 200 miles without a track; but, as they were short of rations, 'they could not wait until we came through, as we had only just left the MacDonnell Range 300 miles back. So Chawner decided to go on to Daly Waters. Leaving Harvey's camp in the beginning of May, and after a great loss of time, got to the Burke, where they met Mr Alfred Giles on his way to Mr Harvey's camp with a party,' wrote John Lewis.

Alfred Giles was about to pilot a Mr Roberts and party to Tennant Creek:

We warned him on that occasion concerning the hostility of the natives along the Newcastle. Subsequently events proved such warnings to be justified, although apparently unheeded, for it appeared that Chawner reached the North Newcastle, the same spot where Mr Roberts was attacked, when the savages tried to prevent him watering his horses, and on rushing to his cart for his firearms seized a loaded and cocked double-barrelled gun by the muzzle and discharged its contents through his left hand.

It was with great difficulty they stopped the bleeding.

With their carts packed with an amazing variety of goods, hawkers followed the settlers out west—sometimes even catching up with the explorers.

Lewis takes up the story:

After travelling north again for about ten miles the natives refused to let them take their horses to water; they attacked them, following them for about twelve miles. Up to this time the little blackboy had followed the track of Alfred Giles, but, being hard pushed by the natives, was unable to continue to do so, and they got too far to the westward. Finding that they were wrong, they had left the cart at North Newcastle, and, most fortunately for them. Had they crossed the plains a little further south they would most likely have been lost to the world. Mr Burton and Mr King were very kind to Chawner. The former was on his way southwards, and when he reached the place where the cart had been left he found the natives cutting it to pieces with an axe while others were digging up his stores. Mr Burton kindly picked up the goods, dried the clothes, and disposed of some of them to his party, and sent a list of those he had sold to Chawner.

Young Alfred Giles later took the cart to the intrepid salesmen where they waited at Daly Waters. In this little saga we are speaking of a man crossing arid and desert lands for a distance of 1,000 miles.

PAPA BOUGHT FOUR CARS

If they had not appeared to be so fragile, delicate and lady-like-of-the-period, the Corrick family girls could be called dauntless and invincible. In 1911, when few cars were in Australia—and fewer drivers— the Corrick family, Papa, Mama, brother Leonard, and seven sisters, had returned from one of their triumphant concert tours abroad. 'In our absence rail fares had gone up and this angered Papa.' Elsie was the baby and lived until 1978.

Papa saw four Ford motor cars in a shop in Adelaide and went straight in and bought them. The salesman explained that there were few roads yet outside the cities suitable for the horseless carriages but Father merely replied that in some countries we had travelled in there were not even tracks, and, anyway, we had been conveyed in rickshaws, gharries, sampans, carts and coaches, so poor roads and Ford cars were unlikely to worry us. We bought a single seater for the agent, a tourer for most of the family, and two lorries to carry our costume baskets, musical instruments and rolls of red arras to decorate the stage. Then we set off.

If aeroplanes had been in without a doubt our father would have expected us to climb into the cockpit and take off without any instruction at all. When he bought those first cars in Adelaide he didn't forecast any difficulty, even though none of us had ever driven a car.

Papa Corrick bought four cars and expected the girls—without instruction—to drive them. Here they are in the sticky mud that passed for the road to Mildura.

Above: The Corrick family. As well as playing musical instruments, they danced, sang, acted excerpts from well-known plays, and performed comedy sketches.

Right: Well-known in Europe and Asia, the Corrick family was equally popular with Australian outback audiences.

The 'Marvellous Corricks' thus became one of the earliest troupes of entertainers in the Southern Hemisphere to be motorised.

Professor Corrick had taught piano and violin and as each of his children was born he selected the musical instrument he or she would play. It wasn't always the accepted instrument of the period for the girls—Ruby, for instance, was taught the cornet. But she became so proficient that a London reviewer, writing in the *Observer* in 1904 said: 'Until we heard Miss Ruby Corrick play last night, we had not known that the cornet was a solo instrument. She proved otherwise. She is worthy of a place in a crack Guards band'.

Others played the clarinet, saxophone, cello, violin, viola, mellophone, flute, oboe, organ and piano. The *Statesman*, Calcutta, India, reported, 'Each member of this family is a star in his or her own right'.

Elsie played the violin, piano and organ, and, as well, wrote music and lyrics, rendered monologues, and danced. 'When Father bought the fleet of cars we become proficient in motoring, also. Ruby, the cornet player, was a splendid driver, but more important, she was an inspired mechanic. I travelled with her, but as a relief and self-starter—the crankhandle was my responsibility.'

The first journey in the cars ended with the vehicles being put on a train: 'In the desert of the north-east of South Australia we just couldn't carry enough water, so had to give in and freight them over the sand plains.'

But soon the family knew all about being a motorised troupe! There were no proper roads, only bush tracks. And when there were no tracks they made them.

THE MARVELLOUS CORRICK FAMILY ENTERTAINERS

7 - ARTISTS - 7
EACH ARTISTE A STAR

: Vocalists :
Instrumentalists

7 - ARTISTS - 7
EACH ARTISTE A STAR

Chimesringers
Society Dancers
ETC.

MISS ELSIE CORRICK, Lyric Soprano

OPINIONS OF THE PRESS:

"PUNCH," MELBOURNE, VICTORIA, AUSTRALIA.

The Corricks furnish a unique illustration of heredity and consanguinity, being singularly and collectively specially gifted with the same artistic abilities distinctly superior to any similar organisation. Their bill of fare surpasses anything hitherto submitted for the great amusement loving public.

"BEXHILL-ON-SEA OBSERVER," ENGLAND, March 20th.

There is something about the Corrick Family that is altogether different from the majority of musical families with which the English public are familiar. Every member is a real artist. A more select and charming entertainment could not be desired.

OPINIONS OF THE PRESS.

"BRISBANE COURIER," QUEENSLAND, January 29th.

Miss Elsie Corrick has a splendid soprano voice, and sang her numbers most beautifully. The young singer was recalled again and again.

"REGISTER," ADELAIDE, S. AUSTRALIA, November 29th.

Miss Ruby Corrick's achievements on the cornet and mellaphone won for her an enviable reputation as a lady instrumentalist. Her solos were treated with a sympathetic touch that evoked rounds of applause.

The Corrick Entertainers

Violiniste and Soprano—MISS ELSIE CORRICK. Flute and Piccolo—MISS AMY CORRICK.
Clarionet and Saxaphone—MR. LEONARD CORRICK. Cornet and Mellaphone—MISS RUBY CORRICK. Pianiste—MISS CORRICK.
Baritone—MR. JAMES CALDWELL. Comedian—MR. JACK BONNY.

THE CORRICKS
In their Delightful Quaker Girl Sketch.

Mr. JACK BONNY
English Character Comedian

"ADVERTISER," ADELAIDE, SOUTH AUSTRALIA, October 14th, says:

Mr. Jack Bonny (the Fool of the Family), a clever English Character Comedian, hit the taste of all classes with his witty sallies, his turn being provocative of enthusiastic recall.

THE CORRICKS
In their Humorous Sketch "Sunshades."

POPULAR PRICES - Children, Half-Price

Doors open at 7.30 — To commence at 8 o'clock

When we went to Mildura (Victoria), we headed up to the Murray River and, in the dark of night, drove along between the trees, dodging great red gums, hoping we wouldn't slip into that deep river.

Next day it rained, and we went on through thick, slippery mud. It got wedged between our wheels and the mudguards and we had to get out and drag the car clear with our hands. We bogged scores of times, and then we had to get out and push. At one time all the four cars were bogged together. We girls wore white shoes and stockings, so after a while we took these off, but then Jessie saw a centipede, so we put them back on.

The two lorries had no back mudguards and the undercarriage had constantly to be freed of mud. Of course, we had a great load on all the vehicles, and when we ploughed down into mud we went deep. But when we reached town it was worth the trials of the bush. Everyone came out to stare. The horses and cattle took fright; but the people who would be our audience stopped to look at us.

The 'Marvellous Corricks' played at places as far apart as Meekatharra in Western Australia, Winton in Queensland, Brewarrina in NSW, and Hobart. This itinerary in itself must have been unusual for a group at the height of their fame in England, South-East Asia, New Zealand and the capital cities of Australia.

In India they had played at the military halls of the great regiments of the day—at Cawnpore, Peshawar, Poona, and at the Khyber Pass—and dined with rajahs. They wore dresses embroidered in India with butterflies' wings, and others made in Paris designed by Queen Mary's dressmaker. Their decorum and gentility were spoken of in the same degree as was their talent, yet they left the theatres of the cities and headed off to the inland, as if it were expected of them.

At Winton, the crowds to see them were such that their agent wrote, 'People were trying to gaze under the cracks beneath the doors. I saw one woman lie full length on the dirty footpath to enable her to look under the door'.

They saw more than the one aspect of the social pattern of their days:

Though in India rajahs came to meet the Corricks, that wasn't the only side of the country we saw. One day we were in gharries being pulled down the streets of Rangoon, and rioting mutineers erupted in the area. My sisters got down on the floor of the gharry, and got out their silver-backed hairbrushes to defend themselves if the need arose.

For young, attractive girls, there was a much greater fear than mutiny in India or the rigours of the outback.

My eldest sister, Alice, the 'golden-throated soprano', had left a sweetheart behind in New Zealand.

After a few years, Alice hoped that Father would replace her with another soprano, but by the time we eventually got back to New Zealand Alice found her beau had grown weary of waiting for Papa to find a replacement and had married someone else. We were all aware of this danger.

When the troupe disbanded after the outbreak of World War I, most of the family settled in Launceston. Elsie taught music, played the organ at her church, and spent every night behind the screen playing the piano accompaniments to the silent movies. She began to despair of ever meeting a young man.

Above: In later years the close-knit family kept up the habit of travelling together with one of the girls at the wheel.

Above left: The East-West railway was under construction when the Corrick family returned home to Australia from one overseas tour. Like other entertainers, the family did a publicity stunt at the line.

Below left: Ethel Corrick was billed as 'The Dainty Comedienne'.

Right: Mary Watson, in her attempt to save herself, her babe, and her Chinese servant, took to sea in a cut-down iron tank—only to drift helplessly through a maze of low-lying sandy islets off the north Queensland coast. (Mary Watson, p. 237)

Overleaf: Some parts of the outback use three horses per day per man. In far western Queensland up to five horses a day are needed in the heat and the fast exhausting work on camp muster.

Below right: There were seven Corrick girls but only one boy, so an 'outsider' joined them for duologues such as this.

Below: As each child was born, Papa decided which musical instruments she or he would play.

'I'll be playing behind a silent screen till the day I die,' she lamented. All the girls she knew were going to dances and all she did was play the piano—alone.

Then the war ended. Soldiers were coming home.

One night three boys just back from the war came round to meet 'The Corricks'—they were fans of our family concert group. One had hot socks on.

He asked me what the staple industry of Launceston was. I thought he was tremendously sophisticated.

Then he hired a horse and trap and we went for a drive. He began to sing. He sang well. You know the rest.

('Hot socks', though they would not be considered bright today, were a departure from the conventional plain black socks formerly worn by men. Some had—horror of horrors—coloured clocks.)

Elsie and Stan Tilley were married and had six children.

In 1932, when Mama Corrick was eighty years old, the citizens of Launceston honoured the family with a 'Command Performance'. Thus in a city hall booked out before the day, the Corricks gave their final concert. On stage was Mama Corrick (Papa had died some years before), six of her musical children, and Elsie's son, young Norman Tilley, a third generation trouper who played a violin.

Even then, when the girls who had been the belles of many a foreign country were middle-aged, their decorum and courtesy charmed the audience. Alice, the 'golden-throated soprano', was to sing a duet with her eighty-year-old mother. Elsie was standing in the wings. 'Alice and mother stood side by side and began to sing *Love's Dream Is Over* and after the first few bars my sister Alice stepped back a pace and left our mother in the centre stage. The audience cheered.'

The stamina and élan of these remarkable women combined to give them heart and backbone that was concealed beneath butterfly wings and dresses from Paris.

THE BISHOP WITH 150 WIVES

Francis Xavier Gsell, Bishop of the Diocese of Northern Australia, was a man who had 150 wives. Half of the world knew about it.

In 1948 when Monsignor Fulton Sheen and Cardinal Spellman of the USA were visiting Australia they recognised Gsell at a conference and were delighted. 'The Bishop with a hundred and fifty wives!' they shouted. They doubtless knew that he had been commanded in audience before the Pope in Rome to defend the charge. The Holy Father, after listening to his story said, '*Oui, je comprends. Vous les achetez pour les deliverer?*' ('Yes, I understand. You buy them to save them?')

Gsell had bought the girls rather than let them be taken against their will by the old men of the tribe, as custom dictated. Earlier, he had written, 'It is always to me a sad sight to see these poor little mites of from eight to ten years becoming the playthings of old greybeards whose other, older wives, too often make them drudges, while he, himself, thinks nothing of making them the object of shameful trading'.

And then, one day, a little girl, Martina, came running to him and begged him to help her. An old man had come to claim her. 'I have come to fetch my wife.' Martina cried, 'Oh, help me, Father. I do not want to go with this old man, he is ugly.' Gsell could do nothing. He knew he must not interfere with tribal law. He watched her, sobbing, leave the mission with the old man. She was marched for forty miles away from the mission, not willingly, and on arrival at the camp refused to show the submission his other wives demanded; she resisted the approaches of the old man and he drove a spear through her leg. This, by tribal law, was justified. Somehow she managed to escape, and despite her wound managed to get back to the mission.

There she waited, well aware of the enormity of her flight. This was no longer a matter between man and wife. It was now a matter for the whole tribe. She knew they would now be gathered and would be working themselves up with shouts and yells as they put on their war paint and got ready their spears and nulla-nullas, and began the march on the mission.

Gsell was powerless. 'She believes, poor little one, that I can save her. But it is not possible. When they take her this time she is lost. If she runs away often enough she may be eligible for a divorce.' A husband of this tribe could defend a divorce by throwing no more than twelve spears at his girl-wife who is permitted to move, but not to run. Gsell knew only one girl who had been successful in this trial by ordeal. She had told him that her husband had been so old and shaky and blind he couldn't throw his spears properly.

So, the French priest stood there facing the tribesmen. 'Help me, God!' he demanded. And help came in a peculiar way. He had an inspiration: as the warriors were tired and hungry after their march, he would feed them. He spread out all the food the mission could rake together. And when they had done with eating the tribesmen lay down to sleep it off. Gsell had gained a little time. He determined, 'I will save Martina and so I will save other little girls who come to me.'

Left: Crosses on Babel Island, Bass Strait, erected in memory of seamen lost in the wild waters of the straits. (Mayday, p. 243)

Below left: When tied up at a wharf the little coastal tramps of Bass Strait appear quaint to onlookers, but once out, servicing the lonely islands, they are on their own, and their men are known to be among the toughest and bravest in Australia. (Mayday, p. 243)

Bishop Gsell all set to pack across miles of his diocese in northern Australia.

He decided to buy Martina. It was not the custom of the tribe to sell a girl outright, only to lend her to a man. In this way she remains useful for further exchange. But Gsell proceeded with great cunning.

On a long table in front of the mission house he set out everything he could think of that would attract the sleeping men. There was a blanket, a sack of flour, a sharp knife, and a hatchet; a mirror, a teapot, some gay beads, tobacco and pipes; brightly coloured cotton material, tins of meat, and cans of treacle. All the while the well-filled men slept on. Gsell, wide-awake, afraid and alert, waited behind a fence, out of sight.

He was going to ask a high price for these goods. If they wanted them they must pay with tribal custom. He must not appear too anxious to sell. He must make no mistake at all or Martina and the girls who would come after her were surely lost.

The sleepers began to awake. They saw the table, nudged their sleeping partners awake, approached the table, then crowded over it, chattering, gazing longingly at the riches, 'trembling with desire'.

Gsell, from his hiding place, waited, afraid to appear eager. Then, 'I drew myself up to my full height and attempted to look majestic. I stalked towards them, a great man (I hoped I looked), I advanced like a regal being.' He needn't have bothered with the majestic approach. They couldn't take their eyes off the tables. He had them. But could he get the girl?

In the annals of missionary endeavour this moment ranks with the most tense. One culture standing toe to toe with another, tribal law. On the one hand, if the men sold him the girl they could be punished by their tribal elders. If Gsell tried to protect the girl or interfere with tribal custom he may, by white man's law, be forced to leave his mission, may indeed have his mission disbanded. The least that could happen to him would be an outcry down south that would have repercussions in parliament.

The man who finished up as the Bishop with 150 wives was sold Martina, his first 'wife'. After long deliberations and discussions as to how to gain the gifts, yet salve their conscience in this defiance of tribal custom, as well as placate the elders, the tribe came to a decision. The 'hairy, anonymous old man who had claimed Martina as wife, quite justly according to native law', came to where Gsell stood waiting, and praying. 'We sell the girl,' said the old man. 'On condition. You must keep her for yourself always; she must not be passed on to any other man.'

Gsell merely answered, 'I am glad you decide to sell. Take everything and I'll take the girl.' He didn't mention the conditions and in their eagerness to possess the goods the tribe ignored the exception.

This may have been the end of the affair for the natives but for Gsell came a 'please explain'. And not one only. First, the Commissioner for the Northern Territory and then Canberra sent a 'please explain purchase of women'—the word had sped south. Then, the questions from farther afield, from his religious superiors.

Gsell, while coping with explanations, had another problem on his hands: other girls began to seek asylum. Soon he had a goodly number. When the tribe saw there was no attempt to wean the girls away from the native way of life, apart from this one point, and that Gsell was willing, indeed anxious, that they should marry young men of the tribe, all doubts fled. Gsell received so many offers of 'wives' that he was forced to limit his business.

One very old man, a bearded Methuselah, came carrying a four-day-old baby in his arms; it was his wife, by tribal custom. 'Father, I have come to sell you my wife,' he explained. 'I am too old for it. I've got beyond it.' (Gsell, when he was Bishop of the Diocese many years later told this story with Gallic wit.) The old man explained that if he could sell the baby, his wife, he would have something for his old age. So, a very young 'wife' was added to the collection. The harem had women of all ages. One poor old crone who, like the old bearded Methuselah, claimed, 'I am too old for it' was allowed to stay, almost a sort of divorce, when Gsell learnt that her husband had several younger wives to care for his needs.

A school had to be established for the 'wives' and in time courtship would begin. Gsell was puzzled when it did start. He found striplings lying about his mission, on their backs, singing at the top of their voices. When the voices of these boys fell silent, the girls' treble would begin in the mission. The children knew how to court, tribal fashion.

The story of the first marriage is now part of the lore of the northern area. Trestle tables beneath a poinciana tree that blazed with crimson flowers, vases of blossom on the tables between piled plates of waffles and syrup, fresh beef and tinned beef, lolly water and sweets. All the tribe turned up for it.

Called to Rome to report to the Pope, the Bishop must have found it difficult to describe to Europeans the duties of a clergyman in the outback.

MATTHIAS

There have been few acts of bravery in the cause of war on this continent, but one that happened during World War II is memorable.

The first Japanese Zero shot down on Australian soil brought a measure of fame to a small Aboriginal settlement. When its pilot was captured by a young man of the tribe a Darwin journalist reported the event, and delighted a country that hadn't had much to delight it for two months since Japan entered the war.

The plane had been hit over Darwin during the first big raid in February 1942. The pilot headed out to sea but his craft was doomed. Aboriginal women on Melville Island, seventy miles north of Darwin, saw the plane crash in the bush at what has been known ever since as Zero Hill. They ran to tell their men-folk who set out to search for it.

They found the plane easily and tracked the pilot who had headed into the bush. It was Aboriginal bushcraft against Japanese pilot and the end was not long coming up. Matthias, a young boy, stepped up to the pilot and said, 'Stick 'em up allasame Hopalong Cassidy.' He then took the enemy into custody.

The remnants of the plane have been brought to the settlement at Snake Bay and Tiwi children at the school mime its doomed flight from Darwin, its spiralling crash, and the final challenge of Matthias.

On Melville Island, 'Matthias' plane' remains as a monument to a small boy's capture of a Japanese pilot in World War II.

THE DIARY OF MARY WATSON

Few diaries can clutch the heart as that of twenty-one-year-old Mary Watson. Her brief words—a dozen or so entries made in pencil on loose pages, now in Brisbane's Oxley Library—contain an indomitable courage, resourcefulness, devotion to her baby and her Chinese servant, a presence of mind in time of disaster and endurance that could scarcely be surpassed.

The diary has no end. It just stops, and we are left mourning the loss of a young woman in a situation so outlandish that even today scarcely anyone has visited the spot.

Mary was well educated, and when she emigrated with her Cornish parents to Queensland in 1877, she opened a private school in Cooktown. Mary is said to have been 'reserved, nervous and delicate', but she attracted friends because she was a talented pianist. A Scots seaman, 'Captain' Robert E. Watson, wooed her and on 30 May 1880 wed her. He took her to live on tiny Lizard Island. If Cooktown was remote and difficult of access how much more was the small island in the Coral Reef area, twenty miles northeast of Cape Flattery. Here Robert Watson had a bêche-de-mer station he shared with P. C. Fuller, his partner. (Bêche-de-mer—or trepang— is the sea-slug that is a delicacy much prized as an ingredient in Oriental cookery). The two fishermen brought the bêche-de-mer to the island from the fishing grounds and boiled and dried it in a square iron ship's tank.

On 3 June 1881 a son was born, Thomas Ferrier (they called him Ferrier), and in September, Robert Watson and his partner set off for the bêche-de-mer grounds at Knight Island, 200 miles away. Here they intended to start another fishing station. They left Mary and the baby on the island with two Chinese servants, Ah Sam and Ah Leong (who supplied fresh food from their farm nearby), a rifle, a revolver and ammunition.

Part of Mary's diary later found on Lizard Island gives us the prologue to the tragedy:

September 27, 1881—Blowing gale of wind S.E. Ah Sam saw smoke in S. direction, supposed to be from native camp. Steamer bound north very close about 6 pm. Corea I think.
September 28—Blowing strong S.E. breeze.
September 29—Blowing strong breeze S.E. although not so hard as yesterday. No eggs. Ah Leong killed by the blacks over at the farm. Ah Sam found his hat which is the only proof.
September 30—Natives down at the beach at 7 pm. Fired off rifle and revolver and they went away.
October 1—Natives speared Ah Sam, four places in the right side, and three on the shoulder. Got three spears from the natives. Saw ten men altogether.

There was no boat on the island, no contact with the mainland. The Cooktown *Courier* reported some unease later in the month, when a ship arrived in Cooktown having passed the Lizard Island on 17 October: '. . .

Bêche-de-mer fishing was a lucrative trade on the northern coast and islands of Australia. The sea delicacy was then boiled in an iron tank and laid out to dry in the sun.

Cooktown, Mary Watson's home before she married.

bush fires were numerous, and on nearing land signals were made but no answer received. Observing that the door of the hut was open, with two blackfellows about, he (the captain) sailed on.' Three days later, 20 October, another vessel saw '. . . eight or ten native canoes hauled up on the beach, and about forty blacks on the Lizard Island where a bush fire was raging'. On 21 October HMS *Conflict* set off with five police troopers for Lizard Island, intending to return on Sunday 23 October if all was well; 'in the meantime further intelligence is awaited in Cooktown with much anxiety'.

It was this party who found the few sheets of notepaper written on with lead pencil, that made up the first part of Mary's diary. But they could find no trace of the young woman, her baby Ferrier, or the Chinese Ah Sam.

It was three months before their fate was known; only then did the story of Mary Watson's incomparable calm and commonsense under fearful pressure emerge.

On 2 October Mary became aware she could no longer defend Lizard Island from the blacks, and sought around for some means of escape. With no boat on the island she decided on the iron tank in which the bêche-de-mer had been treated, and she and the wounded Ah Sam moved it to the water. (It is likely she did most of the moving as Ah Sam was severely wounded in side and shoulder.)

The heroine of Lizard Island, Mary Watson.

She gathered what would be necessary on a voyage she knew would be dictated not by her hand but by the vagaries of wind and sea. She took clothes for the baby, tins of preserved milk, tins of sardines and preserved meats, a small bag of rice, some groats, a pillow for the baby's head and an umbrella to keep the sun from him.

As well she took what money and trinkets she owned and a few pieces of jewellery from better days. She packed all these necessaries in a trunk, which she stowed in the small cut-down tank. Then, armed with her revolver, Mary carried baby Ferrier and helped Ah Sam to the tank. They managed to get it afloat and made their escape.

They drifted all the first night, 2 October, and the next day landed on a bare reef. Her departure from Lizard Island was well planned: all she now needed was to float and paddle to a place where fresh water could be found.

When Captain Watson returned to Lizard Island after his trip north to the bêche-de-mer grounds, he realised that his wife, child and the house-boy, Ah Sam, had made their escape in the cut-down tank as it was missing. He set off immediately to search the nearby islands, the 'whole of his attention directed to sighting the "pot" or "tank".'

For three months the fate of Mary, Ferrier and Ah Sam was unknown. Then, on Sunday morning, 22 January 1882, when the bêche-de-mer

The cut-down ship's iron tank (photographed from above) in which Mary Watson so bravely set off with her babe and the wounded Ah Sam. This relic is now in the Queensland Museum.

schooner *Kate Kearney* arrived at Cooktown from the Northern fisheries, Captain Bremner reported:

On Thursday afternoon (19th instant, 1882) Captain Bremner was endeavouring to beat south to No. 4 Howick (islet), but was unable to fetch it and brought up for the night at No. 5, where his black boys caught some seasonable fish and were allowed to land for the purpose of cooking them. One of the boys who had wandered inland in search of eggs returned with a scared face, and a rather indistinct story of having seen 'um white dead fellow', and under his guidance the party discovered on the south-east beach, the partially decomposed remains of Ah Sam, Mrs Watson's servant. Continuing their search they found, not far distant from the corpse, in a small lagoon close to the Mangrove scrub, the tank, or rather three-quarter tank (used as a bêche-de-mer boiler) missed from the Lizard, half filled with water by recent rains, which, when emptied, disclosed the remains of the missing lady and her little child, together with two boxes. One belonged to the Chinaman. The other contained a few articles of clothing for the baby, Mrs Watson's gold watch and money, tins of preserved milk, tins of sardines and of preserved meats, a small bag of rice, some groats, and close to her side a cap, and a revolver loaded at full cock, together with a number of cartridges. She was lying on her back with her poor baby resting on her decomposed arm, and the diary which the brave lady had managed to write to the last, and which is given below, tells how she, in order to escape from her savage foes, had boldly trusted herself to the elements and the mercy of God in one of the frailest barks which ever bore a living freight, and had drifted forty miles over the torrid sea to die from thirst on an arid and uninhabited coral isle within 10 miles of the mainland. It tells of wonderful presence of mind under trying circumstances, to find that she had even taken a pillow for her babe's head to rest on and an umbrella with which to shield it from the tropical sun. The last entry in the diary found at the Lizards mentioned that Ah Sam had been speared, but he was probably nursed by his mistress and was reserved for a more lingering death.

The few pencil-written sheets of note paper that made the second part of the diary and which was found in the tank by her body tell the story:

Left Lizard Island October 2nd, 1881 (Sunday afternoon) in tank. Got about three miles or four from the Lizards.

October 4—Made for the sand bank off the Lizards, but could not reach it. Got on a reef.

October 5—Remained on the reef all day on the look-out for a boat, but saw none.

October 6—Very calm morning. Able to pull the tank up to an island with three small mountains on it. Ah Sam went ashore to try and get water, as ours was done. There were natives camped there, so we were afraid to go far away. We had to wait return of tide. Anchored under the mangroves; got on the reef. Very calm.

October 7—Made for another Island four or five miles from the one spoken of yesterday. Ashore, but could not find any water. Cooked some rice and clam-fish. Moderate S.E. breeze. Stayed here all night. Saw a steamer bound north. Hoisted Ferrier's white and pink wrap but did not answer us.

October 8—Changed anchorage of boat as the wind was freshening. Went down to a kind of little lake on the same island (this done last night). Remained here all day looking out for a boat; did not see any. Very cold night; blowing very hard. No water.

October 9—Brought the tank ashore as far as possible with this morning's tide. Made camp all day under the trees. Blowing very hard. No water. Gave Ferrier a dip in the sea; he is showing symptoms of thirst, and I took a dip myself. Ah Sam and self very parched with thirst. Ferrier is showing symptoms.

October 10—Ferrier very bad with inflammation; very much alarmed. No fresh water, and no more milk, but condensed. Self very weak; really thought I would have died last night (Sunday).

October 11—Still all alive. Ferrier very much better this morning. Self feeling very weak. I think it will rain today; clouds very heavy; wind not quite so hard.

No rain. Morning fine weather. Ah Sam preparing to die. Have not seen him since 9. Ferrier more cheerful. Self not feeling at all well. Have not seen any boat of any description. No water. Nearly dead with thirst.

She had no word of reproach for the living, did not write of fear of the awful death awaiting her by spear, thirst or the sea; she is reticent to the end. Her joy in baby Ferrier seeming 'more cheerful' and her understanding of the man when she writes 'Ah Sam is preparing to die' is very touching and suggests an understanding few had at that time. The *Courier* writers believed that the 'clouds' the young mother saw thickening as if presaging rain may have been 'the dimming vision of eternal night stealing over her', because, while she lived, there was no rain; but, by an awful irony, after their deaths from thirst, the tank half filled with fresh rain water which washed over the bodies of Mary and Ferrier.

Through the six days the fugitives survived after their arrival on the uninhabited island, their sufferings must have been agonising, but Mary makes no mention of them in her diary, except in her final entry—and then as information, not complaint: 'Nearly dead with thirst'. For the most part she is concerned with the health of her four-months-old baby, and that of her servant. Day by day she wrote firmly, calmly in her diary, entering what to us now is a piteous tale.

The death of Ah Sam seems to have added only more nobility to the end of the three castaways. From the position in which his body was found 'it is evident that when he felt his end approaching he crawled away to the meagre shelter of a dwarf tree that he might neither intrude on the privacy of his mistress, nor pain her with the sight of his suffering'. The rifle and bandages were found beside his body. His instinctive chivalry was in keeping with the rest of the tragic, yet dignified story.

The news was terrible for the isolated town that had known the young girl. One man wrote:

> God knoweth and judgeth, aye, for the best,
> But His judgments sometimes are hard to bear,
> And I wish He had managed that woman to spare—
> A mother of heroes for our new home.

The Cooktown people appreciated how close to rescue Mary had brought the trio.

The *Courier* lamented that but for:

The unfortunate circumstance of No. 5 Howick Island containing no water the fugitives would no doubt have been saved; ... for, not withstanding the terrible danger which menaced them, there was no panic or flurry about their departure, and the tank was well stored with provisions, while Mrs Watson even took with her a box containing her spare clothing and account-books. If the lives of the party could have been prolonged for a few days they would certainly have been rescued, for the island upon which they had taken refuge lies right in the track of steamers, and small sailing vessels frequently cruise about near the group. Mrs Watson says in her diary that she saw one steamer pass, and that signals were made, but that they failed to attract attention. This might very easily be the case, for as the island is uninhabited no special attention would be paid to it in passing, and as the land lies very low, signals unless hoisted on a flag-pole or in some such way, would be very likely to escape the notice of the unobservant. That this particular vessel did not keep a sharper look-out is much to be deplored. Life and death were in the balance, and death turned the scale.

Irony piled on irony: 'It does at first seem strange', said a newspaper report, 'that the bodies should not have been previously discovered. More especially as Captain Watson had sailed around the island whilst searching for his wife and child, but the tank was so effectively hidden by mangroves that it was not discernible.'

On Sunday, 29 January 1882, the people of Cooktown honoured 'the memory of a lady whose name will always be associated with the nobility of her sex and with the history of the "far North"'. Some 650 people attended the public funeral of Mrs Watson and her baby, and of her faithful servant Ah Sam. So ended the short life of a girl of more than ordinary intelligence, self-reliance and imagination. Her courage and initiative in planning and executing the escape from Lizard Island deserved a better ending than fate had arranged for her. The tank in which she cared so tenderly for Ah Sam and baby Ferrier is preserved in the Queensland Museum, but the great spirit of Mary Watson should be preserved in the heart of every Australian.

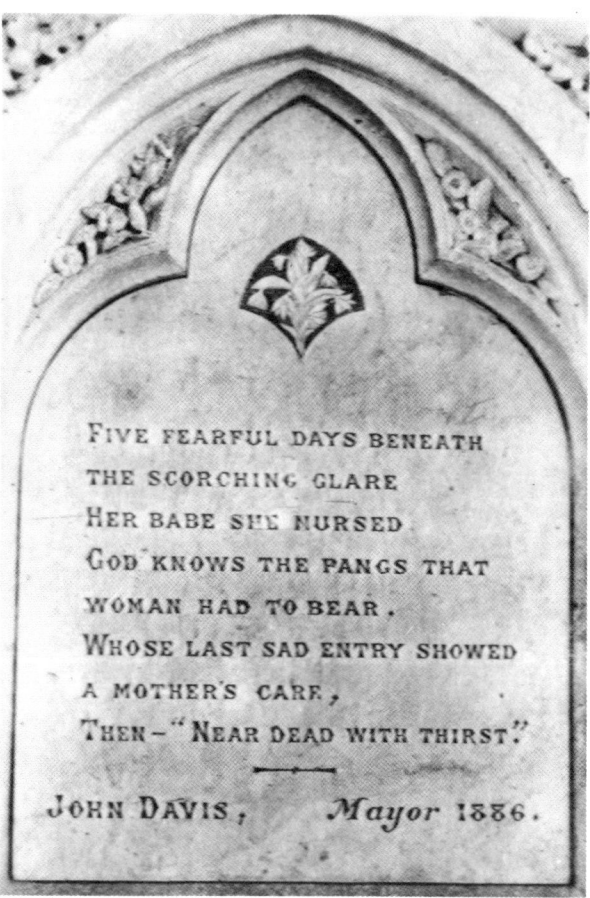

Above: The monument in Cooktown to the brave young mother.

Top: The torment of the young woman touched the hearts of all who read her brief diary.

MAYDAY

The Australian coastline is littered with as many wrecks of gallant ships as adorn the older European shores which have had centuries to collect their cruel trophies. Yet the drama of the sea has always been accepted uneasily here, the death of a ship seeming to be in regions as hostile and only vaguely recognised as are those other inland oceans of sand.

Because of this, the struggles of a dying ship come unexpectedly and painfully to a people who have never consciously accepted that they live on an island and are therefore surrounded by water.

On 17 December 1956, a sixty-ton coastal tramp, the *Willwatch*, was crossing Bass Strait. Her Captain, George McCarthy, was in the tiny box of a wheel-house on deck speaking into his transmitting radio.

It was 7.10 am. 'Fo'c'sle full of water,' he called. 'Deck cargo has to be shifted. Am down by the head. Collision bulkhead holed; plugging holes with blankets. Forward bilge pump blocked, aft bilge can't pick up because of angle of ship. Don't worry too much. I think I'll be able to save her.'

At that time she was the only small vessel in the open sea in that part of the Strait. She had left her north-west Tasmanian home port of Ulverstone the

When white men first came to King Island, there was already a wreck there; in the next 200 years the island became encircled with the wrecks of lost ships.

Captain McCarthy was trying to reach Currie Harbour, King Island—the island that is sometimes called the maritime graveyard.

previous day and was heading for Currie, the port of King Island, largest in the chain of islands that stretches northward from the western tip of Tasmania. *Willwatch* had struck the end of the equinoctial gales that always bring heavy seas.

'She's having it on,' they would be saying in the *Willwatch*.

Besides the skipper, Captain George McCarthy (Mac to men in the small ship trade), on board were engineer Peter Hanson, forty-five, deckhands Neville Chitts, twenty, and Anthony Dick, eighteen, and deck boy John Mercer, sixteen.

McCarthy was not only captain and radio officer, he was the only navigator and experienced seaman on the ship. Hanson had spent a short time on ships in Germany before migrating to Australia two years previously. Chitts and Dick had not been on many voyages, while Mercer, who was from a boys' home, had come aboard only a few weeks before; this was his first job.

Willwatch's cargo was the mixed, ludicrous motley that small ships always carry, the cargo that makes them the butt of many jokes as they head for island outposts on their runs. On her deck were three horses in high-sided wooden boxes, some bales of hay, and fifty large drums of petrol. Down below were green timber fenceposts and what was called 'general cargo'— groceries, cases of fruit, and the jumbled bits and pieces island stores and islanders themselves order.

This then was the setting for what must surely be one of the most moving dramas of the sea, a drama in which a widespread audience of radio listeners participated; some were active in the tense unfolding of events, others helpless to do anything but merely follow the course of the tragic happenings as the little ship and its crew went to their deaths.

First report of anything amiss was the call from McCarthy at 7.10 am when he spoke to the ship's agents in Currie. At 7.30 McCarthy called again and said he could still see Three Hummock Island on the Horizon. He didn't say what time *Willwatch* had begun to take in water or what was causing the leak. Perhaps he thought it wasn't necessary, assuming that the agent (who was also the owner) would know.

It wasn't the first time the sixty-four year old ship had been at risk. Several times in the past the King Island Marine Board had lent their pumps to pump *Willwatch*'s forecastle free of water when she had reached Currie after a battle with wind and sea.

Once, McCarthy had dragged the water-heavy ship home to Tasmania across the strait with the forecastle completely flooded, held only by the collision bulkhead. (This bulkhead separates the forecastle or the forepeak from the rest of the ship.) That time, several of the planks had sprung in *Willwatch*.

Now McCarthy thought he could save her again. In any case, he probably decided there would be plenty of time for explanations of causes and effects when he got *Willwatch* safely home.

It was 8.15 am when the official short-wave shore radio stations, VIM (Melbourne) and VIH (Hobart), operated by Overseas Telecommunications, first heard from *Willwatch* that morning. The radio on *Willwatch* could be worked on several frequencies and in sending the earlier messages to Currie, Mac's radio had been on four megacycles.

At 8.15 he switched to six megacycles and that is when *Willwatch*'s plight became known to the listeners, official and otherwise, who tune in on that wave-length at that time.

This is one of the daily times when small ships are called to enable them to receive or send official messages, and to give their positions and weather reports. (Relatives and friends of ships' crews often tune in on their home dual-wave sets at these times to listen for news of those ships in which they are interested. They cannot take any part in the conversation being passed back and forth.) In these set-time calls precedence is given to any ship calling for help.

On the morning of 17 December, when *Willwatch* called up, Bill Watson at VIH Hobart heard him and so did Don Clayton at Melbourne's VIM. Clayton's voice came on: 'Stand by all small ships please. Go ahead *Willwatch*.'

'I'm shipping water,' McCarthy told him. 'Cannot control the vessel. Request a ship to stand by.'

Immediately, Clayton called all ships in the vicinity to report their positions, course and speed. Only the captain of a distressed vessel can requisition a ship to come to its aid, but as yet McCarthy had given neither of the two distress signals laid down by international code: 'Mayday', the spoken word for SOS, or 'Pan Pan Pan', the lesser distress signal.

At 8.25 McCathy's call was: 'Ship lower in water.'

At Hobart, Watson decided his greatest contribution was to stay off the air and keep other ships with unnecessary traffic off the air as well. He arranged for an emergency station to be set up on top of near-by Mount Rumney in the hope of receiving *Willwatch* more clearly, and in case reception in Melbourne deteriorated. But as events went, it was not needed.

In Melbourne Clayton telephoned J. K. Crone, Deputy Director of Navigation and Lighthouses in Victoria, and relayed *Willwatch*'s message. Captain Crone told Clayton to sound the automatic alarm. This is fitted in many of the larger ships that do not have radio operators on twenty-four hour duty and can be actuated automatically by a special signal in cases of emergency, bringing the operators to the alert. It was 8.29 when this was completed.

Next, all ships were asked to report their positions. Few replies came in. Most ships were sheltering. Usually a dozen or more small ships can be contacted around these waters.

The only ones who reported being anywhere near the spot were *Rhonda H*, from Table Cape; *Pandora* and *Tuna* at Port Davey, about 200 miles away but hearing *Willwatch* perfectly; *Peter H* and *Olympic* at Three Hummock Island. VSP was also at Three Hummock Island, but didn't have her radio switched on at that time as the crew were too busy battling the heavy seas to reach the shelter of the island.

Crone asked for *Willwatch*'s position. The answer came back as twenty-five miles north of Cape Rochon on Three Hummock Island. Though *Peter H* was closest to *Willwatch*, various factors made it more practical for

The Willwatch *was one of the last of the wooden cargo vessels that traded around the Bass Strait islands. Many of these ships—including this one, the* Sheerwater, *a sister ship of the* Willwatch—*have been lost in the straits.*

the much larger, sea-going *Olympic* to go as it could cover the distance in less time and more surely.

Owner-skipper 'Dugger' Warren was ready immediately, but estimated it would take him at least three hours to reach *Willwatch*. As he sailed from the shelter of Three Hummock Warren reported gale-force winds, huge seas, and poor visibility. Neither he nor *Willwatch* had radar.

At 8.45 McCarthy reported that though she was hard to control, *Willwatch* was under way again, heading NNE at three knots. To laymen this may seem strange, as that meant he was heading out to open sea, away from land; but to seamen grouped around short-wave it was clear.

The rough weather was coming from SSW, and if McCarthy had turned about and headed back to Tasmania (presuming it would have been possible for him to turn a hard-to-control ship in such a big sea without rolling it over), the little vessel would have been taking the heavy seas on her bow, the place where she was already damaged.

The same would have applied had an attempt been made to run to King Island. McCarthy's only hope was to run before the wind and the sea.

McCarthy did not say at this stage what had happened (and he didn't even to the end). But those who listened and who had worked on small wooden ships thought *Willwatch* had either sprung a plank—old ships sometimes become 'nail-sick' and the *Willwatch* was built in 1895—or 'spewed her caulking', the inelegant but accurate phrase used to describe the ejection of caulking from between the planks when a vessel is 'working' in a heavy sea.

At 8.50 Mac called again. 'Conditions not improving. Seas worsening, wind freshening. May use distress call.'

By 9 o'clock *Olympic* was well under way with a twenty-five to thirty-knot wind howling over her stern. *Willwatch* contacted her on the four megacycle band. 'Position has deteriorated. Men standing by in life jackets. She is well down by the head.' Mac's hopes fluctuated as the weather worsened and then abated briefly. At 9.30 he told VIM: 'Position not desperate. Might be able to make port.'

A little later rising seas and stronger winds caused him to say, 'I don't think we will be able to make it now.' He said the deck cargo was being shifted aft in the hope it would bring *Willwatch*'s head out of the water. As Hanson was below battling to keep the motor going, it left one man and three boys to move fifty big petrol drums and three horseboxes on the rolling, plunging deck.

At 10 am Vic Hardy on *VSP* switched on his radio to send a message home that he was sheltering at Rape Bay on Three Hummock Island, but when he heard that *Willwatch* was in trouble and *Olympic* was going to her aid, he called up the distressed ship.

'Can I do anything, Mac?' Hardy asked.

'I won't say no at a time like this,' McCarthy replied. 'I've got my crew to think of.'

Hardy pulled up his anchor and in his own words 'gave her all she had' as he, too, headed north in the Strait.

In Melbourne, Captain Crone decided that because of the deterioration in the weather and visibility, air support should be sought.

He called up the RAAF and asked them to send a plane to search for *Willwatch* and 'home' rescuing ships to her, but even then it was too late. The end came shortly after. At 10.09 McCarthy said to *Olympic* and *VSP*: 'Position very bad. I'm going to fire a red rocket. It may guide you to me.' Soon after, he called again. '*Willwatch* to *Olympic*. First rocket gone. Did you see anything of it?' But the ships coming to his rescue were still too far away to sight it.

At the same time an Ansett-ANA plane that had left King Island for Tasmania with passengers swung east to join the search to locate *Willwatch*. Passengers were placed at each window and asked to keep a lookout below for a ship.

Then came another call from *Willwatch*, 'Bulwarks awash. Won't last long.' *Olympic* asked if it was possible to launch the life-boat in that sea, and

Below left: These tramp ships carry what to a landsman is a ludicrous cargo—including cattle, horses and sheep on deck—but they have the highest losses of any ships in Australian waters.

Below: The small coastal traders rarely tie up to a jetty but anchor off shore. Their crews do their own loading and unloading.

with the ship down by the head as she was. McCarthy replied, 'We can't free the dinghy.' A little later he said, 'We've freed the dinghy, but can't launch it.' *Olympic* suggested it might float off and McCarthy answered that he and the crew were depending on that.

The next call came at 10.19: 'Decks awash. Don't know how long we will last.' A minute later. 'Position deteriorated even more. Fifty drums have washed over the side.'

Hardy in *VSP* (the noise of his pounding motors would be matching the pounding in his chest) said, 'We're coming fast, Mac.' McCarthy told them he was sending up another rocket. Warren on *Olympic* and Hardy strained their eyes ahead, trying to pierce the spray for the rocket's glow, but they saw nothing.

At 10.30 McCarthy said, 'I've ordered the crew over the side in their life jackets.'

At many points along Tasmania's northern coast and on the mainland word of the sea drama had been passed around and in dozens of private homes dual-wave radios were switched to short wave and tuned to the wave-lengths on which the fight for the life of a little ship and its crew was going on.

In official quarters, such as the Navigation Department in Melbourne and in Currie and Ulverstone, where many relatives and friends of small-ship men are located, in RAAF, airline, ABC and commercial radio stations, little knots of anxious-eyed people followed every development.

These hundreds of listeners, each with his own thoughts, were with George McCarthy, as they stared silently and impotently at their radio sets during his tragic battle.

And seamen in little ships—though no sound of it came from the radios—could hear the noise of the *Willwatch* dying around that lonely figure, the horses screaming as their boxes rolled across the deck, the lashings snapping like bootlaces as the crippled ship leapt and plunged at the mercy of the deep sea waiting to engulf her. As the minutes ticked by, men shouted at their radios. 'Oh God! Where are the boats . . . the planes?'

They were all going at full speed, but they knew that they wouldn't be in time. The Ansett-ANA plane had lost ten minutes circling the *VSP* thinking it to be the *Willwatch*. The RAAF Dakota and Canberra that were sent to search took an hour to muster crews and become airborne. The *VSP* and *Olympic* were still hours away.

At 10.35 Mac's voice came through, 'I'm still here, but I can't hold her now.'

He had kept a rocket for the very end. 'I'm going to let it go now,' he said.

Hardy said later, 'He was the coolest man I ever knew. When "Dugger" and I told him we hadn't seen his last rocket, he remained as he had been all the time, perfectly calm.'

Finally at 10.37 there was a lot of static and noise, then Mac spoke through it: 'It looks as if this is it . . . see you later . . . cheerio.' There was nothing more.

Again and again, Melbourne called, 'VIM to *Willwatch*. VIM to *Willwatch*. Come in *Willwatch*. Come in *Willwatch*.'

At 11 o'clock the Ansett-ANA plane flew over the *Willwatch*'s last known position, but there was nothing to be seen on the empty sea. At 12.45 the RAAF Canberra bomber sighted wreckage and drums floating in the water, but no sign of crew or dinghy. Later in the day the RAAF plane dropped red markers nearby to guide *Olympic* and *VSP*.

Meanwhile many Tasmanians and fishermen from Eden on the New South Wales coast right around to Adelaide still clustered around their radios. On King Island hundreds of people stood outside the office of the

Having it on' as they call it on the small ships in Bass Strait.

ship's agent waiting for news. The searching ships were in contact with the planes overhead, messages such as these passing between them: '*VSP* from Lincoln. *VSP* from Lincoln. There's something about 200 yards ahead on your port bow,' and 'Lincoln from *VSP*. Lincoln from *VSP*. We're passing through wreckage ... but there's only wreckage. One forty-four gallon drum, one door, one life jacket. That is all. That is all.'

A pressure cooker, some cases of apples, some bales of hay, a fencepost showed up, a pathetic little collection of flotsam.

The boats searched all that day and three RAAF planes swept 6,193 square miles in a 'creeping line ahead', 500 feet above the water. But neither *Willwatch*'s crew nor the dinghy were ever seen again. Still men sat staring at the radio.

At 7.30 that night it was blowing even harder. 'Dugger' Warren called up Vic Hardy. 'Look Vic, the way she's blowing they could be 20 miles from here if they got the dinghy afloat. I reckon we might as well go with it. What do you reckon?' he said. Hardy answered, 'Yes, Dugger. We'll go with the weather in wide circles. It's about all we can do.'

So, through the dusk and the darkness, the crews of the two small ships peered out across the heaving seas, all the time heading away with the weather. Next day *VSP* and *Olympic* retired and other small ships took over, but finally all searching was abandoned.

A lifebelt, a tarpaulin, and later, wooden hatch covers were washed up in Westernport, far to the eastward of where *Willwatch* foundered. That was all.

Strangely enough, one of the few people around the Tasmanian coast who had not been drawn into the crowds listening to *Willwatch*'s battle against the seas was McCarthy's wife Lillian, who lived at Spreyton, a small village not far from Ulverstone. She knew of her tragic loss only when she tuned in to the ABC midday news bulletin on 17 December and heard that *Willwatch* had gone as well as practically all hope for her crew.

She sat looking at the radio for a long, long time—she doesn't know how long. 'Then I went to tell the others, the four who must know.'

That wasn't easy, because the oldest of the four was Sharon, five, then came Michael and David, and the youngest, Stephen, the seventeen-day-old baby in her arms.

'Something's gone wrong,' she told them. 'Daddy won't be bringing his ship home.'

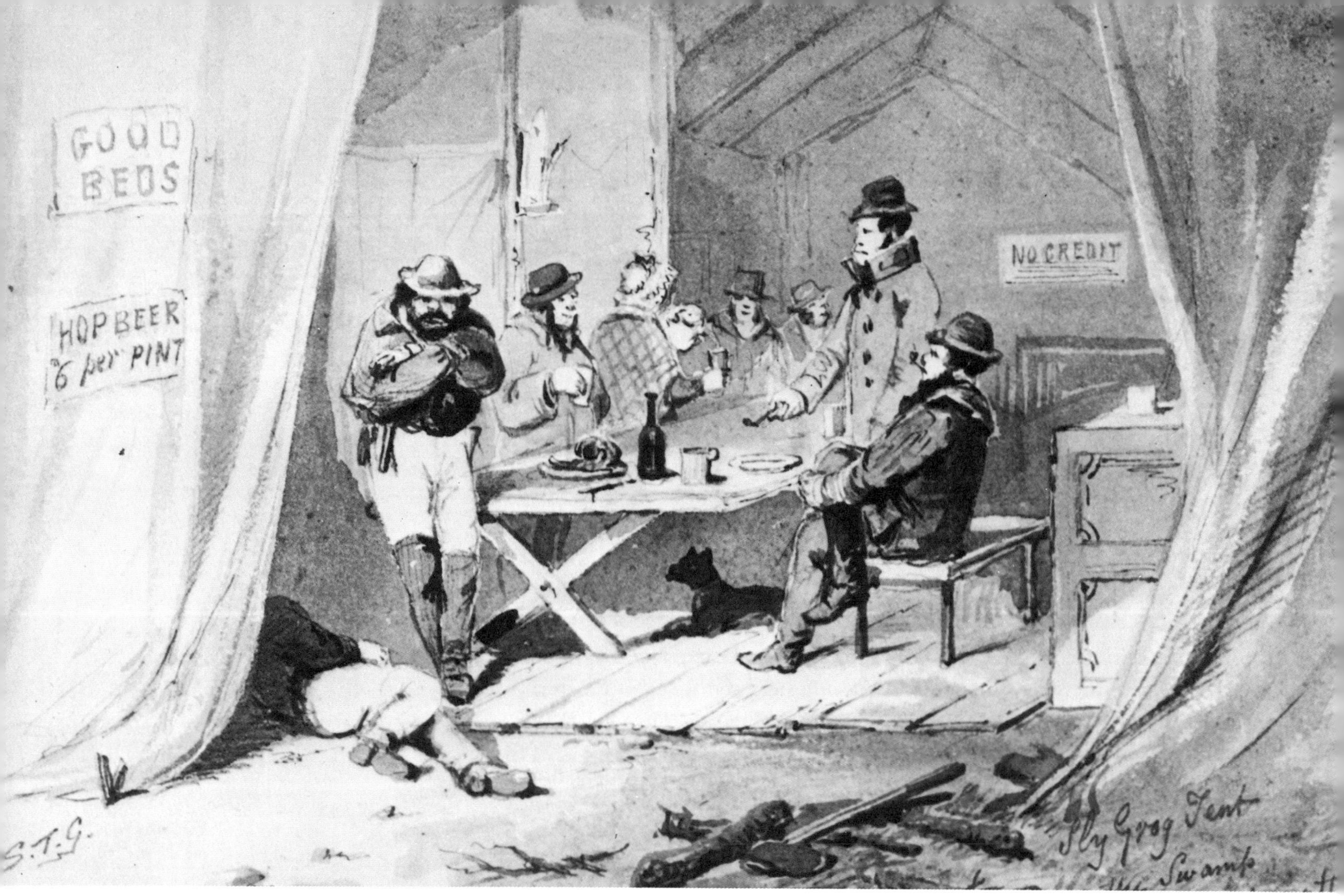

Age and class and race and occupation play no part in heroism. It is an act that can be spontaneous or performed after counting the cost. The heart of the matter is that it is done, whatever the cost.

PUBLISHED SOURCES

The author wishes to acknowledge the following sources:

Poems
'Courage', R. D. Fitzgerald, *Poetry in Australia*, Vision Press, Sydney, 1923; 'The Travelling P.O.', 'The Tracks We Used to Ride', A. B. Paterson, *The Man from Snowy River and Other Verses*, Angus & Robertson, Sydney, 1896; 'The Women of the West', *The Collected Verse of George Essex Evans* (Memorial Edition), Angus & Robertson, Sydney, 1928; 'Where the Dead Men Lie', Barcroft Boake, *Where the Dead Men Lie and Other Poems*, Angus & Robertson, Sydney, 1897; 'Past Carin'', Henry Lawson, *In the Days When the World Was Wide and Other Verses*, Angus & Robertson, Sydney, 1900; 'Bush Girl', Henry Lawson, *The Skyline Riders and Other Verses*, Fergusson & Mitchell, Sydney, 1910; 'The Bush Fire', Henry Lawson, *When I was King and Other Verses*, Angus & Robertson, Sydney, 1905; 'The Bush-Lost Children', Henry Lawson, *Joe Wilson and His Mates*, Angus & Robertson, London, 1913.

General
Australian Dictionary of Biography, Vols 1–6, Melbourne University Press, Melbourne, 1966–76
Australian Encyclopaedia, Vols 1–6, 2nd ed. (1963), 3rd ed. (1977), Grolier Society of Australia, Sydney

Individual stories
'The Anti-Hero', *Empire Review*, Vol. 9, 1905; 'Battlefronts of Outback', *Austral Wheel*, May 1898; 'Black Thursday', *The Chronicles of Early Melbourne 1835–52*; 'Garryowen' (E. Finn), Fergusson & Mitchell, Sydney, 1888; 'Bob the Dog', *Adelaide Observer*, 20 April 1889, 3 August 1895; 'The Bush-Lost Babies', *Australian Tales and Sketches*, Marcus Clarke, A. & W. Bruce, Melbourne, 1896; *Illustrated Melbourne Post*, 22 September 1864; *The Leader*, 8 April 1905; 'Lady Mit the Veil or 3,000 Miles Sidesaddle', *Australasian*, 16 February 1924; 'Mary Watson', *Australasian Sketcher*, 25 February 1882; M. B. P. Watson Diary, Oxley Library, Brisbane; *Mrs Watson, a Cooktown Heroine (pamphlet, author unknown)*, Port Douglas, c. 1891; 'Mother Buntine', *Book of Memoirs (pamphlet)*, J. J. O'Connor, publisher unknown; 'Operation Flood', *Flood Mitigation in NSW*, A. F. Reddoch & A. K. Milston, quoted by Ronald McKie, *A.M.*, March–April, 1955; *Sydney Morning Herald*, 20–28 February 1955; 'The Overland Telegraph', *Exploring in the Seventies and the Construction of the Overland Telegraph Line*, Alfred Giles, W. K. Thomas & Co., Adelaide, 1926; 'Paraway', *Packhorse and Waterhole*, G. Buchanan, Angus & Robertson, Sydney, 1933; 'Starlight', *Brisbane Courier*, 18 February, 17 April 1873; *Captain Starlight, Reckless Rascal of Robbery Under Arms*, Francis Patrick Clune, Hawthorn Press, Melbourne, 1945; 'Tommy Windich', *John Forrest's Journals*, Sampson Low, Martson, Low & Searle, London, 1875; 'The Travelling P.O.', Francis Murray, *People*, 25 March 1964; *Australasian Sketcher*, 20 May 1882; *We of the Never-Never*, Mrs Aeneas Gunn, Hutchinson, London, 1908.

SOURCES OF ILLUSTRATIONS

The author gratefully acknowledges the assistance of the following organisations:

Abbreviations: AGNSW (Art Gallery of New South Wales); AGSA (Art Gallery of South Australia); ANG (Australian National Gallery); DG (Dixson Galleries, State Library of New South Wales); DL (Dixson Library, State Library of New South Wales); IAM (Illustrated Australian Magazine); IAN (Illustrated Australian News); IMP (Illustrated Melbourne Post); JSBLWAH (JS Battye Library of Western Australian History); LTCSLV (LaTrobe Collection, State Library of Victoria); ML (Mitchell Library, State Library of New South Wales); NGV (National Gallery of Victoria); NL (National Library of Australia); SAA (South Australian Archives); RNKNL (Rex Nan Kivell Collection, National Library of Australia).

Illustrations not listed below are in the personal collection of the author.

Front jacket: Reg Morrison; Back jacket: David Moore; Endpapers: David Moore; Page 1: *Weekly Times*, 26 September 1908; 2–3: 'Irrigation Lake, Wimmera, 1949–50', Arthur Boyd, NGV; 6–7: IAN; 8 & 9 left: LTCSLV; 9 right: RNKNL; 9 left: NL; 10 left, below: NL; 10 right, below: NL; 11: NL; 12: G. C. Mundy, *Our Antipodes*, Bentley, 1855; 13 top: G. Grey, Journals of Two Expeditions; 13 below: *Australasian Sketcher*, 20 May 1882; 14 top: Royal Historical Society of Victoria; 14 below: LTCSLV; 15 top: Royal Historical Society of Victoria; 15 below: *Australian Sketchbook*, S. T. Gill, 1875, LTCSLV; 16: Miss D. Derham; 17: LTCSLV; 18: David Moore; 19: SAA; 20: SAA; 21: Sydney Morning Herald; 22: SAA; 23 top: SAA; 23 below: Australian Information Service; 25: *Sydney Mail*, 21 December 1889; 28: IAN; 29: *Australasian Sketcher*, 25 May 1882; 30 below: State Rail Authority of New South Wales; 30 top right: SAA; 31: SAA; 32 below: SAA; 35 & 36: David Moore; 38: SAA; 39 middle and below: SAA; 40 top: SAA; 40 below: JSBLWAH; 41 below: SAA; 42: SAA; 44: Department of Education, NSW; 45 above: LTCSLV; 45 below: NL; 46 above: LTCSLV; 48: LTCSLV; 49: LTCSLV; 50: LTCSLV; 51: IAM; 53 above: 'Bushmen Watering Horses in the Desert of Australia', George Hamilton, RNKNL; 53 below: 'Travelling through the Brush and Sandridges', S. T. Gill, August 1846, AGSA; 54 & 55: David Moore; 56: David Moore; 59: LTCSLV; 60: LTCSLV; 61: IAM; 63 top: NL; 63 below: LSBLWAH; 65: JSBLWAH; 66: IAN; 68: IAN; 69: IAN; 71, 72 & 73: Bush Brothers of Australia; 75 right: *Bulletin*, 8 October 1887; 75 left: SAA; 73: 'Swagsman on the Road Mt Charlson', S. T. Gill, DG; 74 above: David Moore; 77 above: *Lone Hand*, 1 March 1911; 77 below: SAA; 78: SAA; 79: Victorian Railways; 81: *Weekly Times*, 26 September 1908; 82: *Lone Hand*, 1 March 1911; 83 left: *Lone Hand*, 1 March 1911; 83 right: *Australasian Sketcher*, 17 February 1882; 85: *Austral Wheel*, March 1888; 86: *Austral Wheel*, June 1897; 87: *Mercury*; 90: SAA; 91: David Moore; 9: David Moore; 93: SAA; 94 top: JSBLWAH; 95: NL; 99: 'Horrocks' first interview with Hostile Blacks', S. T. Gill, NL; 100: RNKNL; 101: 'Homeward Bound', S. T. Gill, DL; 103: 'Night', S. T. Gill, ANG; 105: *Australasian Sketcher*, 23 September 1882; 106: *Cassell's Picturesque Australasia*, London, 1887; 107 top: *Illustrated London News*; 107 below: *Illustrated London News*; 'Drove of Cattle by Pond in Bush', S. T. Gill, RNKNL; 109 top: 'Rounding up a Straggler', Frank Mahony,

AGNSW; 110: 'Contributions insisted upon Voluntary principals despised', S. T. Gill, LTCSLV; 122: 'A bush race in Darling Downs', R. A. Lindsey, RNKNL; 123: *Australasian Sketcher*; 128: David Moore; 138: 'Mounted Police and Prisoner', S. T. Gill, DL; 139: JSBLWAH; 140: NL; 141 left: 'Leading from Stocks to Paxton's Lode Burra', S. T. Gill, RNKNL; 143: JSBLWAH; 144: JSBLWAH; 145: JSBLWAH; 147: LTCSLV; 149: *Leader*; 150: IMP; 151 top: *Australian Sketchbook*, S. T. Gill, 1875, LTCSLV; 151 below: *Leader*; 153: 'The Lost Child', Frederick McCubbin, NGV; 154–5: 'A Bush Burial', Frederick McCubbin, Geelong Art Gallery; 156: Detail from 'The Pioneer', Frederick McCubbin, NGV; 157: 'Bush Scenes', S. T. Gill, ML; 158; 158 left: ML; 158 right: NL; 159 top: ML; 159 below: LTCSLV; 160 above: 'Stockman's Hut Victoria', S. T. Gill, DL; 160 below: LTCSLV; 161: 'Scene at Hut Door', S. T. Gill, NL; 162 top: 'Mt Crawford S.A.', S. T. Gill, RNKNL; 162 right middle: NL; 162 right bottom: NL; 162 left: LTCSLV; 165 top: NL; 165 below: Australian Information Service; 166: David Moore; 168: *Queenslander*; 169–73: Herald & Weekly Times; 174: LTCSLV; 177: 'A Fallen Monarch', N. J. Caire, AGNSW; 178: Herald & Weekly Times; 180: Herald & Weekly Times; 183–4: Australian Information Service; 185: Herald & Weekly Times; 186: NL; 187: Herald & Weekly Times; 189: IAN; 190 top: 'Might versus Right', S. T. Gill, DL; 190 below: LTCSLV; 191–2: LTCSLV; 193 above: 'Chinese on Way to Goldfields', S. C. Brees, LTCSLV; 193 below: LTCSLV; 194–5: *Australasian*; 196: 'A Bush Funeral', S. T. Gill, DL; 199–200: *Weekly Courier*, Launceston; 205: State Library of Tasmania; 207: *Parade*; 208: LTCSLV; 209: NL; 210: 'The Hermit's Camp near Marysville', N. J. Caire, AGNSW; 213–17: NL; 218: Herald & Weekly Times; 220: *Australasian Sketcher*; 229: 'The Morning Tide', Leslie Rees, collection of the University of Sydney; 230 & 231: David Moore; 234 & 235: LTCSLV; 238 & 239: Oxley Memorial Library; 240: Queensland Museum; 241: Oxley Memorial Library; 250 & 251: S. T. Gill paintings and sketches: ML, DL, LTCSLV, AGSA, Ballarat Fine Art Gallery; 252: 'Night Out' S. T. Gill, NL.

OLD BOTANY BAY

"I'm old
Botany Bay;
Stiff in the joints,
Little to say.

I am he
Who paved the way,
That you may walk
At your ease today;

I was the conscript
Sent to hell
To make in the desert
The living well;

I bore the heat,
I blazed the track—
Furrowed and bloody
Upon my back.

I split the rock;
I felled the tree;
The nation was—
Because of me!"

*Old Botany Bay
Taking the sun
From day to day . . .
Shame on the mouth
That would deny
The knotted hands
That set us high!*

Mary Gilmore